THE POLITICAL ECONOMY OF ARGENTINA, 1880–1946

THE POLITICAL ECONOMY OF ARGENTINA 1880–1946

Edited by
Guido di Tella
and
D. C. M. Platt

St. Martin's Press   New York

© St Antony's College, Oxford, 1986

All rights reserved. For information, write:
St. Martin's Press, Inc., 175 Fifth Avenue, New York, NY 10010
Printed in Hong Kong
Published in the United Kingdom by The Macmillan Press Ltd.
First published in the United States of America in 1986

ISBN 0-312-62252-X

Library of Congress Cataloging in Publication Data
Main entry under title:
The Political economy of Argentina, 1880–1946.
Includes index.
1. Argentina–Economic policy.   I. Tella, Guido, 1931–   .
II. Platt, D. C.M. (Desmond Christopher St Martin), 1934   .
HC175.P62   1985   338.982   85–11896
ISBN 0-312-62252-X

To Raúl Prebisch
Elder Statesman of the Emerging Nations

Contents

List of Tables ix
Editors' Note and Publishers' Note x
Preface xi
Notes on the Contributors xiii

1 Domestic Finance in the Growth of Buenos Aires, 1880–1914   1
 D. C. M. Platt

2 The Relationship between Labour and Capital in Rural Argentina, 1880–1914   15
 Joseph S. Tulchin

3 The Argentine Export Economy: Intimations of Mortality, 1894–1930   39
 Tulio Halperin

4 The Argentine Economy, 1890–1914: Some Salient Features   60
 David Rock

5 Free Trade in One (Primary Producing) Country: the Case of Argentina in the 1920s   74
 A. O'Connell

6 The Economic Formulae of the 1930s: a Reassessment   95
 Peter Alhadeff

7 Economic Controversies in Argentina from the 1920s to the 1940s   120
 Guido di Tella

8	Argentine Economic Policies since the 1930s: Recollections *Raúl Prebisch*	133
9	The Origin of Argentina's Sterling Balances, 1939–43 *Jorge Fodor*	154
10	The United States, Britain and Argentina in the Years immediately after the Second World War *C. A. MacDonald*	183
	Postscript and Conclusions *Guido di Tella and D. C. M. Platt*	201
	Index	213

List of Tables

2.1	Capital invested in agriculture (by Pampean region), 1914	25
6.1	Real expenditure, 1928–39	97
6.2	Public expenditure and budgetary results as a proportion of total production, 1928–39	99
6.3	Annual debt service as a proportion of export value, public expenditure and revenue, 1929–36	101
6.4	Domestic and foreign composition of the annual service of the public debt, 1929–37	103
6.5	Money in circulation and means of payment, 1929–40	106
9.1	Variations in means of payments, 1939–44	177

Editors' Note

This book is the second in the St Antony's/Macmillan series to be devoted to the economic and social history of modern Argentina. The first volume – Platt and di Tella (eds and contrs), *Argentina, Australia and Canada: Studies in Comparative Development, 1870–1965* – was published in 1985. The editors hope that subsequent volumes will include a follow-up on the political economy of Argentina since 1946, a further comparative work on social experiments in regions of recent European settlement (Argentina, Australia and Canada, 1880–1940), and an analysis of the relative position of Britain and the United States in Argentina during and after the Second World War. Other volumes, prepared and edited by Argentine scholars, are planned in the Republic for themes such as communications, finance and banking, industrialisation, and the development of the pastoral and agricultural sectors.

Publishers' Note

The volume is published with the aid of a grant from the Latin American Publications Fund.

Preface

In substance, this book is the outcome of a conference held at St Antony's College, Oxford, in July 1981. The conference discussed the political economy of Argentina for the first half of the twentieth century, a period of critical importance to the Republic during which Argentina moved from an optimism induced by great expansion to the doubts and vacillations which have since preoccupied us all. The papers and subsequent discussion brought together both academics who had worked on developments in Argentina over the period and a group of distinguished public servants who had played a leading role during the later decades. The interaction was interesting, more particularly in the shape of the reactions of public servants to the inferences and conclusions of academics on their behaviour and motivation at the time. As Prebisch pointed out, scholars are better informed today about some aspects of the past even than the leading actors of the time. While contemporaries had to guess the intentions of others, we know today, from local and foreign sources, rather more about what these intentions might actually have been.

In the first part of the book we publish four papers for the years before the First World War. They consider the role of domestic and foreign finance in the expansion of Buenos Aires, the differences in labour and capital usage between the various kinds of agricultural frontier, the emergence of doubt as to the possibility of continuing the geographical expansion of the frontier, and the position arrived at by the Argentine economy just before the First World War. The papers were contributed by D. C. M. Platt, Joseph S. Tulchin, Tulio Halperín and David Rock respectively.

The conference then turned its attention to the inter-war years, to the policies of the 1920s and 1930s, and to the analysis of the economic controversies which surrounded both the transitory nature of agricultural expansion and the need for alternative paths of development for the national economy. The academic argument was presented by Arturo O'Connell, Peter Alhadeff and Guido di Tella, and it contrasts with what Raúl Prebisch, a leading policy-maker at the time, was able to tell us about what he and his group wanted to do, and actually did. The flavour to be derived from the recollections of perceptive contemporaries, public figures of the day, was of exceptional interest to the conference participants, as, we hope and expect, it will be also to the readers of this volume.

The last section of the book discusses the problems of Argentina during the Second World War and its immediate aftermath. It focuses on the financial problems which emerged between Argentina and Britain during the War (Jorge Fodor), and on the changing, triangular relationship between the United States, Britain and Argentina induced and promoted both by Britain's economic decline and by the appearance, in the Southern Cone, of a totally novel degree of North American interest and concern (C. A. MacDonald).

The volume ends with a postscript in which the editors bring together some of the main strands and isolate both the significant areas of agreement and some of the points which remain in dispute.

The editors are glad to take this opportunity to thank St Antony's College (and its Latin American Centre) for having sponsored the conference. They are grateful to the Nuffield Foundation, to the Latin American Publications Fund, and to the Committee of the Argentine Friends of Oxford (Buenos Aires) for their generous support. They thank the contributors and participants for their time and expertise, Adolfo Gurrieri for editing Chapter 8, and Celia Szusterman for her share in the preparation, sub-editing and publication of this volume. They are grateful, in particular, to Raúl Prebisch, elder statesman of the emerging nations, to whom this book is dedicated.

St Antony's College	Guido di Tella
Oxford	D. C. M. Platt

Notes on the Contributors

Peter Alhadeff is a researcher at the Torcuato di Tella Institute, Buenos Aires.

Jorge Fodor is Professor of Modern History at the University of Modena.

Tulio Halperín is Professor of Latin American History at the University of California, Berkeley.

C. A. MacDonald is Lecturer in International Studies at the University of Warwick.

A. O'Connell is a senior researcher at the Torcuato di Tella Institute, Buenos Aires.

D. C. M. Platt is Professor of the History of Latin America at the University of Oxford and Senior Tutor and Fellow of St Antony's College, Oxford.

Raúl Prebisch was until recently Secretary-General of the Economic Commission for Latin America.

David Rock is Professor of Latin American History at the University of California, Santa Barbara.

Guido di Tella is Professor of Economics at the Catholic University and the University of Buenos Aires, and Associate Fellow, St Antony's College, Oxford.

Joseph S. Tulchin is Professor of Latin American History at the University of North Carolina.

1 Domestic Finance in the Growth of Buenos Aires, 1880-1914

D. C. M. PLATT

I

Torcuato de Alvear, the great *intendente* of Buenos Aires, gave finance first priority in his administration; without financial resources there was no hygiene and no improvement – nothing was possible.[1] Nevertheless it remains the case that in the vast literature on urbanisation – a recent bibliography listed over 7000 Latin American items[2] – finance receives barely a mention. Migration, urban transport, housing, planning, slums, hygiene, industry: these are the common coinage of urban history. Finance, the element essential to them all, is missing. Surely, 'money answereth all things.' Without it how can we begin to explain the transformation of Buenos Aires from the *gran aldea* of the 1860s to the metropolis of 1914?

Buenos Aires in the 1860s and 1870s, according to one of its few financial historians (Salvador Alfonso), was still a Spanish colonial city, distinguished from the others only by its greater size and population. Its paving, lighting, hygiene/hospitals, transportation, public establishments, *paseos*, police and public education were all imperfect, in fact, utterly deficient. By the time Alfonso himself was writing (in 1905) he could legitimately describe Buenos Aires as the first city of South America, well on its way to rivalling, some day, the most important cities of Europe.[3]

Sherlock Holmes once reminded us that it is a capital sin to theorise before one has data, and this may be the time and the place to produce a few figures, if only to achieve some sense of scale. The population of Buenos Aires rose from 177,787 in 1869 to 1,575,814 in 1914.[4] An annual growth rate of 5.8 per cent for the city's population during the quinquennium 1904–9 made Buenos Aires second only to Hamburg (6.1 per cent) as the fastest growing major city in the Western world, ahead even of New York at 5.7 per cent. Chicago is often compared to Buenos Aires, yet Chicago's population, in the late 1900s, was growing at the rate of only 1.4 per cent. The population of Buenos Aires was much smaller than that of contemporary London (4.8 million in 1907) or New York (4.1 million in 1906), but the rate of expansion was faster, and the population of Buenos Aires, by the 1900s, was not far behind that of St Petersburg (1.9 million in 1900) or Vienna (1.8 million in the same year); Chicago and Berlin were larger by about 500,000 apiece.[5] However, the density of the population of Buenos Aires was lower than that of the great majority of important cities – 66 inhabitants per hectare, by contrast with 158 in London, and no less than 343 in Paris.[6] And lower density meant extended and expensive urban services.

II

Any city that chose to expand at the rate of Buenos Aires had to find a great deal of money. How was this achieved? Naturally there are many ways in which a city can finance its own growth, provided that it is content to grow at a normal rate. But the growth of Buenos Aires was entirely abnormal. Whatever the contribution of domestic resources – and I shall be looking in this chapter more particularly at the domestic contribution – Buenos Aires could not avoid an appeal to a wider constituency, usually abroad.

This was a *national* problem for the Argentine Republic. The general expenses of the Federal Government absorbed virtually the whole of current revenue. The cost of the national programme of public works shortly before the First World War was estimated at 100 million pesos, yet the budget for 1912 could offer public works only 4 per cent of total revenue (14 million pesos). The Minister of Finance, José María Rosa, made it perfectly plain that the nation would have to borrow to meet both extraordinary expenditures and the major part of its commitment to public works.[7]

It was certainly the case, in the decades before 1914, that both the Argentine nation and the municipality of Buenos Aires had to be prepared to apply to the international capital market for funds. But

Argentina's credit was good, and there was a logic in spreading the burden of modernisation to those future generations who might expect to benefit most. The *intendente* Alberto Casares, surveying (early in the twentieth century) the city's programme of urgent and necessary public improvements – new *avenidas*, a modern municipal office, hospitals, public baths, workers' housing, new *plazas* and public gardens, drains, or whatever – explained that it was impossible and unjust to demand that the cost of these should fall entirely on the present generation; it should be shared with future generations, and for this the perfect mechanism was a loan which could be serviced out of current revenue.[8]

The argument for loans was well appreciated at the time. For Salvador Alfonso, loans were advantageous and legitimate when they were raised for operations of long-term utility and of a size that could not be met by ordinary revenues; loans raised to cancel past debts must be financed from ordinary revenues. In principle this was right. In practice, the major part of the loans raised in the past had been intended to meet existing debts – the 1882 loan unified the consolidated debt and incorporated the floating debt; the national government loan of ten million pesos in 1890 was intended to pay off half the floating debt and extinguish the lottery loan of 1889. By contrast, the loan proposal which Alfonso himself was canvassing – for 45 million gold pesos (£9 million) – was intended for objectives of permanent interest, to be serviced by ordinary revenues. These included the construction of a *gran avenida* to cross the city from north to south, the taming or canalisation of the city's *arroyos*, the installation of rubbish disposal ovens and crematoria, an increase in slaughterhouses and municipal markets, the construction of hospitals and of houses for workers, the creation of new *paseos*, *plazas*, and *avenidas*.[9] The loan was rejected by Congress.

Loans – that is, productive loans, for 'money is like muck, not good unless it be spread' – were an obvious and sensible way of raising money for extraordinary purposes. Meanwhile the routine expenditure of the Municipality was channelled into street lighting, cleaning, public assistance, paving and *paseos*. The total net debt incurred by the Municipality from 1882 to 1910 was somewhere in the region of £10 million.[10] It was funded, to a large extent, from abroad. But it remained only a small part of the cost of modern Buenos Aires, and a small proportion of city finance. Baron Haussman, after all, had raised infinitely more for the beautification and modernisation of Paris. The City of Paris Loans, merely to January 1868, reached 1.2 billion francs (£48 million).[11]

III

Who, then, paid for the expansion of Buenos Aires? This paper points to the largest resource – private, domestic finance.

The relative size of the contribution of domestic capital may be a cause of some surprise. Most would probably agree that the loans for the beautification of Paris were taken almost entirely by French investors – these were domestic loans, in a rich country. But if one could find that elusive character, the man on the street, nowadays in metropolitan Buenos Aires, his most likely answer to the kind of question I am asking would be that the money for the great expansion of Buenos Aires before the First World War came from abroad, mainly from Britain.

My point is that although the more ostentatious elements of city modernisation – public utilities, in particular – required a great deal of money in a short time, and were therefore financed necessarily from the major money markets of the world, the really massive expenditure – on housing and paving – was piecemeal, long-term and domestic. The conclusion is not peculiar to Buenos Aires; it applies equally to major city development elsewhere. After all, the Argentines just before the First World War were not a notably poor people. The total national wealth of Argentina in 1916 has been estimated at 33,988 million pesos m/n (just under £3 billion). Such a figure is meaningless on its own, but if one compares the nine million citizens of Argentina in 1916 with North Americans and Frenchmen for more or less the same date it will be found (at least in Martínez's figures) that the national wealth per capita works out at £374 for the United States, £205 for France, but £333 for Argentina.[12] And the rate of growth for Argentina was astonishing, as astonishing as anything else in that remarkable country. National wealth grew from the £568 million estimated (or rather, underestimated) in the 1895 national census,[13] to the Martínez estimate of just under £3 billion in 1916.

IV

We might now take a look at some of the figures for housing – and I think that it would be reasonable to suppose that housing was paid for at home by the residents of Buenos Aires, native or foreign. Admittedly figures for the number of houses constructed are an imperfect guide; they take no account of size, location, and quality of construction. But, bearing this in mind, the 1869 census showed 20,858 houses both in the city itself and the two suburbs, Flores and Belgrano, which were later to be incorporated within the city boundary; the census of 1887 brought the number up to 33,804.[14] By 1904 there were 82,540 houses, and in 1909 (as registered in the city census of that year) 111,135 houses. The greatest increase between the censuses of 1904 and 1909 had been in houses made of brick and stone, although 91,257 out of the total of 111,135 (82 per cent) were still one-storey.[15] Buenos Aires was not yet a city of *rascacielos* (skyscrapers) like the cities of the United States, but between the two censuses there had, in fact, been an enormous increase in multi-storey buildings.

Obviously it was real estate that was capturing by far the greater part of Argentina's domestic disposable capital for the 1900s and up to 1915. The sums were enormous. Sales of real estate realised in Buenos Aires from 1901 to 1915 inclusive amounted to 3 billion pesos m/n (£264 million).[16] Mortgage operations in the city of Buenos Aires (foreign in part, but mostly domestic), which had accounted for 22 million pesos m/n in 1903, had risen to 206 million pesos m/n (£18 million) in 1911.[17] Sales of rural real estate over the same period, for Argentina as a whole, were 3.4 billion pesos m/n (£300 million), and sales of urban property other than in Buenos Aires added another 980 million pesos m/n (£86 million). The total sale of real estate in Argentina, 1901–1915, was £650 million, nearly half of which was in Buenos Aires.[18]

It is figures such as these that we might bear in mind in preserving some sense of proportion when deaing, say, with foreign investment in Argentine public utilities, or foreign holdings in the bonds of the municipal debt. Property transactions and mortgages were the essence of Argentina's domestic finance. During 1911, which was not a peak year, operations on the Buenos Aires *Bolsa* amounted to 307 million pesos m/n (£27 million), of which more than half, 170 million pesos, were in national and provincial mortgage bonds.[19]

The phenomenon is not difficult to understand for any part of the Western world, let alone Argentina at this particular period; increased land values in Buenos Aires and the concentration of resources in urban real estate were matched precisely abroad. Windfall gains in land values attracted much capital, so that, even when alternative areas of the economy found themselves starved of capital, urban development experienced no difficulty in obtaining what it needed from the domestic investor. Enrique Ruiz Guiñazú cited two foreign examples. The land area of the Borough of Fulham was valued at £2.5 million in 1886; by 1904 the valuation had more than doubled to £5.2 million. For New York Ruiz Guiñazú quoted the case of a lot (10 by 13 metres) on the corner of Broadway and Wall Street, which had been worth £3655 in 1827, £80,000 in 1898, and £140,000 in 1905.[20]

As I have said, Argentine citizens in the 1900s were not so very much poorer, per capita, than the citizens of the United States, and they had less incentive or opportunity to invest other than in real estate. It is no surprise, then, that they put their money into the expansion of Buenos Aires. Eugenio García cannot be wrong when he said, in 1917, that Argentine domestic capital, until the date of writing, had been absorbed almost entirely in the huge development of the pastoral and agricultural industry, in feverish speculation in land values, and in the high income to be earned from mortgage finance.[21]

V

Apart from building, which was the major expense of an expanding city, private and municipal resources were channelled into the widening of streets, the construction of *avenidas*, the lay-out of public parks, and, above all, paving. Because of rising property values, the heavy expense of street widening and improvement could, in large part, be met by domestic finance. Some of the municipal loans offered on international markets included modernisation of this kind among their objectives. But the greater part of this heavy programme of public works was met at home.

The economics are simple enough, and they were shared by evolving cities generally. Barcelona in the last decades of the nineteenth century managed to transform itself into a city grander than Buenos Aires because it was authorised by Spanish law to expropriate (with compensation) the territory which it needed for streets, together with land on each side to the extent of 20 *varas* (17.3 metres). By the sale, subsequently, of expropriated land, Barcelona recovered more than it lost.[22]

This, really, was the point. Massive city development could ultimately pay for itself through the increment in land values created by improved streets, sites, and properties. Compensation might even be total, as it was with the Avenue de l' Opéra in Paris, by which the city of Paris actually made a profit of 47 million francs (£1.9 million).[23] But such expectations were seldom fulfilled. Torcuato de Alvear managed to persuade himself that his favourite project, the Avenida de Mayo, a great and largely pointless avenue westward from the Casa Rosada (the Presidential mansion), would pay for itself simply by augmented land values.

Existing proprietors, Alvear thought, would be eager not only to make a free grant of the land necessary for the Avenida, but also to take a share of the indemnification of those proprietors whose interests were actually prejudiced.[24] Alvear was wrong. The Loan of 1884, which was intended to provide an adequate float for the Avenida de Mayo, and which had brought a total of 2.88 million pesos m/n (£420,000) to the Municipality, fell far short of what was required. When the *intendente* Francisco Bollini was writing, in the autumn of 1893, the expense of the Avenida to the Municipality had risen already to 10.6 million pesos m/n (£640,000),[25] and the cost was to go much higher before the Avenida was completed. Amongst other things, proprietors were less generous and far-sighted than Alvear had anticipated, and Congress less helpful in legislating an appropriate law of expropriation.

All the same, the financial base of planning for city lay-out, for all expanding cities, continued to be the improved site values of the properties adjoining the enlarged streets. In some respects Buenos Aires was better placed than a city like London. London's lay-out was irregular and unpredictable, and sites were often ill-adapted and insufficient for drastic road-widening. Buenos Aires, like most Spanish colonial cities, was planned on a grid system – *cuadras* of 150 *varas* (blocks of 129.9 metres). A lay-out of this kind provided very deep sites, for which the loss of up to 15 metres was amply compensated by a new facade on a busy, improved highway. Furthermore, for Buenos Aires during much of the period I describe, part even of the central portions of the city was still of relatively insubstantial, one-storey construction that presented few problems for demolition and reconstruction, sometimes no more indeed than wooden buildings on *fincas* (small farms).

Perhaps I may be allowed to illustrate what I am saying from the example of the Diagonales – those massive (and again pretty pointless) *avenidas* running south/west and north/west diagonally from the Plaza de Mayo. Like the Avenida de Mayo, the earliest phases (when the work was started and no revenue received) were financed from abroad, by bank advances of £1.32 million negotiated by Ernesto Tornquist y Cía. in Britain and Germany, and by others for 3.75 million francs (£150,000) through Portalis of Paris. These were short-term, for up to two years. Furthermore, the Municipality was authorised by Congress to issue a full, long-term loan (domestic or foreign) of 15 million gold pesos (£3 million) to finance expropriations. Elaborate rules for expropriation were formulated, the essence of which was that there was to be no compensation for parts of a site where the rest of the site remained sufficient in size more than to repay the loss from the proceeds of improved land values. At the same time, the Banco Hipotecario Nacional was to agree to make sufficient funds available, at bank rate, for the reconstruction of the properties, while the Municipality was authorised to issue up to 30 million pesos m/n (£2.6 million) in 5 per cent bonds, to be allocated at face value to proprietors in compensation for expropriation.

I give these details because they illustrate, quite neatly, the different elements in city finance: that is, foreign bank advances for the initial 'float', long-term foreign/domestic loans to finance irrecoverable costs, uncompensated expropriation of the majority of domestic proprietors in anticipation of rising land values, and a large issue of municipal bonds (more or less equal in quantity to the foreign/domestic loans) with which to pay off those proprietors who became entitled to compensation. The 5 per cent municipal bonds, issued at face value, were sold by the expropriated proprietors on the Buenos Aires market for what they could get (probably near face value), either to foreign or to domestic investors.[26]

In the event, it was not possible to raise long-term loans abroad either for the Diagonales or for the contemporary Avenida Norte a Sur; the First World War put a stop to European lending. The continuing liabilities of acquisition and expropriation of the properties required for the Diagonal Norte and the Avenida Norte a Sur were met by the issue and sale of certificates of the Municipal Floating Debt (that is, financed largely at home). And here a point might be made. Arrangements for financing abroad, although often convenient, were liable to disruption from major external upheavals – the Baring crisis of 1890/1, the North American financial crisis of 1907, the European financial crisis of 1913, the First World War itself. Much that was originally planned for the international market came finally to be taken at home. The example may serve simply as yet another reminder of the folly of those who attach overwhelming importance to the role of foreign finance.

Cleveland, Ohio, illustrates the means by which certain forms of city development were financed. The process was not necessarily expensive to the municipality. When Cleveland was faced with the prospect of supplying a number of costly public buildings, the city decided to build a civic centre (buildings, parks, avenues). The only extraordinary expense was the acquisition of the site. Even this was returned to the city in the shape of taxes on the hugely increased value of the neighbouring properties, which had formerly been permitted to decay.

VI

A very considerable element of expenditure incurred in the financing of all cities was the paving of their streets. Where was money to be found? Here too, like the planning and development of the streets, *plazas*, *avenidas*, and parks, some part was obtained from abroad, in the shape of a share in the proceeds of the various municipal loans that found a home in European money markets. But as I have said already, these foreign loans were not of enormous value by comparison with domestic investment in housing, and the same can be said for paving.

The problem of paving was almost overwhelming. Torcuato de Alvear always accepted that paving was a prime responsibility; no city, he said, could prosper without the proper paving of its streets.[27] Yet after all his energetic efforts, about half of the city was still unpaved at the end of the 1880s (2500 *cuadras*), while the remainder (2782 *cuadras*) was often paved very inadequately indeed. Francisco Seeber, one of Alvear's capable successors as *intendente* (May 1889–June 1890), was only too aware of the difficulties. In the old Spanish tradition, the proprietors on each side of the street were responsible for its surface – the entire surface, not simply the pavements as in modern Buenos Aires. It was almost impossible to compel proprietors to fulfil their obligations. House owners were prepared to spend huge sums on the decoration and embellishment of the interiors and exteriors of their houses, 'pero en asegurar una piedra floja, o reparar una rota, no lo hacen, aunque se les amenace con multas y ejecuciones'. The simple solution, practised regularly in Europe and the United States, was to insist that proprietors should be responsible for the initial paving of their streets, after which the Municipality took charge. Seeber preferred this formula and proposed to take the responsibility into the hands of the Municipality of Buenos Aires in return for a small monthly tax. But he could not get the Municipal Council to agree.[28] Nowadays Buenos Aires looks after its road surfaces and discharges its responsibility reasonably well (at least, in the Barrio Norte). Pavements, however, remain at the charge of the individual proprietor, and the condition of the pavements of modern Buenos Aires is a disgrace.

There were, indeed, special problems for a city like Buenos Aires, in the full flood of modernisation. Its road surfaces were always being torn open for the construction of storm drains, sewers, fresh-water pipes, gas mains, telephone lines, electric cables; most of all, they were broken up for the laying of tram lines. In the outlying areas, bullock carts without springs, bearing loads of 1200 kilos on each wheel, tore road surfaces to pieces. Seeber, a conscientious *intendente*, had ridden over as many of the unpaved 2500 *cuadras* as he could, but some were impassable even on horseback; in others, the *carreteros* could move their carts only with the help of ten yoke oxen. For Seeber, the leading issue of his period of office was paving, and it was, as he said of his relations with the politicians even at this stormy period of Argentine political history, 'uno de mis mayores contratiempos'.[29]

Of course, we are not concerned with politics; simply with the origins of the finance for paving, of whatever kind, of the streets of one of the world's great cities. Properly-paved streets raised property values, and this was the route by which access to domestic finance was obtained, just as it was for the other city improvements which I have been discussing. Fear of disease was another – yellow fever and cholera, and then the smallpox, typhus and diphtheria to be encountered from the stagnant water in the ruts and pot-holes of the unpaved or partially-paved streets. Fear of disease was always a powerful (on occasion, *the* powerful) element in the modernisation of Buenos Aires. The first steps towards providing running water and main drainage for the city derived directly from the dreadful yellow fever epidemic of 1871, when 13,614 inhabitants of Buenos Aires lost their lives.[30]

In the colonial city, as I have suggested, the theory was that proprietors paved the street in front of their houses. Little was done. The Law of 1888 put the existing convention on a more regular basis, and paving of an approved kind was made compulsory for every proprietor. Those who already contributed to the direct city tax were expected to pay a third of the cost, while the remaining two-thirds were to be financed by the Municipality from an assigned portion of its revenues.[31] Other laws followed, not always to much effect.

Whether the system was satisfactory or not, my point is that the cost of all this was very high; paving – a basic element in all city development – was both domestically financed and as expensive, over the years, as the more spectacular public utilities financed from abroad. Carlos Morales calculated that the total cost of paving Buenos Aires over the decade 1895–1904 had come to more than 35 million pesos m/n (about £2.7 million). His estimate for the cost of the entire paving of the city, by 1905, was 55 million pesos m/n (about £4.8 million).[32] And although the Municipality contributed some part of this cost, the bulk was paid for by the proprietors.

Shortly after this time the Municipality became much more active in the financing of paving, principally by means of the issue of municipal saving bonds, *bonos de pavimentación*. In 1904 the paved area of the city amounted to 5.9 million square metres. The *vecinos* were still paying the lion's share. Of the 973,000 pesos m/n (£86,000) actually spent on paving in 1903, the Municipality provided 114,000 pesos, the tramway companies 32,000 pesos, and the *vecinos* 827,000 pesos.[33] Paving, at the end of 1910, covered 7.9 million square metres, and perhaps 60 per cent of all roads in the city were properly or provisionally paved.[34] By the end of 1912, 9.2 million square metres were under some kind of paving: 64 per cent granite (cobbles), 14.8 per cent wooden blocks, asphalt and macadam, and 21.2 per cent provisional (grit, gravel, or sand).[35] The investment represented by 5.9 million square metres of granite cobblestones was enormous, and it had been incurred entirely since the first cobbles were laid in 1893.

Some part of this expense (or rather, investment) took the form of municipal loans floated abroad. Another part was subsumed in federal loans which found their way into city finances through the very considerable support which the federal government had given to the city after the adoption of Buenos Aires as federal capital in 1880 – water, drainage, education, police, docks, even the servicing of several city loans. But the bulk of the money was domestic. As a rough calculation, based on the figures supplied by Joaquín de Anchorena (*intendente* from October 1910 to October 1914), the 9.2 million square metres of paving had cost 78.6 million pesos m/n (about £7 million). Spending mounted very rapidly. In 1912 the City issued paving bonds to the extent of 15 million pesos m/n (£1.3 million) face value – or, at 85 per cent issue price, 12.75 million pesos net. These were bonds issued in payment by the Municipality to owners of expropriated property and to the contractors. They were intended to be bought by the citizens concerned, whereupon the proceeds were passed to the contractors, and in fact the city's accounts department reported that about half the cash had actually arrived.[36] In the decade 1903 to 1912, an annual average of 460 thousand square metres was paved each year, with a peak of 1.1 million in 1912.[37]

I must apologise for producing so many figures. Lord Randolph Churchill, sometime Britain's Chancellor of the Exchequer, once said of the decimal point: 'I never could make out what those damned dots meant.' But it is the *scale* of the domestic spending on the modernisation of Buenos Aires which I am trying to indicate. And it was the low density of the population of Buenos Aires – that wide dispersal in one-storey buildings to which I have already referred – that so immensely extended this particular portion of the city budget.

VII

As may already have become apparent, my theme is not simply *municipal* finance – that is, the funds and activities of the Municipality of Buenos Aires. Much of what I have been saying has had nothing to do with the Municipality – the construction of most buildings, the paving of most streets. My purpose has been to establish how the city of Buenos Aires, not the Municipality, managed to finance its expansion during a particular period of its history.

For the years which I am discussing, the Municipality regarded itself as responsible for health, public works (street-widening, paving, *avenidas*, *plazas*, parks, monuments), for street lighting, cleansing, public markets, cemeteries, and social welfare. Public utilities – tramways, gas, electricity – were provided by joint-stock companies. The port of Buenos Aires, as the principal port in the Republic, was administered by the Federal Government. The drainage and water supplies of the capital were also the responsibility of the State. Apart from a very limited amount of worker housing (from about 1908), housing and private building generally were not touched by the Municipality.

In other words, the Municipality provided the services that were not self-financing, that could not be contracted out to private enterprise or paid for by the State as profitable undertakings. In the nineteenth century, this distribution of responsibilities was not unfamiliar anywhere in the Western World.

But may I end by making what may seem to be an obvious point? Great cities, including Buenos Aires, grow primarily out of their own resources; their growth, above all, takes the shape of housing and paving. Perhaps, in the past, we have fixed our attention too exclusively on the glamorous superficialities – the public utilities, the international loans, the Puerto Madero, the top ten per cent for which money had to be found abroad.

NOTES

N.B. During the period covered by this paper, the premium on gold fluctuated from nil to the high point of 3.58 m/n (moneda nacional) to 1 peso oro. Pesos m/n have been converted to £s sterling at the current annual average rate.

1. *Memoria del Presidente de la Comisión Municipal al Consejo, 1880* (Buenos Aires, 1881) p. 5.

2. Martin H. Sable, *Latin American Urbanization: A Guide to the Literature, Organizations and Personnel* (Metuchen, N. J., 1971).
3. Salvador Alfonso, 'Finanzas y administración comunal', *Censo General de la Ciudad de Buenos Aires, 1904* (Buenos Aires, 1906) pp. 239, 241.
4. Alberto B. Martínez, 'Consideraciones sobre los resultados del Tercer Censo Nacional de Población, *Tercer Censo Nacional, 1914*, vol. I (Buenos Aires, 1916) p. 80.
5. Martínez's preface to the *Censo General de la Ciudad de Buenos Aires, 1909*, vol. I (Buenos Aires, 1910) pp. xi–xii.
6. Ibid., pp. xxv–vi.
7. *Memoria del Departamento de Hacienda, 1911*, vol. I (Buenos Aires, 1912) p. xxxvii.
8. *Memoria de la Intendencia Municipal, 1903* (Buenos Aires, 1904) p. 149.
9. Alfonso, 'Finanzas y administración comunal', pp. 251–3.
10. The total net debt (allowing for refunding, etc.) was calculated at 82.2 million pesos (presumably m/n) in the *Memoria del Departamento de Hacienda, 1912* (Buenos Aires, 1913) pp. 476–7: that is, £7.2 million. It is true that many of the new loans were, in fact, simply the cancellation of old debts, so that the net amount would be less than might be expected. But the figure still looks too small, and I have raised it, slightly, in my text.
11. *La Finance* (Brussels), quoted in the 'Commercial History and Review of 1867', p. 38 (attached to *The Economist*, 14 March 1868).
12. Alberto B. Martínez, 'La fortuna colectiva del pueblo argentino', *Tercer Censo Nacional, 1914*, vol. VIII (Buenos Aires, 1917) p. 453.
13. Quoted by ibid., p. 431 (Martínez himself felt that the 1895 figure was much too low).
14. Manuel C. Chueco, 'Estudio sobre los resultados del Censo de Edificación', in *Censo Municipal de Buenos Aires, 1887*, vol. II (Buenos Aires, 1889) p. 73.
15. *Censo General de la Ciudad de Buenos Aires, 1909*, vol. I (Buenos Aires, 1910) p. lxxvi.
16. Martínez, 'La fortuna colectiva', p. 425.
17. *Anuario Estadístico de la Ciudad de Buenos Aires, años 1910 y 1911* (Buenos Aires, 1913) p. xliii.
18. Martínez, 'La fortuna colectiva', p. 425.
19. *Memoria de la Intendencia Municipal, 1911* (Buenos Aires, 1912) p. 369.
20. Enrique Ruiz Guiñazú, 'Finanzas de la Municipalidad de Buenos Aires', *Censo General de la Ciudad de Buenos Aires, 1909*, vol. III (Buenos Aires, 1910) pp. 470–1.
21. Eugenio E. García, 'Consideraciones sobre los resultados del censo de las industrias', *Tercer Censo Nacional, 1914*, vol. VII (Buenos Aires, 1917) p. 23.
22. *Memoria de la Intendencia Municipal, 1889*, vol. I (Buenos Aires, 1891) p. 36.
23. Ibid.
24. Alvear's letter to the Minister of the Interior (Bernardo de Irigoyen, 21 August 1884, reprinted in the *Memoria de la Intendencia Municipal, 1884* (Buenos Aires, 1885) p. 63.
25. *Memoria de la Intendencia Municipal, 1890–92* (Buenos Aires, 1894) p. 124.
26. *Memoria de la Intendencia Municipal, 1912* (Buenos Aires, 1913) pp. vi, 25, 76.

27. Adrián Beccar Varela, *Torcuato de Alvear, primer intendente municipal de la Ciudad de Buenos Aires* (Buenos Aires, 1926) p. 213.
28. *Memoria de la Intendencia Municipal, 1889*, vol. I, p. 43.
29. Ibid, p. 67.
30. M. A. Pellizi, 'Crónica abreviada de la ciudad de Buenos Aires', in the *Censo Municipal de Buenos Aires, 1887*, vol. I, p. 50.
31. Cited in the *Memoria de la Intendencia Municipal, 1888* (Buenos Aires, 1889) pp. xxiv–v.
32. Carlos María Morales, 'Estudio topográfico y edilicio de la Ciudad de Buenos Aires', *Censo General de la Ciudad de Buenos Aires, 1904* (Buenos Aires, 1906) pp. 425–6.
33. *Memoria de la Intendencia Municipal, 1903*, pp. 109–10.
34. *Memoria de la Intendencia Municipal, 1910* (Buenos Aires, 1911) pp. 92–3.
35. *Memoria de la Intendencia Municipal, 1912*, p. vii.
36. Ibid., p. 57.
37. Ibid., p. 60.

2 The Relationship between Labour and Capital in Rural Argentina, 1880–1914

JOSEPH S. TULCHIN

I

The results of the export boom that Argentina experienced in the half century following 1860 are easy enough to measure in economic terms at the national level. Virtually all indices of growth show marked increase.[1] The volume and value of the nation's exports had reached unprecedented levels by the time of the centenary in 1910, bringing great wealth to the nation and to many individuals linked to the export economy. The governing élite and many foreign observers anticipated that the pattern of growth would continue, and that Argentina, within a reasonable period of time, would join the ranks of the world's rich and powerful nations.

The statistics that bred that optimism concealed a complex process. It is wrong to think of the Argentine export economy as an undifferentiated unit organised for production in the same manner from one end of the pampa to the other. That simply was not the case. It is the purpose of this paper to describe the significant differences in social and economic organisation across a series of regions on the pampa, to explain the differences, and to offer some preliminary suggestions concerning the consequences of those regional differences for later economic and political developments. The argument is based upon three propositions drawn from the human ecological paradigm:

1. Adaptation to environment proceeds through the formation of a system of interdependences among the members of a population;

2. System development continues, *ceteris paribus*, to the maximum size and complexity afforded by the existing facilities for transportation and communication; and
3. System development is resumed with the introduction of new information which increases the facility for movement of materials, people, and messages, and continues until the capacity for movement is fully utilised.[2]

Settlement on the pampa occurred at different times and under different geographic conditions. Soil, climate, and access to transportation, both natural and man-made, differed from one location to another. As I explained in great detail in another study,[3] I combined these variables – time of settlement, soil, climate, access to transportation, and migration pattern – to define a set of seven regions on the pampa and to demonstrate how the process of regional differentiation led to sharp distinctions from region to region in access to the export market, access to land ownership and, subsequently, to differentiation according to principal mode of production, size of agricultural unit, ethnic composition of the population, percentage of the population gathered in towns, and land tenancy. In this paper, I want to carry the analysis further and focus on the distribution of labour and capital as facets of the adaptive and growth propositions. But, first, I must describe the regions to be studied (see Map 1).

Region 1: Santa Fe Wheat

The ten central counties of Santa Fe province make up this region. This is the area of earliest and most intense agricultural colonisation – the 'old frontier'. Land here was considered marginal before 1860, less desirable than the established pasture and grazing areas of the north-western portion of Buenos Aires province. Although subsequent experience was to show that it was less than ideal for cereal production, easy access to the Paraná River was sufficient to stimulate the production of exportable cereal grains.

Region 2: Northern Wheat

This region includes the established agricultural settlements stretching north-west from the city of Buenos Aires, 31 counties in Buenos Aires province as well as the easternmost county in Córdoba and two counties in the south-west corner of Santa Fe, 34 counties in all. Land here had

Map 1 Boundaries (Pampa Region)

been used as pasture since the eighteenth century and it was from this area that the herds of criollo cattle moved into the southern counties of Buenos Aires province. The black soil in this region was fertile and there was adequate rainfall. For centuries, access to the major urban market had been by oxcart roads and the Paraná River. The railroad tracks crossed this zone not long after they reached out from Rosario. The towns here were among the oldest in the nation, and the population long settled.

Region 3: Southern Wheat

This is a wedge of land south of the Salado River, stretching from the bay of Samborombón on the east to the north-western corner of Buenos Aires, at the boundary with Córdoba and La Pampa, 20 counties in all. The climate of this region is essentially the same as in Region 2, as is the soil quality in the western counties. The land in the eastern half of the region is low and often floods. The entire region was outside the line of effective settlement until 1850 because of the danger of Indian depredations. The only exceptions to this were some small settlements around forts. This is a transitional zone between the older settlements of Region 2 and the newer establishments on the frontier, opened to railroad service almost as soon as Regions 1 and 2. The Ferrocarril del Sud reached Chascomús in 1884, making the eastern section of the region as accessible to Buenos Aires as the western section of region 2.

Region 4: Littoral-South

Included here are three Buenos Aires counties in the River Plate delta and the 14 counties of Entre Ríos. Seven of the Entre Ríos counties, the southern portion of the province, are criss-crossed by rivers and have essentially the same soil and climate as the three counties of Buenos Aires. The northern seven counties of Entre Ríos share soil and climatic characteristics with the northern counties of Santa Fe, but I have joined them with the other counties in the province because the two major rivers, Paraná and Uruguay, give the province a unifying transportation system and cohesion that has stood the test of many years. Colonisation began here later than in Santa Fe, and settlement tended to hug one river or the other. In the 1880s, a railroad line was laid across the centre of the state, from the capital of Paraná to Concepción del Uruguay, linking the two rivers, but the rivers continued to be the principal link to Buenos Aires as late as 1910.

Region 5: New South

The 22 counties in Buenos Aires province stretching inland, south and west, from the bulge around Mar del Plata along the Lobería hills, comprise this region. Although the natural vegetation is classified as 'hard' grasses, excellent soil fertility and adequate rainfall characterise it. Military campaigns in the 1820s and 1830s had attempted to open the area to settlement, but the Indians recaptured large portions and delayed permanent settlement until the 1870s, when cattlemen moved herds from the western part of Region 2 in search of better grazing. Others settled the region by moving north and east from the rapidly developing city of Bahia Blanca. Access to transportation for commodities was virtually non-existent until the railroad came. The tracks of the Ferrocarril del Sud reached Dolores in 1874 but didn't really penetrate the region until ten years later.

Region 6: Western Wheat

The six counties on the eastern flank of the Córdoba hills were characterised by lower rainfall than the Santa Fe region and dark grey, rather than black, soil. The first trunk line in the country crossed the region en route to the city of Córdoba by 1870, but there was virtually no further construction until 1890. Settlements here date back to the colonial era, but they were sparse until a wave of Italian immigration at the end of the nineteenth century. Immigration produced a pattern of smallholdings unique on the pampa.

Region 7: Frontier Wheat

Included here are the 28 counties of the semi-arid pampa covering the westernmost counties of Buenos Aires province, the eastern tier of counties in the La Pampa territory, and the south of San Luis province. This region is characterised by less fertile soil than any of the other regions, and the rainfall is barely adequate for the commercial production of food staples. Access to markets for commodities was only by railway which arrived in the area late in the 1880s and 1890s. Land in the national territory was distributed by the federal government to veterans of the Indian Wars as payment for meritorious service, and to the railroads as a form of subsidy. Much of this land was accumulated in large units by speculators, who included some of the most prominent landowners in Buenos Aires. Beginning in the 1890s, parcels of land were put on the market and resold in smaller units by colonisation societies and land companies, many of which were affiliated with the railroads.

II

The county level data of the 1914 census are the reflection of numerous individual decisions during the long historical process of settlement and expansion. Here are the summaries of literally millions of decisions of labourers to go out on to the land in search of their fortunes, perhaps only for the harvest season, perhaps for a short period under a rental contract, perhaps to settle either as a labourer, a sharecropper, or a small farmer, eking out a living. These were the decisions on how to employ the available production factors in adapting to the environment, adapting so as to participate more efficiently in the production of agricultural surpluses. These were the decisions that gave shape to the land market and, ultimately, determined how the land was to be used.

At the outset of the period of rapid expansion, the land included in the seven regions I have defined was either unoccupied or occupied by unfenced herds of criollo cattle and sheep, attended irregularly by mobile bands of gauchos. By 1914, the pampa had been settled and fenced. Thanks to the railway, virtually every corner of the zone enjoyed access to the major urban centres of the country and through them to the international market. The dramatic growth of the national economy represented a transition from extensive modes of exploiting the land to ever more intensive forms. The most intensive were highly-mechanised cereal farms and labour-intensive fattening of stock for sale to the new British or American meat packing plants or back to the breeders to improve the quality of their herds. But even the so-called extensive mode of exploitation in 1914 was many times more capital-intensive than the grazing on the same land 50 or even 20 years earlier. In the 1860s there was scarcely any blooded stock on the pampa. By the time of the 1914 census, more than 95 per cent of the cattle in the province of Buenos Aires were in that category. A similar transformation had occurred in sheep raising.

In order to raise such stock, it had been necessary to transform the land, to convert the pasture from the hard native grasses to softer cultivated pasturage. Such improvements represented the investment of considerable amounts of capital. By 1914, the total value of pampean agricultural enterprise, exclusive of land, was 10 billion pesos m/n. Some of these improvements were made through the direct investment of capital. A considerable portion, however, was effected by the use of tenant labour. In a typical situation, a rancher might rent out 100 of his 5000 hectares to a tenant for a period of two, three, or even five years, with the stipulation that the land be left fenced and suitable for planting. By the time of the 1914 census, this transition had been completed in the regions closest to Buenos Aires, and was still going forward on the southern frontier.

The various modes of factor utilisation at the time of the census reflect the decision-making power of those in control of the means of production during the period of rapid expansion. In general terms, it also reflects the influence of different types of export agricultural activity in different regions, demonstrating the variety of adaptation to the environment over time, and the gradual imposition by the government of its control over the territory of the nation, especially the northern and southern frontiers where the presence of nomadic tribes of Indians had made settlement and agriculture all but impossible. This was a matter of significance to those who intended to settle the land and to those who planned to invest their time or money in the production of foodstuffs for export. Relative stability in politics after 1880 undoubtedly played a prominent role in the vertiginous speed of the nation's growth in the succeeding 30 years.

The supply of land, labour and capital had to be increased so that production could rise in response to international demand. It was the conviction of Argentina's leaders after 1860 that production for export was the most rational response to market forces, holding out the promise of an adequate return on investment.

Production data will not indicate whether increases were the result of labour inputs or inputs of capital in the form of machines. We can form a fairly clear impression of which it was by associating the various census characteristics with one another. Wheat farming was closely associated with medium-sized units administered by tenants under relatively stable conditions of land tenure. The same syndrome held true throughout the pampa, although on the southern frontier we know that it was considerably harder for immigrants to secure favourable opportunities in cereal farming. In almost all of the regions, concentrations of population were characterised by smallholdings under the most tenuous tenure conditions and by the cultivation of corn. Many of these high-risk agriculturalists on the old frontier were Spaniards, the late arrivals, whereas in other regions the ethnic composition was more heterogeneous.

But how did this settlement pattern affect investment and production?

Argentine observers at the turn of the century believed that only security of tenure would ensure a disposition to make improvements on parcels under contract, and that higher land values such as prevailed around centres of population were an indication of expectations of higher returns on investment and should be associated with higher levels of investment. Whether or not that was true remains to be seen. In proximity to Buenos Aires, the major port and domestic market, there was a pronounced tendency toward capital-intensive agricultural activities – truck farming and fattening of cattle. While land values undoubtedly were higher in areas of concentrated population, such concentrations required many people who were not engaged in agriculture, and provided lucrative alternatives to agricultural production for so-called, prime real estate. The task, then, is to see how site conditions and settlement patterns influenced the relationship between capital and labour.

The straightforward dichotomy in land use between farming and ranching holds up well enough for investment in livestock, which is greater in Region 5 (24 million pesos)[4] than in any other region, although Region 3 had more money invested in cattle ($18 million vs. $16 million). There were more sheep on the southern and western frontiers than in other regions, sheep farming having virtually disappeared from Santa Fe. The value of machinery was fairly uniform across regions, with Regions 3 and 5 the lowest ($43 million each) and Regions 4 and 7 the highest ($58 million and $56 million). This is a statistical reflection of the burgeoning activity around the port of Bahia Blanca, of the recent settlement of both of these regions, and of the soil which required more machines for the cultivation of crops. There, increases in productivity required greater investment in machines. The pattern is consistent with the experience in the US where farms on the great plains were more heavily mechanised than the older, smaller, family farms of New England.

It is surprising that the oldest agricultural section of the country, around the city of Buenos Aires, should have had the lowest average investment in livestock per county (7 million pesos) especially as there were quite a few fattening establishments and famous *cabañas* (stud farms for prize pedigree stock) in the area. Here is another case in which the regional means obscure the structural complexity of the older settlements, the specialisation of economic activities, and the advanced stage of urbanisation. There were many people in Region 2 who were not engaged in agriculture at all. More useful information will be conveyed by ratios of the amounts invested in machinery or livestock to population, the number of agricultural units or land areas. These ratios can be taken as rough indicators of capital intensity. Here, the specialised nature of fattening in Region 2 and in portions of Region 1 shows up. Both regions had twice as much money invested in livestock per hectare committed to ranching than any other region on the pampa.

	Region						
	1	2	3	4	5	6	7
Livestock value $ (pesos) per hectare in ranching	11.86	11.86	5.90	5.96	4.84	5.17	2.70

On the other hand, the ratios of investment in machinery or livestock to population are as much the expression of high population levels as low investment figures. The lower ratios in Regions 1, 4 and 6 are an indication, also, of widespread smallholdings.

	Region						
	1	2	3	4	5	6	7
Livestock value $ (pesos) per capita	356	614	1 537	549	2 151	464	1 585
Machinery value $ (pesos) per capita	1 382	4 210	3 629	2 539	6 852	1 282	16 611

A more precise sense of capital intensity in farming is derived from the ratio of capital invested in machines to the number of hectares devoted to agriculture or, more specifically, to the cultivation of export staple crops (essentially wheat and corn), even though the census variable refers to all machinery and not merely to those used exclusively for farming. Region 2 was far and away the leader in machine-intensive farming, nearly two-and-a-half times more than the wheat-growing, old frontier. The ratio of machines to hectares planted in export staples carries the comparison one step further. If the agriculture in a region were devoted to the production of export grains, this ratio should approximate the ratio between machinery and all the hectares in a county devoted to any kind of agricultural activity. The greater the difference between the two ratios, the less dedicated the region to export agriculture. The two extremes within the pampean zone are Regions 1 and 6 on the one hand and 5 and 7 on the other, with the former almost totally given over to the cultivation of export staples. Outside the pampa, the tremendous difference between the two ratios indicates the insignificant role of export agriculture anywhere except on the pampa.

	Entire Country	1	2	3	Region 4	5	6	7
Machinery value $ (pesos) per hectare in agriculture	1 186	182	489	173	301	176	92	114
Machinery value $ (pesos) per hectare in export staples	643 000	467	10 000	2 000	4 000	12 000	197	490 000

Other comparative measures of investment in agricultural machinery indicate dramatically lower levels per farm unit in Santa Fe and Córdoba than in any other region. This suggests that the small cereal units so common in densely populated areas were virtually bereft of machines and that even the larger units in the colonies were not highly mechanised. Memoirs and studies of life on the colonies report that such machinery as existed was shared through co-operatives, and that it was common for families to provide all the labour necessary to farm the land.[5] With or without machines, there was an overwhelming dedication on the old frontier to the production of exportable cereal grains. A far higher percentage of the land in Region 1 was cultivated in export staples (55.3 per cent) than in any other region, although every region on the pampa except Region 5 (8.1 per cent) exceeded the national average (9.0 per cent). If we exclude corn, a traditional crop associated with subsistence farming and domestic consumption, the differences are sharper.

Another measure of investment is the capitalisation of agricultural units, the value placed by the administrator on the buildings and other improvements. These data are summarised in Table 2.1. The declared value of all agricultural units on the Santa Fe frontier and in Córdoba

TABLE 2.1 *Capital invested in agriculture, 1914 (by region)*

Investment category	Entire country	1	2	3	4	5	6	7
Total capital stock of all units:	$4 258	$12 818	$5 882	$7 960	$6 929	$6 045	$13 592	$7 072
Capital stock of units by size:								
25 hectares or less	784	1 471	859	497	900	353	462	354
Units 26–50 hectares	310	1 205	446	376	599	179	370	127
Units 51–100 hectares	381	2 266	878	534	893	229	854	269
Units 101–500 hectares	1 025	5 753	1 966	1 736	2 326	1 131	6 414	2 071
Units 501–1000 hectares	280	505	400	626	376	836	1 532	917
Units greater than 1000 hectares	865	1 222	1 117	2 418	1 200	2 590	3 200	2 664

NOTE All figures are the calculated mean for counties in each region, in thousands of pesos, moneda nacional.

was nearly twice that of any other region. For all size categories of units up to 500 hectares, the capitalisation rankings are Regions 1, 4, 2, 3 and 5, with six and seven somewhat of an anomaly. Above 500 hectares, the order is often the reverse, 6, 7, 5, 3, 1, 4, and 2. Taking into account the number of hectares in agriculture, capitalisation levels are highest in Regions 1 and 2 (42 and 40 pesos per hectare), falling off rapidly in the lands of more recent settlement to a low of 12 pesos per hectare in region 7. This does not mean, however, that farming in the newer frontiers was unsupported by capital inputs. As I stated previously, by 1914 even extensive grazing was an enterprise that required considerable resources.

Measured against total population, capitalisation of agricultural units was greatest in Region 7 (654 pesos per capita) and least in Regions 1 and 4 (290 and 255 pesos per capita), which supplies further evidence for the proposition that increases in production in Santa Fe and Entre Ríos – the colonisation zone – were the results of labour inputs, not capital inputs. Similar ratios, such as capitalisation per agricultural unit or per individual engaged in agriculture, place Regions 5 and 3 above 7, with 1, 4 and 6 at the lower end of the scale. These data are entirely consistent with the proposition that the type of economic activity, the settlement patterns and functional differentiation in these various regions were inextricably related. Agriculture in Regions 5 and 3 was primarily ranching, and cereal farming tended to be on larger units than any of the other regions. The amount of capital invested was significant, particularly in terms of the relatively sparse population, though in terms of the unit of productive land it was less intensive than either Regions 1 or 2. Regions 7, 6 and 1 had large numbers of under-capitalised units, together with economically-viable cereal farms that undoubtedly were the principal source of the exportable surpluses that were produced in those regions and were more mechanised than the smallholdings of Santa Fe or Córdoba. Unlike Santa Fe, the cereal farming syndrome in the dry zone was closely associated – statistically, if not geographically – with ranching on vast parcels of land, ranches on which the livestock was worth much less per head than on the same kinds of units in Regions 3 and 5, and which were capitalised at lower levels than in either of the other ranching areas. A similar pattern held in Region 4, reflecting the presence of the fever tick and the depressed price of land, which facilitated the access of the less wealthy to land ownership.

While the distinction between labour intensive and capital intensive regions may be sufficiently clear from the data on capitalisation, additional analysis of the labour supply will help us understand the differentiation in social organisation from region to region. For example, the area around Tandil and Lobería (region 5) was dedicated to extensive agriculture and had no colonies. In fact, as has been shown in other studies, the nature of the credit system, the land market, and the high rate of return on extensive holdings were obstacles in the path of those trying to enter the region and begin a life as independent agriculturalists on modest holdings. It is not surprising, therefore, that greater use was made of wage labour than in any other region on the pampa.

	Region						
	1	2	3	4	5	6	7
Wage Earners as a % of the agricultural labour force	12.8	16.9	20.2	15.7	24.2	13.4	24.3

Those who worked for wages fell into two categories: administrators of ranches and farms, who were paid a salary, and hired hands. The latter constituted by far the larger group – 90 per cent of all those dependent upon wages. In Region 5, more than 22 per cent of those engaged in agriculture were male labourers, nearly twice the proportion of Region 1 (12 per cent). Indeed, in Region 1 there were fewer male employees (2116) than there were administrators of agricultural units (2430). Except perhaps at harvest time, hired hands were not used. Farming was a family or colony affair. Not so on the southern frontier, where there were two employees for every administrator and where there were very nearly as few administrators earning wages (8.4 per cent) as there were in Region 1 (6.7 per cent). Employees and their families constituted over 40 per cent of the agricultural population in Region 5 compared to 17 per cent on the old frontier.[6]

For the most part, the area around the city of Buenos Aires had proportionately as few employees as the old frontier. The major exception was the category of administrators working for wages. In this crude measure of absentee ownership, the oldest settlements ranked first; confirmation that the fattening establishments and other capital intensive forms of agriculture were run by professional managers, that the owners lived in the metropolis and dedicated themselves to politics, the professions or commerce, and that agriculture in this region, unlike either of the frontiers, was considered essentially a form of business. This was especially the case on rented fattening establishments where the capital structure of the enterprise, often based on short-term loans from the Banco de la Nación, most closely approximated commercial establishments.[7]

The sheer magnitude of his investment in agriculture must have affected the attitude of the individual entrepreneur and agriculturalist toward his land and the use he made of it. The owner's stake in land undoubtedly influenced decisions on planting, harvesting, producing for the domestic market or the export market, shifting between cattle herds and cereal grains, making improvements in holdings, the assumption of debt, and the like. One available measure of a county's stake in agriculture is a summary figure representing capital stock plus the total value of machinery and livestock – the total known investment in agriculture in the county less the value of the land itself. We can use this figure and its component elements to compare the nature of investment in the different pampean regions.

The data suggest homogenity across the pampa, especially in comparison with the rest of the country. The calculated means for the countries in each region are remarkably similar. All the regions on the pampa have at least 20 per cent more capital invested in agriculture than the national average.

	Entire Country	Region						
		1	2	3	4	5	6	7
Total capital invested in agriculture (in millions of paper pesos)	57.1	76.3	70.9	73.7	79.9	73.9	83.6	80.2

There was a great deal of capital invested all over the pampa, nearly twice as much as the county average in other sections of the country, and discussion must avoid the trap of considering extensive modes of exploitation as anything approximating 'traditional' in the sense of self-sufficient. Taken in the aggregate, pampean agriculture by 1914 was a commercial enterprise or a variety of commercial enterprises, requiring considerable amounts of capital resources or access to credit.

The capital intensity of export agricultural production can be taken as a reflection of the competition for land use among available sustenance functions, and as an indicator of the distribution of resources in the society. More specifically, it should tell us about the shift between breeding and fattening and farming, thereby providing useful information about the nature of social organisation from region to region. There are several ways to measure capital intensity with the county level census data: controlling for the number of male employees, the number of persons engaged in agriculture, the number of agricultural units and the number of hectares devoted to agriculture in that county.

Taking land as the control, we see that the region around the federal capital had the biggest stake in agriculture per hectare (555 pesos) and that Córdoba had the least (121 pesos). Córdoba was a region that had been devoted to extensive grazing for many years and, at the time of the 1914 census, had only recently attracted large numbers of immigrants; it was in the early stages of breaking up the larger units into very small holdings. These *minifundia* represented insignificant capital investments. Way out on the southern frontier, Region 7, the ratio was very nearly as low (142 pesos), whereas Regions 3 (242 pesos) and 5 (241 pesos) were almost identical to the northern frontier (224 pesos), an indication that in terms of land use, the different forms of export agriculture required similar capital inputs. Obviously, grazing required larger units of land, but as the cost of land was lower in Region 5 than in Regions 1 or 2, the total cost of starting a unit of production directed toward the international market may have been comparable; most of the evidence indicates that the profitability of the larger units was greater than the more intensively cultivated cereal farms on the old frontier, and may even have been greater than in the fattening establishments of Region 2, the most capital-intensive units of production on the pampa.[8]

The differences between old and new frontier are sharpest in ratios of investment to population in agriculture or to employees.

	Region						
	1	2	3	4	5	6	7
Capital invested in agriculture per 1000 population engaged in agriculture	4.6	14	12	9	24	4.4	14.7
Capital invested in agriculture per 100 male employees (in millions of paper pesos)	45	85	72	71.5	92	39	65

In both of these, the immigrant farming areas of Regions 1 and 6 are anywhere from half to one-fifth as capital-intensive. For Region 4, where immigration came late and covered only a portion of the counties, the ratios are half way between the two extremes. In these areas, labour inputs were required to bring the land into production. Since the farmer did not have access to credit, so closely restricted by the state, he had recourse to his labour and the labour of his family. This is a form of investment that is relatively inflexible and cannot be subdivided. The agricultural unit dependent upon labour inputs or the purchase of machinery for increments in its level of production has much less freedom in coping with the market than units dependent upon wage labour, assuming a constant supply, or upon inexpensive capital used to hire machines or bring under-exploited units of land into production. In labour intensive areas, increasing production meant increasing productivity; in areas of extensive cultivation such increases were relatively simpler and quite literally might involve bringing under cultivation or fencing land that had been barely used to graze creole cattle. The distinction between northern and southern frontiers is fully as dramatic when we control for the number of agricultural units. The total capital per unit was six times greater in Region 5 (220) than in either Region 1 (34) or 6 (34), and was even greater than in Region 2 (100) where the units were generally smaller and more intensively exploited.

The southern frontier was the locus of large ranches on which significant capital improvements had been made. There were crucial differences between Regions 5 and 3, reflecting different stages in the transition from traditional grazing to more commercial, more capital-intensive modes of production, either mixed agricultural or the fattening of pedigree stock. Without question, Regions 5 and 7 were dominated by breeders, whereas Region 3 was characterised by a mixture of fatteners and breeders, and Region 2 by the dominance of fatteners on smaller units, many of them rented by entrepreneurs who achieved startling leverage on their investments through inexpensive lines of credit provided by the Banco de la Nación. More than half of all the acreage devoted to ranching in this region was leased. On the southern frontier, cereal farming was an activity most often carried out on fairly large units, certainly larger than the typical farm in Regions 1, 4 or 6, and typically dependent upon wage labour rather than family labour and more disposed to investments in machinery. Purchases of expensive machinery made more sense on larger units. On the smaller units, such investments could not be amortised and over the years a peculiar form of contractual mechanisation evolved so that the expense of the machine could be shared by many of the producers in the area.[9]

These measures of capital intensity have to be related to the demographic characteristics of the community. In statistical terms the adaptation to demographic parameters can be expressed as correlation coefficients between variables measuring investment and variables measuring population. For all three investment categories, capital stock, livestock and machinery, there is a strong positive relationship in Region 5 with total population, which weakens considerably when density of settlement in the county is taken into account. The relationships are as follows:

Capital stock to total population	.75
Capital stock to density	.38
Value of livestock to total population	.61
Value of livestock to density	.18
Number of machines to total population	.68
Number of machines to density	.27

Of course, to some extent these coefficients indicate merely that there was more money where there were more people, or that the larger counties had more capital than the smaller. The absence of significant correlations with density suggests that on the southern frontier the most valuable units of production were not necessarily closest to the towns and the railheads. The time–money cost of transportation was not critical to breeders. The reverse is true for fatteners and the correlation coefficients are quite different in Regions 3 and 2, reflecting the transition to more capital intensive modes of production for which the access to transportation was critical.

As the process of national consolidation unfolded, Argentina's leaders sought first to pacify the hinterland and then to make it accessible to the international market. Once those objectives had been accomplished, they felt the nation's comparative advantage to be an adequate attraction for the labour and capital required to put the fertile land into production. It is interesting that contemporaries of Alberdi in the 1850s and 1860s, and reformers in the Ministry of Agriculture 50 years later, were convinced that a class of land-owning yeomen would be most likely to respond to the European demand for foodstuffs by making investments on their properties to increase productivity. The link between disposition to invest and landownership was assumed. Studies published in the early years of the twentieth century observed the pattern of tenancy that had evolved on the pampa and spoke darkly of a tenant's unwillingness to make investments on land that never could be his or, worse, of the tenant who 'raped' the land to make a profit, without concern for restoring its fertility by the use of fertilisers or crop rotation.[11] Some tenants certainly yearned to own their own parcel and were reluctant to invest more than their labour on the land they rented. But many tenants invested a great deal of capital in their agricultural enterprises, and did so under various tenancy conditions.

Investment in livestock in a county tended to vary inversely with the concentration of short, expensive contracts and with farming contracts written in cash. The only exception to this was in Region 6 where small farming units were carved out of large undercapitalised ranches. Thus, the same strong, positive relationship holds in that region for livestock investment and the concentration of long ranching contracts, whereas in those counties where long term farming contracts were common, investment in livestock tended to be low. In Region 3, the correlation between livestock investment and length of contract is most pronounced ($r = .66$). There is a similar pattern, though slightly less pronounced, in Region 5, where length of contract was correlated with an apparent disposition to improve cattle herds ($r = .42$). The same pattern is repeated across the pampa; the higher the concentration of long contracts, the greater the disposition to increase investment in animals, machines, or buildings, all of which were signs of commitment, of a willingness to take risks in the interests of profit.

The picture changes when the intensity of capital inputs is taken into account. In many of the regions there is a positive relationship between short contracts and contracts written in cash and high rates of investment per hectare. This is particularly pronounced in Region 2 where we know fattening establishments to have been concentrated, where the high price of land required high levels of economic rent, and where earning profits required greater commitments of capital than in other regions. Indeed, the commercial quality of agricultural activity in the area closest to the port of Buenos Aires was such that the intensity of investment was inversely proportional to the concentration of long-term ranching contracts. The relationships are similar but not statistically significant for Regions 3 and 5. In Region 4, the high positive correlation between intensive investment and short or expensive contracts is a function of the differentiation represented by colonisation ($r = .89$). When we take into account the extraordinarily high portion of ranch land in Region 2 that was rented, we might conclude that export agriculture there was based on minimising fixed capital investment. By comparison, out on the southern frontier, in the area more inclined to breeding, the lower incidence of ranching tenancy, together with the higher proportion of the value of livestock to total capital invested, suggests the dominance of an agricultural activity slightly less commercial in its organisation and slightly less flexible in its ability to respond to short term shifts in the market. On the other hand, the use of tenant labour to realise improvements in the land represented a form of saving capital for alternative uses, making the landowner less dependent upon the accessibility of credit.[12]

The landholding pattern, as an indicator of the differentiation in each region, reflects the characteristics of the dominant mode of the region's economic activity, its social structure, and the hierarchy of power among the different activities. On the southern frontier, and in sections of Entre Ríos, owners of large units of land were functionally dominant – theirs was the activity that represented the most efficient adaptation to the environment – and they exercised their dominance in various ways like easier access to credit, higher social status, and greater political influence. In Santa Fe and Córdoba, holders of smaller units were more numerous. The excessively small size of the most common unit in Córdoba, less than 50 hectares, suggests that smallholders could not have generated enough capital to have exercised dominance and were in any case dependent upon others – wholesalers, suppliers, creditors, etc. – to determine their relationship to the market. In the zone of colonies in Santa Fe, the medium-sized cereal unit predominated statistically and functionally, but the dominance of the activity in a national or pampean hierarchy of export agriculture is questionable. The labour intensity of the colonies, and the nature of their social relationships, implied that the individual producer was locked into his activity and scarcely had a realistic option in bad times to continuing his activity and piling up debt; in the medium and long term the producer was dependent upon others to market his product and to provide the capital buffer necessary to withstand sharp adverse movements in prices.

Proximity to the city of Buenos Aires, the nation's principal port and domestic market, together with the quality of the land, drove up the anticipated economic rent payable to agriculture in the northern tier of counties in the province of Buenos Aires, and contributed over time to the subdivision of the larger units and to the dissemination of capital-intensive modes of production. Here, owning large units of land did not of itself confer functional dominance on the producer; he earned it literally by the profits of his enterprise. The peculiar system of ranching tenancy that came to characterise this region by 1914 represents an efficient adaptation to the environment by using state institutions to minimise risk. If the market turned against the tenant fattener, he could sell out and put his capital into other activities. Under these conditions, he avoided making fixed investments on the lands he rented, and restricted his investment as nearly as he could to the purchase of young cows and a tiny permanent staff of administrators. He reduced his fixed capital further by borrowing the money he needed at low rates of interest from the Banco de la Nación. In this region, perhaps more than any other, direct access to bank credit was vital to the maintenance of the profitability of the dominant organizational form, and consequently to the decision-making independence of the individual producer and his exercise of functional dominance.

Out on the southern frontier functional dominance was exercised by the activity of extensive grazing, generally breeding, in combination with commercial farming and, less frequently, with fattening on the improved portions of relatively large units of land. Tenant entrepreneurs were far less common than in the north of the province, and commercial agriculture tended to be an activity for landowners. Assuming he owned the lands he administered, the producer in Regions 3, 5, and 7 had a higher ratio of fixed capital than his compatriot in the north. Given his commitment to the land and to the breeding of cows, he enjoyed far less flexibility in the face of market forces than his northern colleague. However, in the long run, he had open to him the triple alternatives already mentioned – breeding, fattening and the commercial cultivation of cereals. Theoretically, of course, assuming a liquid market for land, he could also sell his holdings and capitalise the investments he had been making over the years. The strong, highly speculative market for land on the pampa for nearly ten years prior to the census undoubtedly served to strengthen the producers' commitment to the land.[13] Following the First World War, when the land market became less frenetic, the ranchers on the southern frontier became the focus of a bitter political debate that threatened to create a sharp sectoral cleavage between fatteners and breeders. At the time of the census, however, the principal distinctions between the two activities were the greater capital intensity of the former and the high rate of return per hectare of the latter. At the same time, the widespread presence of tenancy among fatteners served to inhibit fixed capital investments in that sector as well, leading ultimately to the peculiar pattern of Argentine agriculture in which low productivity has been such a dominant feature.

From this perspective two forms of economic activity on the pampa appear to have enjoyed a clear advantage and to have translated that advantage into other areas of social and political dominance. The first was fattening blooded cattle on medium sized units (from 100 to 1000 hectares), often rented, fairly close to the meat-packing plants and the port of Buenos Aires, and with direct access to low cost official bank credit. The easy credit provided the leverage necessary to ensure the rate of return on a capital-intensive investment, while for tenants the short duration of the contracts provided maximum mobility. The changing structure of European demand, and technological advances in refrigeration during the period of expansion provided this group with a comparative advantage over other modes of production which they exploited to the full, dominating Argentine society and politics during the entire half century of expansion prior to the centennial, and for many years thereafter.

The other form of activity which could adapt best to changes in the international market was ranching on the southern frontier, in Regions 3 and 5, where portions or all of the land had been converted to soft grasses or forage for pedigree stock, and where the labour supply allowed for a relatively rapid switch between grazing and the cultivation of cereal crops. In 1914, this form of mixed commercial agriculture was so new that the census takers failed to provide a separate category for it, an omission corrected in the subsequent agricultural census of 1937. This transitional mode of agriculture, in the combination of capitalisation per unit, the relatively large size of the units, the high concentration of land in a relatively few hands, and the greater reliance upon wage labour, served to maximise the decision-making flexibility of the landowner and increased his ability to react to market forces over the long term. As the structure of demand for the exportable staples changed, those engaged in transitional agriculture were better able than their fellows to adjust their employment of production factors in the effort to satisfy that demand. In the short term, from year to year, their ability to react to changes in price for the products they could or did produce was a function of their access to capital. While less capital-intensive forms of grazing were still highly profitable by 1914, the crisis of the First World War undermined the dominant position in the Argentine hierarchy of those dedicated exclusively to breeding, and, in the 1920s, they began to lose power to those closer to the market in the production sequence, especially the fatteners and those engaged in mixed or transitional agriculture.

Compared to these two modes of production others on the pampa, even if they were ecologically dominant in a particular region, were at a distinct disadvantage in terms of their ability to react to the international market and, as a result, in terms of their capacity to influence decisions at the national level concerning distribution of the society's resources or the relationship of the state to the production process. Where the expansion of agricultural production was accomplished by massive inputs of labour in the form of immigrant settlers (generally sharecroppers or members of a colony), flexibility was restricted to working harder, cultivating the modest parcels of land more intensively or making small, incremental investments in capital stock or machinery. Typically, the colonist on the Santa Fe frontier or in Entre Ríos or La Pampa and the tenant farmer anywhere on the pampa, went to work on the land with little or no capital resources. His start-up costs would be covered by a loan from the colonial *empresario*, the landowner, or, most frequently, a local representative of a commercial firm interested in purchasing the forthcoming crop. The modest producer's ability to make money and accumulate capital was a function of how quickly he could get rid of his burden of debt. By contrast, it has been suggested that holders of large units of unimproved or partially-improved land on the southern frontier, whose land appreciated dramatically as the centennial approached, may have accumulated capital too quickly, in the sense that they made money without additional capital inputs, thereby locking themselves into a pattern of regional differentiation that inhibited their later adjustment to a dramatically changed market after 1930.

Rich or poor, smallholder or largeholder, in any region of the pampa, the producer's capacity to reallocate production factors in response to market forces was a function of his liquidity. On a given parcel of land, discounting unexpected cost-free advances in technology, production could be increased by adding labour, by adding machinery, by upgrading the quality of the herd, or by making other improvements. All of these cost money – money that might be borrowed or accumulated in the form of profits; therefore access to credit became a factor in human ecology just like weather or access to transportation. In such an historical situation, access to credit – indispensable to economic growth – becomes a measure of position in a market hierarchy, and the control over credit becomes an important indicator of power in the export economy and in the society.

Throughout this study I have argued that as social organisation and the distribution of production factors at the local level – measured by the county level data taken from the 1914 census – reflected disparities of power within the community, these disparities were a function of the adaptation of the community's particular mode of production to the international market. I have demonstrated that modes of production varied from region to region for historical and ecological reasons, and that the dominance of one form of organisation over others was the result of entrepreneurial flexibility in the face of external market forces. This flexibility was less the product of any specific relationship between capital and labour than of access to credit and to the international market.

NOTES

1. The most comprehensive discussion of these indices is Carlos F. Díaz Alejandro, *Essays on the Economic History of the Argentine Republic* (New Haven: Yale University Press, 1970).
2. Amos Hawley, 'Human Ecological and Marxian Theory', manuscript.
3. 'El crédito agrario en la Argentina, 1910–1925', *Desarrollo Económico*, no. 71 (Oct.–Dec. 1978).
4. Figures here and below are the calculated means of counties in each region in paper pesos.
5. For example, see Isaac Kaplan, *Recuerdos de un agrario cooperativista*, Alberto Gerchunoff, *Entre Ríos, Mi País*, and Enrique Dickmann, *Recuerdos de un militante socialista*. Studies of the area include Mark Jefferson, *Peopling the Argentina Pampa*, and Carl C. Taylor, *Rural Life in Argentina*. Here, as in so many instances, the calculated means can hide diversity. In Regions 4 and 7, there were colonies cheek by jowl with large ranches and these measurements of capital intensity show unusual range across the counties within each region. The means in such cases is an arbitrary measurement of marginal utility. I shall not include frequency tables because I am concerned with gross distinctions at this juncture.
6. The 1914 census figures on agricultural labour are flawed because of the curious decision by the census takers not to record the category of temporary labourers. A comprehensive study by the Centro de Estudios y Investigaciones Laborales has corrected the census figures by comparing them to similar data from prior and subsequent surveys: see Floreal Forni *et al.*, 'Estructura Ocupacional de Sector Agropecuario Argentino 1914–1969' (Buenos Aires: CEIL, 1977) mimeo.
7. A survey of the records of one important firm, Adolfo Bullrich y Cía., suggests that large consignment firms managed many farms and ranches, particularly in the areas closest to Buenos Aires. These units were run as commercial establishments, with carefully kept, detailed accountancy books. I am grateful to Jorge Bullrich for granting me access to these records. On the commercial character of fattening establishments, see Jorge F. Sábato, 'Agricultura y ganadería en la pampa argentina: 1890–1930' (Buenos Aires: CISEA, 1978), mimeo, who argues that the distinction between fattening and breeding is vital to any understanding of agricultural production in Argentina. As I shall make clear I consider such a dichotomous distinction inadequate and prefer to analyse the commercial character of agricultural production on the basis of regional differences in the employment of production factors.
8. See Flichman, 'Por que Pergamino no es Iowa?' (Buenos Aires: CEDES, 1978).

9. On the contratistas, see Flichman, *La renta del suelo*; F. Forni and Raul H. Bisio, 'Empleo rural en la república argentina 1937–1969' (Buenos Aires: CEIL, 1977), Documento de Trabajo, no. 1.
10. All of these are expressed as Pearson correlation coefficients (*r*).
11. See, among many others, E. Lahitte, *Informes y Estudios*, M. A. Cárcano, *La propiedad de la tierra en la república argentina*, and E. S. Zeballos, *La tierra amena*.
12. See Sábato, 'Agricultura y ganadería', on the differentiation between breeding and fattening as economic activities. For a discussion of functional specialisation and disparities of power among types of community organisation, see Hawley, 'Human Ecology', and Berry and Kasarda, *Contemporary Urban Ecology*.
13. I am grateful to Roberto Cortés Conde for pointing this out to me. This information forms part of his research on the land market in the province of Buenos Aires at the time of the economic boom.

3 The Argentine Export Economy: Intimations of Mortality, 1894–1930

TULIO HALPERÍN

One of the most striking aspects of the retrospective view of that stage of Argentine economic history dominated by the expansion of exports is the consistently gloomy image proposed for a period during which economic growth took place at a speed infrequently paralleled in other areas and periods. The reader would expect this to be a consequence of the disappointing performance of the Argentine economy in more recent times: whatever could be said for the export-dominated stage, it appears obvious that it did not effectively prepare the country's economy to face the more complex challenges that became unavoidable from the Depression.

As I shall show in these pages, this is not quite the case; retrospective gloom was anticipated by an undercurrent of pessimism that can be detected as early as 1894. In that year Estanislao Zeballos, then Argentine representative in Washington, published a report on *La concurrencia universal y la agricultura en ambas Américas* that cast the first doubts on the spontaneous ability of Argentine grain agriculture to hold its own in the world markets, and asked for complex protective policies to ensure its future. This was indeed a new note: 11 years earlier the same Zeballos had offered in *La región del trigo* (the second volume of his *Descripción amena de la República Argentina*)[1] a more panoramic view of the present and future of Argentine agriculture, dominated by a constant admiration for the changes already introduced by agricultural expansion within the very fabric of Argentine society. The rosy panorama opened with the symbolic figure of Doña Eulogia Llanos, the aristocratic lady from Zeballos' native town of Rosario, on the Paraná river, who had led a life of more than Roman simplicity in blissful ignorance of the world. Changes started to happen; Rosario was flooded with trade and foreigners, Doña Eulogia's elder son lost a valuable section of his *estancia* needed for the railway line from Rosario to Córdoba; her younger son had his fleet of carts put out of business by the same railway. Doña Eulogia herself, who made her bread and her soap like a Roman matron and, very much in the style of Rosario, sold it to the public, could not survive the competition of bakery bread and imported soap. In desperation, she solemnly removed the engraved portrait of President Mitre from its place of honour in her spartan parlour and threw it into the well: he was guilty of the destruction of the town and province that Doña Eulogia knew and loved. Ten years later, Zeballos went back to his native town, and it was indeed a new and splendid city; only Doña Eulogia's parlour was as spartan as it had been ten years earlier. But Doña Eulogia was a new woman: she was now a wealthy real-estate owner, her children were prosperous merchants in the new agricultural colony of Candelaria, and her elder son had sold his *estancia* at an incredibly high price; General Mitre's portrait, none the worse for its period in the well, was back in its place of honour.

Doña Eulogia and the entire nation marched then towards a future of infinitely expanding vistas of growing prosperity and greatness. This, Zeballos tells us, is a true story; it is also an exemplary tale anticipating the redemption of a whole nation by agriculture. What is remarkable here is not only the systematic optimism of Zeballos' economic projections, but – perhaps even more – the fact that in his own thinking the quick rise to unheard-of prosperity was a sign of something more complex and valuable: namely, the rise to a new stage of civilisation unknown to Argentina in the past and only dimly anticipated in its present.

This remarkable approach to the expansion of grain agriculture, that saw it both as an economic and as an existential alternative to stock raising, was already well entrenched in Argentine ideological tradition when Zeballos wrote his *Región del Trigo*. Since the late eighteenth century, a narrowly economic view of the opportunities for the Pampa region barely held its own against a more complex perspective that favoured agriculture not as the most desirable economic use of the regional resources but as a precondition for the emergence of a civilised lifestyle. In the 1780s the Bishop of Córdoba, fray José Antonio de San Alberto, offered perhaps the first rough draft of a view of Argentine problems that Sarmiento was to describe more vividly and, together with Alberdi, was to focus on the issue of population. In the countryside, San Alberto discovered with horror, there were not enough people to sustain a network of social relations, 'cada vecino es un pueblo aparte'.² These preconceptions found their way into the writings of the Enlightenment economists: in the opinion of Hipólito Vieytes, in the first decade of the new century, economic forces left to themselves would impose an almost total concentration on stock raising, which could not support a happy, polished, numerous and prosperous rural population. He called for the Crown, the Church and learned men to join in an effort to create a more complex economy and society on the pampa. The opposite view was held by don Félix de Azara; in his opinion the region was destined by nature to stock raising and, by concentrating on this activity, it would achieve the only kind of prosperity really available – a paradoxical prosperity that would make it possible to sustain a minuscule population well provided with the basic necessities of life, but not with the amenities available even to the poor in less marginal areas.³

The two alternative approaches were inherited by the independent Republic. From 1820 on, while the pastoral economy developed vigorously, the worsening political crisis gave a new urgency to the arguments in favour of the first view: in the opinion of the enemies of Rosas, the whole nation had paid a heavy price for allowing the country dwellers to live in backwardness, isolation and squalor, and these were the social consequences of the kind of stock raising economy that had developed on the pampas. After the fall of Rosas, this viewpoint was still dominant, although once in power his enemies found the correction of these inveterate ills less urgent; in 1868 Sarmiento again expressed these basic assumptions in his speech in Chivilcoy, and promised to change the very face of the country by creating a 100 agricultural colonies that would promote a new level of civilisation in the barbarous countryside.

Bartolomé Mitre, Sarmiento's predecessor in the Presidency, in another speech to the Chivilcoy farmers, offered a point-by-point rebuttal of Sarmiento's traditional approach. His argument was basically economic: stock raising had won the day because it was able to integrate land, labour and capital in proportions adequate to their local availability; by doing so it gave the region the chance to create vigorous links with the world economy. But he went beyond economics: Buenos Aires owed its vast territories to its pastoral vocation; cattle had conquered the land as effectively as the arms of Spain. Moreover, the social consequences of a stock raising economy had been much maligned: the rural population of Buenos Aires was not only more productive, but also happier, more free and more prosperous than that of agricultural Chile. The Chivilcoy farmers, according to Mitre, understood their own interests better than Sarmiento. While Sarmiento went on preaching the gospel of agriculture and promising to create 100 wheat-growing Chivilcoys, the farmers had quietly started to raise sheep.[4]

When, finally, grain agriculture began its expansion on the pampa, the almost eschatological view of the prospects it opened for Argentina became only slightly less dominant than in earlier decades. Grain still offered one of the frames of reference employed to understand the specific issues of agricultural development, and its influence can easily be detected in Zeballos' feverish expectations for his province and his country in 1883. From then on it was to be felt mostly as a reminder of a lofty dream that somehow failed to become reality. After the shock of 1891 the pace of agricultural expansion became frantic, but the social context of this expansion diverged more and more from the one foreseen by those who had expected Argentine regeneration to come from agriculture. The prophecy of future greatness gradually gave way to a more gloomy view of the present and the future, but even then the assumptions held by so many illustrious Argentines since Bourbon times were to colour many analyses of the shortcomings of Argentine agriculture.

This influence was now perhaps more pervasive, but it was also more elusive. While, in the past, economic arguments – namely, the comparative advantages of stock raising – were confronted by social, political and cultural ones, the deleterious influence of stock raising on Argentine society – now become an economic argument (the need for the Argentine economy to prepare for a difficult future) – ran very close to a socio-politico-cultural argument that stressed the desirability of reforming social relations in the farmlands in ways that would define a more harmonious, more fair, more civilised national lifestyle. So close were they, indeed, that it was not always clear that they were different, and that the remedies proposed with the first issue in mind were not necessarily the most likely to satisfy the more complex aspirations that inspired the second.

These aspirations went beyond economic prosperity: they centred around the creation of a rural society dominated by a class of prosperous farmers, free both of excessive economic inequalities and of the dead weight of peasant traditionalism. By the late 1890s it had become painfully clear that the kind of society that was emerging in the newly-settled farmlands did not come close to this ambitious model. Differences were to be found in every aspect of rural life, but behind all these manifold shortcomings observers felt the negative influence of the limited access of farmers to landed property; this was the first cause of the disappointing success of the experiment in national regeneration through shifts in dominant agricultural staples.

From the start, farmers tilling their own family-sized plots had been less dominant than the model required: after the 1874 economic crisis they lost some additional terrain to tenant-farmers, and in the 1890s, precisely when Argentina became an important exporter of grain to overseas markets, tenant-farmers emerged as typical on the pampa. While all this was happening, a solid consensus was maintained around the notion that this development was intrinsically wrong. Retrospectively, this may seem surprising: these were times when social conflict was rife in Argentina, and contrasting views on issues related to it were boldly stated, both in favour and against the existing order of things. Not so for grain agriculture: here the evils of *latifundio* were a subject of universal condemnation, and the absence of a more equal, and – so it was assumed – *eo ipso* economically more productive land tenure pattern in the new agricultural regions was also a matter of universal regret.

By the end of this period, Dr Miguel Angel Cárcano offered in his *Evolución histórica del régimen de la tierra pública* an authoritative summation of what, in his view, had been the most important, missed opportunity in Argentine history. While the tone of the book was by no means pessimistic, it stressed the urgency of tackling the land tenure problem before it was too late. In his prologue, Eleodoro Lobos – a respected, Conservative, senior statesman – stressed the consensus that supported Cárcano's conclusion; 'the extremist and the conservative tendencies in Argentine politics today', he said, 'share in this aspiration'.[5]

This consensus was not the result of the belated adoption by the conservatives of views first introduced by the extremists. The opposite is the case: dissatisfaction with a land tenure pattern dominated by large properties was – as we have already seen – present from very early in the ideological tradition on which the Argentine conservative creed had been built. While this is true, it is also true that, if Argentina had a dominant class, this was the landowning class. The very fact that the aspiration for a new society based on a vast class of independent farmers survived for so long without challenge is indeed surprising. Even more surprising is that when some members of the landed élite, overcoming the disinclination towards intellectual exertion so common among them, took part in the debate, it was to join in the at first hopeful and later melancholy chorus that sang the praise of rural democracy.

This very fact, however, would suggest that, while this almost religious faith in the redemptive social value of farming in family plots could not fail to influence actual policy proposals, its influence was to be felt more ambiguously than the often blunt condemnation of the existing conditions would lead one to expect.

Roberto Campolieti's writings offer a conveniently complete inventory of the main themes explored in detail by critics of the conditions under which agriculture expanded from the 1890s. These writings cover three decades, from 1897 to 1929, during which the Italian agronomist advanced essentially the same basic thoughts, adapted each time to changing circumstances, and – more superficially – to a changing frame of intellectual reference. At their core one finds Campolieti's awareness of the intrinsic fragility of extensive agriculture, in which low land productivity was balanced by the low price of land (by international standards): it was of course extremely vulnerable to the land price boom that its very success was to cause. Campolieti's weakness lay in his inability to reach an equally clear economic picture of the alternatives he proposed to this prospect of doom: he was of course sure that the way out of this dilemma was to be found in more intensive agriculture, but he was not ready to explore the economic preconditions for the heavy investment that it would need: what he had to offer were homilies to landowners and city dwellers who must modify their lifestyle to save such capital as agricultural modernisation required. These exhortations are not uninteresting in that they reflect a change in the ideological climate of the country: by 1914 the idle and spendthrift land rentier was his main target. By 1929 he reserved his most scathing condemnation for the urban consumer of imported luxury goods, thus echoing the protectionist ideas that were now becoming fashionable.

But if Campolieti's solutions were vague, moralistic and on the whole based on a very shaky understanding of the economic mechanisms he wanted to put in motion, his view of the basic problem of agriculture gained clarity with time: in the prologue to his *La organización de la agricultura argentina (ensayo de política agraria)*, he put it more limpidly and succinctly than ever before: the cause is 'la valorización de la tierra que tuvo lugar de 1903 a 1910',[6] and the persistence thereafter of the style of agricultural production fashioned in the era of cheap land had now closed for ever.

This shrewd but, after all, simple insight was no doubt available to agricultural experts at the Ministerio de Agricultura, created in 1895: if they did not dwell on it as insistently as Campolieti, it is perhaps because they felt less at home in the analytical-speculative explorations that attracted the Italian agronomist, and preferred to engage in more down-to-earth examinations of agricultural conditions in the several productive regions of Buenos Aires, Santa Fe and Córdoba. They probably did not rate Campolieti's contributions very highly; while he explicitly dismissed theirs as too empirical and unsystematic.

Even so, it is not difficult to discover behind these monographic studies of a crop, a region or an issue, produced in such abundance by the agronomists of the Ministerio in the first two decades of its existence, a common view of the basic problems of Argentine grain agriculture – or rather, a set of only partially concurrent views, differing less in their inventory of problems than in the assessment of their seriousness and the links between them.

Among these agronomists the most influential – not exclusively because of his bureaucratic seniority – was Emilio Lahitte: he was also the least pessimistic about the future and least prone to offer too harsh an indictment against the land tenure system dominant on the pampa (and for that matter against any other aspect of the social arrangements linked with grain production and marketing). It is tempting to associate this reluctance to engage in social criticism with his success in the new technical bureaucratic establishment; but at least in his first writings Lahitte conveyed in the most guarded terms his refusal to find anything pathologically wrong in the existing agrarian system: his caution is understandable, since the Minister to whom his reports were addressed, Dr Wenceslao Escalante, was already on record as a severe critic of that system (although he admitted regretfully that it could be modified only gradually). In 1901 the massive survey of Argentine agriculture launched by the Ministry was also permeated by this mood of melancholy disapproval, very clearly reflected in the section on the province of Buenos Aires, written by Carlos Girola.

Lahitte's view was rather that, while a lot of things were undoubtedly wrong with grain agriculture, nothing fundamental was at stake. The land tenure system was not the issue. In 1905 he remarked that 'económicamente . . . esta repartición de la tierra no ha de ser tan fundamentalmente desequilibrada como se ha dado a entender',[7] since it had not stood in the way of the incredibly successful expansion still prevailing. True, it would be desirable for the tenant to be able to buy land; but this could be achieved under existing conditions, although with growing difficulties that Lahitte proposed to alleviate through improvements designed to diminish the cost of production, transportation and marketing of grain.

In Lahitte's opinion all of these improvements were easier to introduce and required much less sweeping changes than most critics suggested. Further expansion of production would require, on the other hand, very heavy investment in 'medios de transporte terrestres y fluviales, obras de irrigación, construcción y ensanche de puertos *con todos sus anexos*'[8] (Lahitte's emphasis).

Lahitte's optimism was thus far from complacent. It was predicated on a very ambitious – and expensive – programme of public works, and on a return to subsidised immigration by which additional labour might be supplied. The desired outcome would be to stimulate a return to 'colonisation' (in the peculiar, Argentine sense of breaking up of large estates into family-sized farms to be sold to aspiring agriculturalists), and a gradual phasing out of the tenant-farming and share-cropping arrangements already dominant.

To this extent, Lahitte shares the thrust of the critics who make the radical reorganisation of the land tenure system the precondition for stable prosperity in Argentina's grain agriculture. There are, however, at least two features in his analysis that make his approach less typical. The first in his almost total identification with the landowning interest. Changes were needed, but the landowners were not to pay for them. The ambitious plan of public works would have put the burden on the taxpayer; the same was true of subsidised immigration; the land interest was notoriously undertaxed by comparison with other producers and with the consumers (mostly urban) of imported goods.

The second is that Lahitte apparently did not consider the need for improvement to be a matter of any real urgency. Only five months after having submitted his lengthy report on land tenure, in a shorter report on the prospects of the 1905/6 harvest Lahitte totally ignored the issues he had so recently explored. True, in the Argentine farmlands, 'la anormalidad parece ser una condición normal de la producción agrícola',[9] but far from seeing in this anomaly a cause for concern, he looked at it with a kind of embarrassed pride as the price that had to be paid for the extraordinary pace of agricultural progress. The next harvest promised to be the largest in the short history of Argentine overseas exports, and care should be taken that labour would be available when needed; this was the gist of his advice.

This lack of urgency helps to explain some obvious shortcomings in Lahitte's proposals that were not so carefully thought out as his analyses of current conditions. How could a man who knew so well the technical and economic realities of growing grain propose, for example, a moratorium on the opening of new land, intended to accelerate the transition to a more productive kind of agriculture? He knew, of course, only too well that as long as new land was actually available no Argentine government would be able to muster the technical ability and political authority to impose such a moratorium.

Reform-mongering was not Lahitte's forte, and his heart was not in it. Precisely because this was so, the fact that he joined in the chorus of the reform-mongers shows again to what extent the planning of drastic reforms (or reforms that could pass for drastic) was then considered one of the basic duties of the new breed of agricultural experts. And, for all his instinctive moderation, his proposals were not dissimilar to others advanced with more enthusiasm in the first years of the new century.

In 1904, Florencio T. Molinas followed a line of thought parallel to that of Lahitte, but he chose to lay stress on suggestively different points. He also advocated a return to colonisation, and offered a spirited defence of the 'empresario de colonización' – this much maligned agent of agricultural progress, who was 'útil para el agricultor porque está interesado en [su] adelanto . . . dependiendo por completo [su] prosperidad del resultado de los cultivos, le incumbe ayudar con sus recursos y sus consejos al agricultor'. This flattering portrait contrasts with Molinas' stern condemnation of the *fainéant* landowners who rent their land to farmers:

> Estos propietarios que se limitan a percibir sus rentas al fin de año, constituyen una clase que enriquece el curso natural de las cosas con una completa actitud pasiva de su parte . . . disfruta de aquella supervalia de la tierra creada por la colectividad que la fecunda.[10]

Behind the flattery to the *empresario de colonización* lies stern advice to the landowners. If they wanted to survive they had to become entrepreneurs; they had to be prepared to offer the technical assistance and credit needed by fledgling agriculturalists, to whom they should sell family-sized plots in long instalments. Policies that would make life increasingly difficult for rentier landowners should be introduced. A higher tax should be imposed on land; the *contribución territorial* on a family plot at that time was less than the indirect taxes paid by an average farmer's family on the yerba, rice and sugar it consumed, and also lower than the yearly licence fees for carts and other vehicles.

Molinas was thus ready to burden the landowners with a more complex, more onerous and on the whole less pleasant task than Lahitte. But with him, again, there are reasons to wonder how serious his proposals for reform really were. In 1910 he published *La colonización argentina y las industrias agropecuarias*,[11] in which he fell easily into the triumphalist tone so characteristic of the first centennial of Argentina's existence as a free nation. He was again ready to admit that Argentine agriculture did not follow the most advanced productive techniques, but he argued that there were sound economic reasons for that apparent shortcoming. True, tenant-farmers were greater in number than independent producers, but their profits would permit them to buy land. True, these affluent tenant-farmers depended for credit on local merchants who imposed stiff conditions and charged interest rates several times higher than the bank rate, but this was less unfair than it sounded, since lending money and advancing goods on the guarantee of future harvests were extremely risky. Some real causes of complaint and concern *did* exist, and on second thoughts they seemed linked to the primitive organisation of transportation, marketing and credit, rather than to the land tenure system. Even here, Molinas felt confident that the co-operative movement, then making what he saw as a promising start in Argentine farmlands, would take care of the outstanding problems.

In 1904 a return to colonisation could still be considered a viable alternative, and not only for the purpose of offering an apology for the existing rural order. Karl Kaerger, an excellent rural expert attached to Germany's Foreign Office, also saw tenant-farming as a stepping stone in the immigrant's road to independent farming, with share-cropping (an ever more frequent arrangement) an earlier step in the same direction; he even considered this gradual approach advisable for those immigrants who brought with them enough capital to buy land on arrival: it would eliminate the risks inherent in re-learning their trade in the exotic context of pampean agriculture. And – leaving aside Lahitte's partially apologetic aspiration – we can no doubt trust him when he tells us that in many cases sharecroppers were new immigrants brought to the farmlands through the initiative of tenants. Tenants sublet part of their plots as a way of playing for bigger stakes in the lottery of pampean agriculture, with the purchase of a farm of their own as their final goal. While probably not a few of these tenants had at least as much in mind the return to a life of modest leisure in their country of origin as any permanent settlement as independent farmers in Argentina, it was still true that property was an available alternative for a not insignificant number of farmers who were both tenacious and lucky.

By 1910 all this argument had acquired an aura of unreality, so well reflected in the vague optimism of Molinas' writing of that year. Very soon other authors would express a different mood, more attuned to the new circumstances. A very distinguished example of this new approach was *The Land We Live On*,[12] a short pamphlet published in 1914 by Herbert Gibson (later knighted), also known as Heriberto Gibson, a widely and deservedly respected Anglo-Argentine agricultural expert whose technical services were much appreciated by both the British and the Argentine governments. In Gibson's opinion the state of Argentine agriculture gave cause for urgent alarm. Tenant-farming in itself was not the culprit: but the shortcomings on the one hand of tenants devoid of capital and expertise and, on the other hand, of landowners who had the resources but not the will to supply the amenities and improvements that would attract a better class of tenant, went a long way to explaining why rented land was so much less productive in Argentina than in England, where a very forward-looking agriculture had developed on the basis of tenant-farming.

But while Gibson was not complacent in the way he looked at the problem, his main purpose was less to suggest what should be done to solve it than what should not be done. The notion that heavier taxes on land would force the landowner to put his rural assets to better use was wrong and dangerous; pushed to the limit it would bring about state ownership of land, with no real advantage for the tenant. He sidestepped the suggestion that there was something wrong in existing marketing and credit arrangements by offering a spirited defence of the *pulpero* that carefully ignored the fact that this (in his opinion) much maligned pioneer of agricultural progress had already become a fully-controlled agent of the grain exporting firms.

The solutions that Gibson offered were essentially exhortatory. The tenants should exercise more thrift, the landowners should be made aware that their practice of renting land in leases as short as the market would bear, and without any improvements, not only detracted from their potential profits but gradually eroded their own capital: it forced their tenants to pursue, as a matter of survival, an extremely exploitative agriculture that destroyed the fertility of their land.

Gibson's solution was really no solution at all. For all his readiness to admit the dangerous shortcomings of Argentine agriculture, what he offered was an oblique defence of the status quo. What makes it interesting is no doubt the implicit assumption that the land tenure pattern dominated by tenant-farming had become a feature in Argentine farmland.

The acknowledgement that this was indeed the case also inspired a literature less apologetic than Gibson. Damián M. Torino, a former Minister of Agriculture, had already in 1912 accepted the general acknowledgement of the need for drastic reform that was to be described with approval in 1916 by Eleodoro Lobos. As Torino explained at length in his *El problema del inmigrante y el problema agrario en la Argentina*,[13] the culprit was indeed the *latifundio*; this legacy of the Spanish and pastoral dark ages of Argentina should of course be eliminated. But Dr Torino, so eloquent in denouncing its deadly grip on economy and society, does not say how this necessary reform might be achieved: he promised to do so in a later chapter of his book, but somehow forgot.

As might be expected, Juan B. Justo, the founder of the Argentine Socialist party, was more ready to offer drastic remedies. He diagnosed the illness in terms very close to those preferred by those Conservative politicians who until now had taken charge of the agricultural policies of the state, such as Escalante, Torino or Lobos. The difference, however, was more evident in matters of policy than ideology. Anibal Arcondo has very rightly pointed out in a recent article that Justo's views on the agrarian question owed nothing to Kautsky's attempt to apply to it the Marxian notions on the functioning (and the developmental trends of) the modern industrial economy.[14] Whether this should be held against Justo – as apparently Arcondo is inclined to do – is a wholly different matter: it seems now rather clear, after all, that at least some of the current trouble in socialist agriculture is due to the influence of Kautsky's views on those who called him a renegade. But neither was Justo a follower of Henry George, as Arcondo also apparently suggests: he of course did not share in Henry George's debased, Ricardian approach, and he was never a believer in the single tax. Arcondo was not the first Argentine to propose, as a solution to agriculture's woes, a higher tax on land that would force landowners to devote it to more productive uses and, by stopping the rise in prices, make it more easily available to farmers eager to own their plots.

This of course had an additional consequence, disturbing to many: it would diminish the economic power of the landowners. For Justo, this was in itself a desirable development: in his opinion the Argentine landowners were distinguished as a group by a total lack of entrepreneurial inclinations and abilities, and by a short-sighted, self-serving use of their awesome political influence. Justo, then, was not very far removed from an almost universal consensus when he denounced the landowner as the culprit and suggested that he should pay for the necessary changes; he overstepped its boundaries only when he offered a precise legislative plan to impose these painful readjustments on the landowning class.

Not everybody agreed, however, that the landowner was indeed the culprit. A less popular, alternative view had been advanced by some since early in the new century; both Lahitte and Molinas were aware of this alternative – Lahitte when he declared that improvements in transportation, marketing and credit were a precondition of the final, painless victory of *colonización* over tenant-farming, and Molinas when he recognised in his 1910 study problems in these areas that (he hoped) the future success of the co-operative movement would eliminate.

The interest in these areas was in part stimulated by a growing attention to developments in United States agriculture. This in turn was linked to the increasing acceptance, among observers and critics of conditions in Argentina, of the notion that the country was having some, at least partial, success in achieving the goal proposed by Sarmiento (who had suggested that any Latin American country which did not want in future to be swallowed by the United States should strive to imitate this formidable neighbour). Apparently, it had succeeded most in sharing not a few of the problems that plagued the great northern democracy; and policy discussions then current in the United States were recognised as of new relevance to Argentine circumstances.

In this vein, President Roque Sáenz Peña launched in 1910 a spirited campaign denouncing the dangers that the trusts posed to the Argentine economy, explicitly inspired by Theodore Roosevelt's crusade against the 'malefactors of great wealth'. And even when they rejected the American example, Argentine politicians recognised it as their natural frame of reference. Thus Juan B. Justo, when proclaiming his party's unflinching support for a sound and stable currency, hastened to acknowledge that the democratic and progressive forces in the United States rallied in support of the opposite alternative. It was so – he reminded Argentines – because a strong currency was advocated by the financial interest to keep the small producers in its thrall. In Argentina a debased currency was the instrument of the landed oligarchy in raising its profits from exports, reducing its debts to the state banks that had lavishly financed its unproductive as well as its productive expenditures, and depressing real wages.

With respect to social issues in the grain-growing farmlands, the comparison is with similar areas in the United States. In the US – while tenant farming was not unknown – the tenants were not distinct as a social group from the land-holding farmers: pitched battles against both grain trading firms and railways encouraged a shift of emphasis from the land tenure issues to those linked with the rise in the 1890s of grain exporters who monopolised the trade, or alleged high tariffs and deficient service from the railways, or the absence of a formal credit system available to farmers.

Similar issues were explored caustically by Hert T. Holm in his 1914 pamphlet, 'Agriculture in Argentina: National Wealth Prostituted; A Plea for Safe and Scientific Methods'. The gist of his argument was anticipated in his even shriller subtitles: 'The truth about our agricultural prosperity/Is it a myth?/500,000,000 pesos annual wastage/The farmers' hopeless handicap/Which is it to be, ruin or reform?/Elevators: an absolute economic necessity/Urgent government action imperative.'[15]

Holm saw exploitative and wasteful transport, marketing and credit systems as the main cause of the stagnation that threatened Argentine agriculture. Its very shortcomings were artfully employed to keep the farmer under the control of an unholy alliance of railway and export companies, while the local merchants (the only source of credit genuinely available to the small producer) acted as agent for both. Thanks to these shortcomings, the farmer could not, even after an exceptionally large harvest, dispense with the extremely expensive mercantile credit that he needed to face the next agricultural cycle. More credit from the state banks did not really help; it only fed the existing credit system. Legal reforms such as warrants or *prenda agraria* could not offer the farmer direct access to bank credit; their only effect was to tighten the grip of his creditors. Only the creation of a network of local and central silos and elevators would introduce the changes that were now urgent, and this in two different ways: first, by preserving the only valuable asset the farmer could offer as collateral (which was of course his harvest), it would finally offer him access to bank credit; second, by offering this protection it would make it possible for the farmer to participate more actively in the speculative aspects of the grain trade. As long as abnormally high interest rates and quick deterioration forced the farmer to dispose of his grain as soon as it was harvested, the grain exporters could play the speculative game unilaterally against the farmer's interest, and with devastating effect. And, Holm optimistically concluded, building such a network would be much less costly than the profiteers from the status quo would like the public to believe.

Most of the arguments offered by Justo and Holm were far from new: what was new was rather the impassioned urgency with which they were now advanced. Why this urgency? In 1912 – a year of good harvests, after a succession of very poor ones, but also a year of extremely disappointing prices – a tenant-farmers' strike that had started in the Santa Fe maize belt expanded into the farmlands in Buenos Aires. Córdoba and La Pampa. Here at last was a sign if not of the final crisis that (according to its critics) Argentine agriculture would be able to surmount only by drastic reform, at least of a crisis serious enough to require some reaccommodation within the agricultural economy. The movement left a permanent legacy: a network of farmers' leagues associated with the Federación Agraria Argentina, which, while really vigorous only in some districts, made their presence felt in almost all.

The permanence of the leagues was one of the signs of the coming of age of a more or less stabilised rural society. Until 1912 agricultural Argentina was considered still to be a pioneer area, where the agents in charge of the different economic functions linked with agriculture had kept only the most tenuous and fleeting links with these functions (ready to abandon them and the area in response to both success and failure). From the start, this image exaggerated some of the social features of agricultural expansion on the pampas, and ignored others perhaps no less important. But it was probably only in the few years before 1912 that accelerated changes in the farmlands made the stereotype completely misleading. The global rise in land prices indicated by Campolieti underlay these changes, and thanks to Roberto Cortés Conde's admirable *El progreso argentino* we can now gauge and understand them better.[16] As Cortés Conde clearly demonstrates, *valorización* of land was linked with the closing of the agricultural frontier: by 1912 the railway had reached – indeed overstepped – the furthest boundaries of the area naturally endowed for grain agriculture under current technology. The massive rush into new land, started in 1870, and frantically accelerated from the 1890s, was finally over. The consequences of this new situation were made harsher for the farmers by the emergence in areas of later settlement of a new breed of landowners who wanted to be something more than rentiers: in western Buenos Aires as well as in south-western Córdoba, grain agriculture was mostly integrated into the stock raising *estancia* in a system of mixed cultures that precluded any sale of agricultural land in family-size plots. While in areas of older settlement *valorización* made the acquisition of family farms ever more difficult in the pioneer areas that had offered in the past a more affordable alternative, land was still available for rent but very seldom for purchase.

Underlying *valorización* and its manifold consequences was of course the relentless pressure of farmers for new land to till under any conditions, a pressure that forced them to pay most of the price for more expensive land while weathering the negative consequences of an unimproved transportation and marketing system. Their bargaining position was constantly eroded by growing numbers. New immigrants, ever more numerous because – among other things – of much cheaper oceanic fares, competed for land with the new generations raised by the large *colono* families in the areas of earlier agricultural settlement. For both, the only solution available was increasing exploitation of their own and their families' labour. This solution could not however solve the basic problems of Argentine agriculture because impoverished farmers did not share the peasants' resilience in the face of economic adversity. They still needed money or credit to purchase seeds, to rent agricultural equipment, and to pay for the seasonal labour required at harvest time.

Paradoxically, hired hands were still scarce and expensive. As Justo acutely remarked, Argentine agriculture had managed to combine the drawbacks of both plethora and scarcity of labour. Casual labour was an extremely unattractive alternative for the resident population of the farmlands; what was available was mostly made up of seasonal migrants from cities and towns and from the poorer interior provinces, and of trans-oceanic temporary workers who moved to Argentina at harvest time; even with cheap oceanic transportation, daily wages during the comparatively short harvest season had to be kept fairly high to induce them to come.

The 1912 crisis did indeed reflect the intrinsic weakness of the agrarian system that had developed in the littoral and the pampa. Neither landowners nor merchants had taken charge of the entrepreneurial function; it was still left (by default) to tenant-farmers with very little capital of their own, and to share-croppers destitute of any productive assets beyond their labour. The viability of the system depended on the ability of the most marginal among these producers to make ends meet, which in their case and by 1912 meant no more than ensuring their own and their families' subsistence, with enough credit left to face the next agricultural cycle. By 1912 not even this modest goal was apparently attainable for all farmers.

Some kind of reform was needed, then, simply for survival. At the same time, however, the emergence of a group movement (and later an organisation) of the tenant-farmers suggests that the opportunity for reform from above, practicable so long as society in the farmlands had not consolidated itself along fairly well-defined lines, had already been allowed to pass. When asked to suggest courses of action in response to the agricultural conflict, Lahitte referred the Minister of Agriculture rather curtly to his previous reports, where the conditions that gave rise to conflict were described – he asserted – with prophetic accuracy; as for solutions, the best would be to allow the conflicting interests to solve their differences in their own way.

Already, in the course of conflict, Justo had said essentially the same: his preference was sustained by the hope that the newly-mobilised farmers would lend more strength to the reformist positions he had supported for so long, and with such limited success. This was, however, not to happen: reforms were indeed introduced, but they were far less sweeping and radical than even the most moderate critics had declared necessary to ensure the continuing vitality of Argentine agriculture.

This triumph of extreme moderation was achieved against a new political background. In 1912 the universal male franchise – as old as the Republic – was given new relevance by an electoral law that made fraud extremely difficult and established the secret ballot; the loose conservative coalition that had ruled the country since 1890 was on its way out, even if it was not yet aware of it; the future belonged to the radicals, thanks to their mastery of the new game of mass politics. In the maize-growing districts of Buenos Aires, still ruled by Conservatives, Justo's socialists were able to provide political guidance to the tenants' leagues. But in Santa Fe, the core of the Argentine farmland, a radical administration was offering protection and direction to the strikers; there Dr J. Daniel Infante, a recent convert from anarchism, joined the position of Minister of *Gobierno* in charge of provincial police to that of attorney for the leagues (a circumstance that perhaps helps to explain the quick and uneventful success of the tenants' movement in that province). As Justo was soon to discover, the alliance with a political organisation able to offer such support held attractions that the socialist leader's limited influence in Congress could not match.

Infante's pamphlet on *El problema agrario* offers some keys to the radicals' success in using social conflict to their political advantage: it reflects their ability to combine a lofty refusal to acknowledge any rent in the seamless web of Argentine society with an uncannily shrewd understanding of the far from harmonious ways in which this society actually worked. Infante starts conventionally enough by looking for culprits in the agricultural crisis, but very soon changes his path. The real issue, he averred, was not who the guilty party might be, but whom should the tenants choose as their target. Should they attack the marketing, transportation and credit system? This would mean joining battle against 'los ferrocarriles, los acarreadores, los bolseros y los gobiernos . . . cuatro luchas y de qué género y con qué enemigos.'[17] On the whole, the tenants did the sensible thing in challenging merely the landowners. Just how sensible, Infante does not care to dwell upon: he neglects to mention, for instance, the fact that the local merchants – by that time no more than a *longa manus* for the grain export companies – usually offered their store as a meeting place for the strikers' committees, and even chaired some of them.

This kind of tenants' movement very much anticipated the kind of reform brought about by its success. The outcome was disappointing to agrarian reformers, who frequently attributed it to the cunningly disguised social conservatism of the Radicals. They were right, in that the Radical party never was (and never pretended to be) committed to systematic social reform: but they managed to ignore other perhaps equally important aspects of the situation.

While the Radical administrations were frequently accused of social paralysis by sometimes brilliant but on the whole powerless critics to their left, those who preferred to accuse them of reckless if not wilful indifference to the very survival of the existing social order, while frequently much less articulate, were much more powerful and influential within Argentine society. More importantly, the pressure for more radical change from the very social groups on whose behalf the leftist critics were speaking, was extremely weak. Gibson was not wrong when he asserted that the only people he knew who favoured the single tax were city-dwellers, and the socialists – for all their tenacious efforts to bring their message to the farmlands – could not make any significant dent in the farmers' allegiance to the Federación Agraria and its unwritten but working alliance with the Radical administrations.

What was this alliance giving the farmers? Very little indeed, and what it gave came slowly and gradually – a minimum term for leases, limited compensation for some improvements introduced by tenants, and almost nothing else. Until 1930 the disgruntled conservative opposition denounced this agrarian legislation as mischievous demagoguery, but this was apparently a reaction to many electoral defeats rather than an expression of sincere alarm at the social impact of the new rural policies. After 1930, when the Conservatives regained power by courtesy of the military (who had ousted the Radicals), they continued and expanded these policies, so much so that the two basic features of the Peronist solution to the land tenure question – stability for tenants and a freeze in rents – were in fact a Conservative legacy; both had been established in 1942 to shelter grain producers from the impact of trade disturbances created by the Second World War.

In all fairness, the Conservatives could not be accused of demagoguery – since they systematically and brazenly faked election results, they did not need to indulge in such tactics – and obviously they did not have the tenants' interests at heart. But, for all the electoral dividends that the Radicals had been able to obtain from their agrarian policies, it can be argued that the tenants and their welfare were not the paramount consideration for them either. What these exceedingly mild reforms tried to secure was the survival of Argentine grain agriculture by keeping the tenants and share-croppers (the weakest and most important link in the productive chain) barely in business.

Implicit in these policies was the reconciliation with the socioeconomic order created in the farmlands by 50 years of blind travail. This is also the implicit point of departure for Alejandro Bunge's careful exploration of strengths and weaknesses in the Argentine economy in the 1920s. Bunge's early career is very similar to that of the experts of the Ministry of Agriculture under the last Conservative administrations; he had brought to the publications of the state statistical office, of which he was in charge, a new depth and sophistication (among others, his 'Riqueza y Renta de la Argentina', published in 1914, offered a pioneering calculation of the GNP).[18] In 1916 the first Radical administration dispensed with his brilliant services; in 1922 the second Radical president, Alvear, restored him to his former position in the bureaucracy. But whether in the government's service or not, Bunge could see the state no longer as the agency for shaping a still formless society. The kind of social engineering that turn-of-the-century technical bureaucracies had considered as such an important part of their privileges and duties, was now made impossible by the emergence of a more mature society, where conflicts had acquired new vigour and sharpness. Whether as a member of the technical bureaucracy of the state or as a private economist, Bunge – for all his contempt for electoral politics – was as much a politician as Infante, and he virtually acknowledged this fact when he proudly described himself not as a scholar or a scientist, but as a man of action.

By way of his publications Bunge very deliberately intended to take part in the struggle to define the future course of change in Argentine society. Sometimes this went against what later proved to be the case; thus, most of what he wrote on the subject of railways followed too closely the viewpoint of the companies to reflect that original contribution which was his hallmark when he was more free in directing his own line of thought. But his militant identification with social groups and economic interests that – while under-represented in the new political order based on mass electoral organisations – had managed to keep most of their awesome economic power and influence on Argentine society, had also more positive consequences: it helped Bunge to achieve an admirably rich and nuanced view of the workings of the Argentine economy at a transitional moment in its development, a view that – for all its wealth of significant detail – was organised around a few issues and dilemmas, the enormous significance of which he was by then almost alone in perceiving. He was thus able to offer a programme for future action that accurately defined the basic problems – and anticipated not a few of the solutions – that were to dominate the Argentine economy in the next three decades.

At the centre of Bunge's view of the predicament of the Argentine economy was the notion that agriculture had pretty much fulfilled and exhausted its role as that leading sector the growth of which underlay the remarkable progress of the previous half century. While agricultural stagnation was in his opinion at the core of the economy's problems, he looked elsewhere for solutions. The rural sector was for him an established fact, and the changes he proposed centred on other areas that had now to make up for its unavoidable shortcomings. Industry in particular should be expected to absorb the excess of manual workers that every new generation unloaded on the labour market; farmlands could no longer meet the demand. Industry should also compensate, by substituting its own products for at least some of the important consumer goods, for the increasing inability of agricultural exports to pay for all the inputs (imports, government loans, private capital investment) that Argentina had traditionally received from overseas.

This perceptive analysis marks the last stage in the dissipation of a cherished national dream: the redemption of Argentina, born again as a new society and a new economy in the deserted pampa. But Bunge's sober, disenchanted view reflects a moment no less transitional in the development of the view that Argentina had of itself. Today Bunge is honoured as a prophet of a new faith: the belief that industrialisation will create a new Argentina, thus cancelling the dark heritage of the agricultural past. The advice offered by President Mitre more than a century ago – namely, to accept the fact that Argentina cannot be very different from what God and the Argentines have already made it – is apparently as abhorrent to his compatriots today as when it was first advanced.

NOTES

1. Estanislao S. Zeballos, *Descripción amena de la República Argentina: La región del trigo*, vol. II (Buenos Aires, 1883) pp. 14–22 and 38–40.
2. *Cartas pastorales del Illustrísimo y Reverendísimo Sr. D. Fr. José de San Alberto* (Madrid, 1793) p. 3.
3. Felix de Azara, *Memoria sobre el estado rural del Río de la Plata y otros informes* (Buenos Aires, 1943) pp. 16–17.
4. Bartolomé Mitre, 'Discurso de Chivilcoy, pronunciado el 25 de octubre de 1868 en el banquete popular que le ofreció el pueblo de Chivilcoy, con motivo de la feliz terminación de su presidencia constitucional', *Arengas* (Buenos Aires, 1889).
5. 'Las tendencias extremas y conservadoras de la política argentina coinciden

en estos días en la misma aspiración', in Miguel Angel Cárcano, *Evolución histórica del régimen de la tierra pública, 1810–1916* (Buenos Aires, 3rd edn 1972) p. xxxi.
6. Ing. Agr. Roberto Campolieti, *La organización de la agricultura argentina (ensayo de política agraria)* (Buenos Aires, [?1929]) p. 7.
7. E. Lahitte, 'La propriedad rural. Ventas, Hipotecas, Colonización, Latifundio', *Boletín del Ministerio de Agricultura* (hereafter *BMA*), III (June 1905) pp. 72–104 and p. 101.
8. Ibid., p. 102 fn. 7.
9. E. Lahitte, in *BMA*, IV (Dec. 1905) pp. 70ff.
10. Florencio T. Molinas, 'Informe agrícola sobre la provincia de Santa Fe y colonización interprovincial', *BMA*, II (Dec. 1904) pp. 35–45.
11. F. T. Molinas, *La colonización argentina y las industrias agro-pecuarias: Año 1910* (Buenos Aires, 1910).
12. Herbert Gibson, *The Land We Live On* (Buenos Aires, 1914).
13. Damián M. Torino, *El problema del inmigrante y el problema de la tierra en la Argentina* (Buenos Aires, 1912) pp. 96–7.
14. Anibal Arcondo, 'El conflicto agrario argentino de 1912 – ensayo de interpretación', *Desarollo Económico*, XX (1980) pp. 351–81.
15. Hert T. Holm, *Agriculture in Argentina: National Wealth Prostituted. A Plea for Safe and Scientific Methods* (Buenos Aires, 1914).
16. Roberto Cortés Conde, *El Progreso Argentino, 1880–1914* (Buenos Aires, 1979).
17. J. Daniel Infante, *El Problema Agrario* (Rosario, [?1912]).
18. Alejandro Bunge, 'Riqueza y renta de la Argentina', in *La economía argentina: La conciencia nacional y el problema económico*, vol. I (Buenos Aires, 1928) p. 200.

4 The Argentine Economy, 1890–1914: Some Salient Features

DAVID ROCK

The modern political economy of Argentina dates from around 1860. At this point came the first of the great export booms led by wool, and the formation of a national state. From this time forward Argentina's population and its chief cities grew rapidly. Its lands were settled by European immigrants. It drew in foreign capital for the development of its railways and a wide variety of urban amenities: tramways, sewage and gas works, and, later on, electricity. Production, now integrally linked with world markets, underwent rapid expansion. This economy persisted largely unchanged until the coming of the world depression in 1930.

Within the whole 70-year span between 1860 and 1930, the period which best exemplifies this dominant quality of expansion and growth is that between the depression of 1890 and the outbreak of the First World War in 1914. At this point the pace of change and development was fastest, and confidence in the country's potentialities at its highest. This period, before all others, was Argentina's great step forward. The country embarked into the twentieth century on a wave of promise and prosperity which had few equals throughout the world.

Yet the 1890s began inauspiciously in the midst of financial collapse, caused mainly by recent overborrowing from aborad, and with the threat of political breakdown. Soon after the financial crisis struck in 1890, an attempted revolution brought the overthrow of President Miguel Juárez Celman. Afterwards came several more lean and gruelling years. After Juárez's fall his immediate successors as president, Carlos Pellegrini and Luis Sáenz Peña, struggled to avoid default on the foreign debt. For some time the government could do little but attend to this issue, while battening down on renewed expressions of political discontent. The depression deepened in 1891. The gold premium, which measured the depreciation of the paper peso against gold, increased from an average of 151 per cent in 1890 to 287 per cent the following year. In January 1891 Pellegrini successfuly persuaded the government's main creditor, the British merchant banking house Baring Brothers, to accept a moratorium on large slices of the debt. The year 1892 marked some improvement. However, the following year brought more difficulties when the wheat harvest failed. Export earnings, whence came the resources to settle the foreign debt, plummeted steeply once more. In 1893 the Sáenz Peña government was obliged to renegotiate the external debt once more, and to seek further postponements on its interest repayments. With the 'Romero Deal' (*Arreglo Romero*), as it was known after the Minister of Finance who led the negotiations, many interest charges were deferred until 1898, and amortisation repayments delayed until 1901. Another result of this renegotiation was that the national government assumed responsibility for debts of the provinces contracted during the past decade. But it did so on condition that the provinces surrender control over several local revenues and taxes. The crisis of the early 1890s thus released new centripetal impulses and reinforced the concentration of power in Buenos Aires, which had been a sailent feature of the period since 1860.[1]

Despite the severity of the depression, the longer-term outlook was not unfavourable. Once the debt problem had been brought under control, there was every possibility that expansion could be quickly renewed. This depression did not produce major shifts in world trade, nor a redistribution of international economic power. Although commodity export prices had fallen, the crisis was, at root, financial in nature. Its effects were more severe among borrowers in Latin America than among the industrial countries. In the 1890s Argentina still possessed an enormous land reserve in the pampaean region suitable for export production. As was the case under similar circumstances in the 1870s, the way to surmount the depression was to increase production and exports. Here the high gold premium which prevailed during the depression began to prove itself a disguised blessing, since it meant that local costs of production fell faster in gold terms than commodity prices on the world market. As this margin widened, it fostered opportunities for profit and incentives to increase production. Recovery was also assisted by the completion of railway construction at the height of the depression, which had been contracted and financed in the late 1880s. Between 1890 and 1892 the railway track length grew more than a quarter. The cultivated area increased with it from 2.4 million to almost 4.9 million hectares between 1888 and 1895.

Recovery was also based on agriculture, particularly upon wheat. Exports of wheat which were less than 250,000 tons in the 1880s climbed to 1.6 million and beyond in 1894 and subsequent years. Before 1890 the value of wheat exports had never exceeded 1 million gold pesos. In the years afterwards it rapidly ascended to more than 20 million. Earlier wheat farming had been largely concentrated in the central region of Santa Fe, the site of the first colonies of Europeans. By the late 1890s the southern parts of the province had moved to the forefront. With the construction of new railroads and large grain elevators in Rosario, the acreage devoted to wheat in Santa Fe tripled between 1887 and 1897. Wheat farming also spread to the west and south of the province of Buenos Aires, into eastern Córdoba and to the now developing territory of La Pampa. With the opening of the southern regions of Buenos Aires and La Pampa, Bahía Blanca, the Atlantic port which served the new wheat trade, underwent swift growth to rival that of Rosario in the north. By 1904, less than 30 years since Argentina had been a wheat importer, this same cereal had outstripped wool to become the most valuable of the country's exports.[2]

What remained of the depression had ebbed away by 1896. During the quinquennium beginning that year export prices were around 25 per cent higher than the average for 1890–5. With the renewal of prosperity the government found itself able to resume interest and amortisation payments on its outstanding debts well before the time appointed by the 1893 agreement. Instead of falling continually, the peso now began to appreciate against the world's major currencies, the gold premium declining from an average of 257 per cent in 1894 to 125 per cent in 1899. At this point in 1899 after a lapse of almost 20 years Argentina returned to the gold standard. This step was taken by the government mainly in response to pressure from exporting interests, who as the gold premium fell were now faced by rising domestic costs and a shrinkage of the earlier margin between costs and returns from selling abroad. The readoption of the gold standard was intended also to express a new commitment to financial stability and rectitude and a final break with the tradition of deliberate manipulations of the national currency. Henceforth domestic currency issues were to be regulated automatically and independently of government interference by fluctuations in gold reserves and the balance of payments. A Conversion Board was introduced to release or withdraw paper money in accordance with the level of gold reserves at the fixed ratio of 0.44 gold pesos per paper peso. By 1902 a sufficient metallic reserve had been accumulated to make the system workable, and it persisted almost unchanged until 1914.[3]

From 1895 Argentina underwent nearly two decades of uninterrupted, sustained expansion. Despite two brief trade recessions in 1899 and 1907, gross national product increased at a roughly constant 6 per cent annual rate.[4] Between the Second National Census of 1895 and the Third of 1914 population doubled, rising from 3.9 million to 7.8 million. By this point population growth was concentrated overwhelmingly in the eastern littoral region. Between 1895 and 1914 the city of Buenos Aires grew from 660,000 inhabitants to 1.5 million. Growth in the provinces of Buenos Aires, Santa Fe and Córdoba was at a roughly similar rate. In Buenos Aires population rose from 900,000 to a little over 2 million, in Santa Fe from 400,000 to almost 900,000, and in Córdoba from 350,000 to 735,000. On the other hand in many parts of the interior growth was almost nil. Over the same period La Rioja's population, for example, increased from only 79,000 to 83,000, and Jujuy's from 76,000 to 80,000.[5]

Population growth was due in part to a rising birth-rate and a falling death-rate. But the main factor was a renewed and massive wave of immigration from Southern Europe. Having ceased in 1890, immigration resumed in 1891. It thus preceded recovery from the depression, although during the 1890s net immigration at around 50,000 annually was under half the immediate pre-depression period of the late 1880s. Immigration increased rapidly around 1904. From this time forward until 1914 the annual balance of immigrants over emigrants exceeded 100,000. By the latter year there were almost 1 million Italians in Argentina and 800,000 Spaniards. Aside from the always substantial Uruguayan population of Buenos Aires, the next largest groups were Russians (including Poles and Finns), of whom there were around 94,000 in 1914, the French with 86,000, and Ottoman Turks (mostly Syrians and Lebanese) with almost 80,000.

During the wheat boom of the 1890s many immigrants became pampa farmers. But soon afterwards the trend which had characterised the 1880s reasserted itself, and the majority of immigrants settled in the cities. Between 1895 and 1914 the rural population increased from 2.3 million to 3.3 million, but that of the cities and towns from 1.6 million to 4.6 million. In the city of Buenos Aires by 1914 the foreign population was almost as large as the native, while foreign-born men substantially outnumbered natives. The same patterns prevailed in Rosario and Bahía Blanca. In the province of Buenos Aires there were about half as many foreigners as natives. Foreigners were three-fifths in Santa Fe and about a quarter in Córdoba. Again immigration was almost entirely confined to the littoral region. Outside the pampa the proportion of foreign-born in 1914 in San Luis and Tucumán was only one tenth, and except for Mendoza, one twenty-fifth or much less elsewhere in the interior.[6]

Another feature of this period was a spectacular growth of foreign trade. In 1893, a year of harvest failure, the value of exports was less than 100 million gold pesos. By 1903 this had increased to 203 million and to 519 million by 1913, a fivefold increase in 20 years. Imports grew at a parallel rate from a depressed 96 million in 1893 to 496 million in 1913. Foreign trade as a whole, a mere 190 million in 1893, exceeded 1000 million in 1913. Overseas trade values thus expanded at a rate more than double the rise in population. From a per capita average of around 50 gold pesos in the early 1890s, trade had climbed to 132 gold pesos in 1913. The increase in export earnings immediately after 1895 was due principally to rising world prices. But after 1900 favourable price trends were augmented by renewed advances in production. After 1901 export earnings grew at a 7.5 per cent annual rate, of which roughly 3 per cent was due to rising prices and the rest to increased volumes.

During this period Argentina's main trading partner was Great Britain. To Britain went at least 20 per cent of Argentina's exports and in some years, such as 1907, as much as 40 per cent. From Britain came usually around one-third of Argentina's imports. By 1913 a sizeable trade had also developed with Germany, although it amounted to only half that with Britain. In 1913 Argentina exported goods to Germany valued at 84 million gold pesos, while its imports from that country were worth more than 62 million pesos. There was also flourishing commerce with France, Belgium, the Netherlands, and Italy. Transatlantic trade now greatly outstripped any commercial ties Argentina possessed within Latin America. Exports to Bolivia worth 1.4 million gold pesos in 1885 had declined to 266,000 by 1914. There were substantial exports of wheat and flour to Brazil, and large imports of coffee. However, trade with Brazil was less than one-sixth of that with Britain. By 1914 Argentina had thus become the primary exporter *par excellence*, intimately linked with the industrial economies of Western Europe. Britain took its meat and a large proportion of its cereals, Germany its unwashed wool, France its sheepskins. 90 per cent of Argentina's exports were primary goods produced in the pampean region; more than 85 per cent of them went to Western Europe.

Along with the growth in export production was a parallel expansion in the cultivated land area, which also grew fivefold during this period. In 1895 land under cultivation amounted to less than 5 million hectares;

in 1914 it was 24 million. Between 1895 and 1914 there was a tripling of the land planted to wheat (and a sextupling by comparison with 1888), a quadrupling of that used for maize and a quintupling of that for linseed. After the great expansion of wheat farming in the early 1890s came similar growth in maize production. With maize Argentina now became the world's largest exporter. In 1912 and 1913 exports of maize reached almost 5 million tons. Exports of linseed also climbed from a little over 100,000 tons in the early 1890s to more than 1 million in 1913. By 1913 all these crops had become major export earners. Wheat and maize each regularly produced 100 million gold pesos and linseed around 50 million.

Among imports coal for use on the railways was the largest item, adding up to around 10 per cent of the total. By 1914 there were also substantial imports of petroleum products, *yerba mate* from Brazil, and a wide range of finished textile, metallurgical and other manufactured items. The United Kingdom was the source of coal, railway materials, and most finished metal and textile goods. Italy had now established itself as a large exporter of dyed cotton cloth to Argentina. The Germans won dominance in the rapidly expanding trade in machinery and electrical goods. The United States, which had become the main outlet for Argentina's cattle hides and ranked seventh among its trading partners, had as yet little stake in the market for manufactured goods, but was Argentina's main supplier of oil.[7]

During the early 1890s, when the country was struggling with the debts it had incurred under Juárez Celman, it received little new foreign investment. The mid-1890s thus saw a pronounced lull in new railway construction. British investment resumed on a large scale after 1900. It then reached a climactic peak between 1904 and 1913. During this brief period Argentina received almost as many funds from Britain as throughout the whole of the nineteenth century. Following the Baring crisis, investment patterns underwent a substantial change. Henceforth relatively little came in the form of public loans to the government. The private railway companies now swallowed the lion's share. Capital invested in railways rose from 346 million gold pesos in 1890 to 1358 million in 1913. Between 1894 and 1914 the railway track length more than doubled to reach 33,000 kilometres. Meanwhile railway cargoes increased from 5 million tons to 42 million, and railway revenues rose from 8 million gold pesos to 52 million. This sum amounted to about one-third of the total revenues of the national government in 1913 and around one-half in the depressed year which followed.

A turning point in the history of Argentina's railways during this period came in 1907 with the adoption of a new code known after its main congressional proponent as the Mitre Law (*Ley Mitre*). This legislation abolished the old profit guarantee system used since the 1860s, and instead exempted the railways from duties on imported equipment and materials. Within limits determined by profit levels and the ratios between investment and operating costs, the law also left the companies free to set their own freight and passenger rates. The aim of the new code was to increase the rate of railway construction. It proved enormously successful. Between 1907 and 1914 the system grew at an annual average of 1100 miles.

Besides its capital from Britain, after 1900 Argentina also received substantial investment funds from France and Germany. The French had a modest role in railway construction, while the Germans came to dominate a newly-developing electricity system. Nevertheless in 1913 more than 60 per cent of foreign investment in Argentina was British; British investment in Argentina was also about 10 per cent of the total Britain invested abroad. In the developed eastern core of the country British influence was almost ubiquitous. In 1898 British engineers completed the construction of a deep-draught port in Buenos Aires. Here and in several other cities they also developed lengthy tramway networks and a multitude of gas and sewage companies.[8]

Numerous other indicators attested to the great advances made during this period. Between 1895 and 1914 manufacturing establishments throughout the Republic doubled in number, while capital invested in them increased by five times. The manufacturing sector now embraced a great diversity of activities from flour or meat-packing plants to bakeries, laundries or blacksmiths, shoe factories, brick and soap works, hat factories and tanneries. Dairying, insignificant in 1890, had become a major industry by 1914. Between 1895 and 1914 flour milling expanded by four times, sugar refining by three times, beer output by eight times, wine tenfold. From the introduction of the Conversion Law in 1899 money in circulation climbed from 295 million paper pesos to 823 million in 1913. After a shaky start, the Banco de la Nación Argentina founded by Pellegrini in 1891 to replace its bankrupt predecessor, the Banco Nacional, was issuing discounts and advances in 1910 valued at 360 million paper pesos, a tenfold increase over 1892.

A last major feature of this period was renewed and frequently profound change on the land. After 1900 both sheep farming and agriculture, the dominant activities of the past two generations, became increasingly subordinate to a renascent cattle economy. While sheep were largely displaced southwards from the pampa into Patagonia, much of the land hitherto reserved exclusively for agriculture was converted to a new type of mixed farming in which cereals, fodder crops and cattle pasturing were combined on a rotationary basis. Mixed farming of this type also became the most prevalent form among the new lands recently opened to settlement and development. After 1900, although production of the cereal staples continued to expand, their growth was overshadowed by a vast increase in lucerne or alfalfa output, the main source of cattle fodder. By 1914, after a tenfold increase in production in the past 20 years, alfalfa occupied a larger land area than wheat. Along with this came a rapid transformation of Argentina's cattle stock. Over much of the pampa after 1900 the creole breeds which had occupied the land since the late sixteenth century largely disappeared. In their place came high quality breeds imported from Britain, mainly Shorthorns and Herefords.

The source of all this lay in the introduction of meat-packing plants employing newly developed refrigeration techniques which enabled the export of a new range of beef products. The coming of the *frigorífico* to Argentina was due almost entirely to exogenous conditions. Until 1900 the international beef trade was composed overwhelmingly of exports from the United States to Britain. However, as the domestic market in the United States grew, the exportable surplus steadily dwindled, obliging the British to seek out alternative sources of supply. For a time Britain responded by increasing its imports of live cattle, many of them from Argentina. But in 1900, in an effort to prevent the spread of foot-and-mouth disease, this trade was banned. At this point several British meat-packing companies were set up in Argentina, both to develop frozen meat shipments to Britain and to provision British troops in South Africa during the Boer War.

From these beginnings Argentina swiftly overtook the United States as the major supplier of beef to Britain. The trade grew most rapidly after 1907 following the advent in Argentina of American meat-packing interests based originally in Chicago. The Americans brought with them new techniques. They could chill as well as freeze beef, and this enabled them to ship much higher quality products. Soon chilled beef dominated the industry and by 1914 made up around three-quarters of total meat exports. The coming of chilled beef also boosted investments in higher quality stock. By 1914 creole herds were largely confined to marginal zones, mostly to the north in Corrientes and Entre Ríos. Beyond this it also prompted a specialisation of functions among ranchers, separating them into an outer ring of breeders and an inner core of fatteners close to the *frigoríficos* of Buenos Aires and La Plata. The former sold to the latter, who in turn dealt directly with the packers.

The arrival of the American meat-packers represented the first major investment liaison between Argentina and the United States. By 1914 American companies, headed by Armour and Swift, controlled between a half and two-thirds of Argentina's beef exports, leaving the British share at under 30 per cent. Yet although Americans now dominated the industry, more than four-fifths of Argentina's beef exports continued to be sent to the United Kingdom. Opposition from the farm lobby and popular campaigns in the United States against the Chicago 'meat-trust', prevented the meat-packers from gaining access to the American market for their River Plate subsidiaries. But if unpopular in their homeland, during these early years the Americans were held in high regard by Argentina's cattle ranchers. To consolidate themselves against British competition, they paid high prices for the stock they purchased. For several years after 1907 Argentine ranchers thus profited handsomely from the 'meat wars' between the rival segments of the industry.[9]

By 1914 Argentina had enjoyed almost 20 years of prodigal, breathtaking expansion. It grew upon the triple exogenous impulse of favourable foreign markets for its exports, foreign labour and foreign capital. Throughout this period by continually augmenting its exports of farm products Argentina had shared in the prosperity emanating from the urbanisation and industrialisation of Western Europe. In 1914 around one-third of its population was foreign-born, and 80 per cent either immigrants or descended from arrivals since 1850. By this time immigrants had become a substantial majority among urban manufacturers, rural tenants, and workers in the cities and the pampa. Foreign investment amounted to half the total capital stock, and was valued at two-and-a-half times gross national product. British investors alone owned around 80 per cent of the Argentine railway system, large tracts of its land, most of its tramways and urban utility companies, some of its meat-packing plants and industries.[10]

By 1914 per capita incomes in Argentina compared with Germany and the Low Countries, and were higher than Spain, Italy, Sweden and Switzerland. Buenos Aires, with its 1.5 million inhabitants, and having grown at an average rate of 6.5 per cent since 1869, was now the second most populous city of the Atlantic sea-board after New York. It was also by far the largest capital city throughout Latin America, having for now at least left Rio, Mexico City, Santiago and the rest trailing far behind. As a society of white immigrants undergoing almost breakneck economic growth, Argentina no longer seemed part of Latin America.

In the great compendium it issued on the Republic's affairs in 1911, Lloyd's Bank of London pointed out that until around 1903 the value of foreign trade in Argentina and Brazil was broadly equal; by 1909

Argentina's had grown by half as much again above its leading rival in the sub-continent. By 1911 per capita foreign trade in Argentina was almost six times the average in the rest of Latin America. Except for entrepôts like Holland and Belgium, no country in the world imported more goods per head of population than Argentina. Also by 1911 foreign trade had attained a magnitude greater than Canada's and was already a quarter that of the United States. Argentina had catapulted itself into the ranks of the world's leading cereal and meat producers. It was the largest exporter of maize and linseed. It was second in wool, and third in live cattle and horses. If it ranked only sixth as a producer of wheat, it was still the third, and in some years the second, largest exporter. Despite competition from cattle for the land, the expansion of wheat production after 1900 was faster than in Canada. Among Lloyd's contributors in 1911 were heady optimists eager to extrapolate from the immediate past and to predict that the value of cereal products would again double during the next decade; only 50 million of a possible 80 million acres were as yet under the plough.[11]

Yet the euphoria of these years was sometimes tempered by a sense that Argentina still had an enormous distance to traverse. Among the many European observers who now visited the country, and eagerly debated its accomplishments, there was general agreement that the age of infancy was passed; not so that of adolescence. Maturity beckoned in the shape of still greater ministrations of Capital and Labour. A population of less than 8 million in a land mass the same magnitude as the whole of continental Europe between the Baltic, the Mediterranean and the Danube estuary, still left much to be accomplished. If much of this land was destined forever to remain a near-empty desert, nevertheless British observers would soberly reflect that if Argentina should ever acquire the same population density as England at that time, it would embrace no less than 450 million people. To have infused the Republic with a new population; to have constructed there one of the largest railway systems in the world; to have endowed Buenos Aires and Rosario with the most advanced port facilities; these and other cities from Bahía Blanca to Salta, with tramways, gas, water and electricity plants was undoubtedly a considerable achievement. Yet it still left the country far short of fulfilling the goals proclaimed by the country's leaders since 1880. The generation of 1880 had looked to Argentina not merely as a leader in Latin America but as an antipodean counterweight to the United States. It aspired to a Republic of 100 million people or more, at least tenfold its present number, imbued throughout with the vitality of its eastern core.[12]

For the most part in 1914 change and development were visible only in the capital and its immediate pampa hinterland. Beyond this 500 mile radius, most of the interior, without funds for irrigation works and lacking its due share of new population from the coming of the immigrants, remained in moribund backwardness. Despite the prevailing optimism over the country's future, it now seemed doubtful whether change would continue to encompass fully the regions beyond the pampa. In 1913 a new depression brought to an end the inflow of immigrants and capital. If in part this signalled the impending European crisis soon to erupt in war, it also illustrated that Argentina was nearing saturation point in its capacity to attract resources from abroad. For some time past the best land in Argentina had already been brought into production. What remained promised far more meagre returns to investors and pioneers alike.

Unable to continue its expansion geographically, Argentina seemed no more likely at this point to be capable of industrialising its economy. Although manufacturing had undergone rapid expansion during recent years, it was heavily dependent upon the growth of domestic demand and incomes from exports and the inflow of foreign investments. At this point, despite the wide adoption of steam power, most industrial products were simple handicrafts employing little capital or machinery. Locally-manufactured foodstuffs, for which raw materials were cheap and abundant, were of high quality. It now made little sense to import beers and table wines, or flour and Italian grain-based foods. But these industries were again an outgrowth of the rural export sectors rather than tokens of an incipient industrial economy. By comparison with food manufacturing, the metals and textile industries were much less firm. Local metallurgical plants used imported raw materials, and were thus highly dependent upon low ocean freights. The new textile industry in Buenos Aires likewise used a high proportion of imported raw material. It was also extremely primitive. Rather than in factories, for the most part it functioned on a semi-mercantile 'putting-out' basis among female seamstresses. At this point the textile industry in Argentina was notably less developed than in Brazil. In 1911 Argentina had 9000 spindles and 1200 looms against an estimated 1 million and 35,000 respectively in Brazil.

In 1914 Argentina lacked even the embryos of heavy or capital goods industries. Its relatively scant reserves of coal and iron ore lay in far-flung and presently inaccessible regions, mostly in the far south-west. To begin developing these required enormous capital outlays on which the returns would be negligible or nil for an indeterminate future. Apart from sugar, wines and flour, recent experiments with tariff protection suggested the country had no easy inbuilt capacity to lessen its dependence on imports. Limited markets narrowed the scope for the adoption of advanced technology and economies of scale among industrial producers. The home market was rich but still relatively small. There seemed few opportunities among foreign markets while they remained dominant by the industrial giants of the world.

It was difficult to envisage in Argentina the smooth colligation of industry and agriculture which had underlain the development of the United States. Nor had Argentine society any discernible common quality with early nineteenth century Britain or more recent industrialising nations such as Germany or Japan. Argentina's new urban middle class was made up more of consumers than of petty industrial producers. Its high standard of living was constructed upon the easy and painless flow of foreign imports which had followed the upward expansion of farm exports. Nor did Argentina have the type of labour force suitable for industrial development. Without major changes in the rural sector – rapid natural population growth or a shift into less labour-intensive activities – it would be difficult to recruit an urban labour force from the land. The growth of the labour force thus largely depended on the country's attractiveness to prospective immigrants and its ability to uphold favourable wage differentials against the immigrants' countries of origin. However, primitive accumulation in an effort to industrialise would undoubtedly compress real wages; 1890 had shown that if the wage rate fell, Argentina would swiftly become a net exporter rather than an importer of labour.

In 1914 the immediate future for Argentina thus seemed unlikely to be much of a departure from the immediate past. The country's basic economic structure would remain largely the same, unresponsive to efforts to diversify it. On the other hand, the country no longer enjoyed its earlier advantage of an open frontier of virgin land, which could be cheaply and swiftly opened up to development. This meant that it could no longer respond to depression by increasing production, at least with the same ease of former times. For the future, growth would come at a far more modest pace amidst an increasing inflexibility towards outside market trends.

NOTES

1. For the depression in the early 1890s see Laura Randall, *An Economic History of Argentina in the Twentieth Century* (New York, 1978) pp. 49–56; A. G. Ford, *The Gold Standard 1880–1914: Britain and Argentina* (Oxford, 1962); John H. Williams, *Argentine International Trade under Inconvertible*

Paper Money, 1880–1900 (Harvard, 1920); H. S. Ferns, *Britain and Argentina in the Nineteenth Century* (Oxford, 1960).

2. For wheat farming see James R. Scobie, *Revolution on the Pampas: A Social History of Argentine Wheat* (Austin, Texas, 1964); Fernando Enrique Barba, 'El desarrollo agropecuario de la província de Buenos Aires (1880–1930)', *Investigaciones y Ensayos*, no. 17 (July–Dec. 1974) pp. 210–310.
3. For the Conversion Law of 1899 see Ford, *The Gold Standard*, Williams, *Argentine International Trade*, Randall, *Economic History of Argentina*.
4. The best statistical summary for this period is Ernesto Tornquist and Co. Ltd, *The Economic Development of the Argentine Republic in the Last Fifty Years* (Buenos Aires, 1919); see also Carlos F. Díaz Alejandro, *Essays on the Economic History of the Argentine Republic* (New Haven, 1970) ch. 1; Guido di Tella and Manuel Zymmelman, *Las etapas del desarrollo económico argentino* (Buenos Aires, 1967) pp. 202–93; Ricardo M. Ortíz, *Historia económica de la Argentina*, vol. 2 (Buenos Aires, 1955); Roberto Cortés Conde and Ezequiel Gallo, *La formación de la Argentina moderna* (Buenos Aires, 1967); Jaime Fuchs, *Argentina: su desarrollo capitalista* (Buenos Aires, 1965).
5. For population see the two national censuses of 1895 and 1914; also Zulma Recchini de Lattes, 'El processo de urbanización en la Argentina; distribución, crecimiento y algunas características de la población urbana', *Desarrollo Económico*, vol. 12, no. 48 (Jan.–Mar. 1973) pp. 867–86; Juan C. Elizaga, 'La evolución de la población argentina en los últimos 100 años', *Desarrollo Económico*, vol. 12, no. 48 (Jan.–Mar. 1973) pp. 795–806.
6. For immigration see Gustavo Beyhaut, R. Cortés Conde, H. Gorostegui and Susana Torrado, 'Los inmigrantes en el sistema ocupacional argentino', in Torcuato S. di Tella *et al.*, *Argentina: Sociedad de Masas* (Buenos Aires, 1967) pp. 85–123; Guy Bourde, *Urbanisation et immigration en Amérique Latine, Buenos Aires (XIXe et XXe siècles)* (Paris, 1974); Oscar E. Cornblit, 'Inmigrantes y empresarios en la política Argentina', *Desarrollo Económico*, vol. 6, no. 24 (Jan.–Mar. 1967); Carl Solberg, *Immigration and Nationalism in Argentina and Chile, 1890–1914* (Austin, Texas, 1970); Jorge Schvarzer, 'Algunos rasgos del desarrollo industrial de Buenos Aires' (Buenos Aires, CISEA, 1979) mimeo.; Adolfo Dorfman, *Historia de la industria argentina* (Buenos Aires, 1970); Roberto Cortés Conde, 'Problemas del crecimiento industrial', in di Tella, *Argentina: Sociedad de Masas*; Eduardo F. Jorge, *Industria y concentración económica* (Buenos Aires, 1971); Díaz Alejandro, *Essays*.
7. For foreign trade figures see Tornquist, *Economic Development*.
8. For foreign investment see Ford, *Gold Standard*; Ferns, *Britain and Argentina*; Winthrop R. Wright, *British-owned Railways in Argentina: Their Effect on Economic Nationalism, 1854–1918* (Austin, Texas, 1972); A. E. Bunge, *Ferrocarriles argentinos* (Buenos Aires, 1917); D. C. M. Platt, *Latin America and British Trade, 1806–1914* (London, 1972); Harold J. Peters, *The Foreign Debt of the Argentine Republic* (Baltimore, 1934).
9. For meat see Simon G. Hanson, *Argentine Meat and the British Market, Chapters in the History of the Argentine Meat Industry* (Stanford, 1938); Peter H. Smith, *Politics and Beef in Argentina, Patterns of Conflict and*

Change (New York, 1969); Oscar E. Colman, 'Luchas interburguesas en el agro argentino: la crisis de la carne en el '20', Serie Estudios, no. 12 (Buenos Aires, CICSO, n.d. [?1973]).
10. Cf. United Nations (CEPAL), *El desarrollo económico de la Argentina*, 4 vols (Mexico, 1959); Jorge Schvarzer, 'Algunos rasgos del desarrollo industrial de Buenos Aires' (Buenos Aires, CISEA, 1979) mimeo.; Adolfo Dorfman, *Historia de la industria argentina* (Buenos Aires, 1970); Roberto Cortés Conde, 'Problemas del crecimiento industrial', in di Tella, *Argentina: Sociedad de Masas*; Eduardo F. Jorge, *Industria y concentración económica* (Buenos Aires, 1971); Díaz Alejandro, *Essays*.
11. Cf. Reginald Lloyd (ed.), *Twentieth Century Impressions of Argentina* (London, 1911).
12. Cf. Carlos Pellegrini in Alberto B. Martínez and Maurice Lewandowski, *The Argentine in the Twentieth Century* (London, 1911) p. xv.

5 Free Trade in One (Primary Producing) Country: the Case of Argentina in the 1920s

A. O'CONNELL

I

It is a well-known fact that at the end of the First World War the Argentine Republic ranked among those countries in the world with the highest incomes per head. Starting from a very low base, such a position had been achieved by an accelerated process of growth beginning in the last quarter of the nineteenth century. Everybody also knows that half a century later the Republic was placed much lower in the world income leagues, not to speak of this last decade's performance.

One significant aspect of that earlier process of growth was the extent to which the country opened up to trade and investment with foreign countries, among which Great Britain was particularly important as customer, creditor and direct owner of a large sector of the capital stock of the Republic. Refusal by successive governments to intervene in the economic life of the country – and more particularly actively to regulate foreign trade so as to promote the development of domestic industry beyond an initial programme of support for agricultural activities – has also been regarded as another main characteristic of that period not unrelated to the previous one.

It is not my purpose in this paper to challenge what I think is a rather idealised image of the pre-1914 period, neither is it to discuss whether laissez-faire policies were appropriate or even prevalent in that era. But it is a fact that in Argentina in the 1920s such policies continued to be applied. The country, as a consequence, was caught in the severe

Depression of the inter-war period, completely dependent on the export of half a dozen agricultural goods and on a few markets, foremost among them Great Britain – an economy with a severe foreign exchange problem. Such a circumstance, I would contend, is somewhat connected with the poor growth performance of the Argentine economy since then.

The argument has been advanced that those events were largely unpredictable. But, without the benefit of hindsight, Alejandro Bunge in the early years of the 1920s had already delivered dramatic warnings against maintaining free-trade policies; he forcefully advocated industrial protectionism as the appropriate response to the increasing restrictions that Argentine export staples were facing (and were about to face) in foreign markets:

> Until 1908 or 1910 our policies, which were adapted to British policies, were beneficial in all aspects. Our economic progress has been due largely to our strong commercial links with Britain and other European states. . . . We all know Britain makes great efforts to obtain foodstuffs, protecting the production of her dominions. . . . As a result of Britain's new policies we are left practically outside her commercial orbit . . . the United States, which is interested in attracting all South American countries towards its own commercial orbit . . . needs, nevertheless, to defend its farmers and ranchers. . . . Our new policies are a consequence of new needs which in part have sprung precisely from the changes in economic policy in those countries in whose orbit we moved until recently . . . it is of fundamental importance that our exports should include a larger number of products than to date, thus risks will diminish and our imports will not continue to rise.[1]

Bunge was not alone in correctly pointing out developments in the international division of labour and advocating industrialisation as the way out. In the context of the First and Second National Economic Congresses (Congresos Económicos Nacionales) sponsored by the Confederacíon Argentina del Comercio, de la Industria y de la Producción, which brought together almost all trade and business organisations, one may detect exactly the same preoccupations voiced even by representatives of those sections of society that had traditionally been taken as opposed to industrialisation.[2]

Forty years later, di Tella and Zymmelman revived part of Bunge's thesis by labelling the 1914–33 period as 'the delay'. An opportunity to invest profits derived from agricultural activities in the building up of industry during prosperity was missed.[3]

Opinions might differ about the right course of action to follow once a change in the international division of labour and in the commercial policies of the great powers was detected. But it is difficult to accept that inaction was best. That such a transformation was taking place has in any case first to be unequivocally established. And it is my contention that Bunge was not merely crystal-ball gazing when he arrived at the right diagnosis of the world situation. The information was there for any literate person to read, in newspapers and in other media. It is to such a purpose that this paper is dedicated, that is, to document the unrelenting onward march of protectionism, discrimination and government intervention in economic life – more specifically, in agricultural activities – beginning at the very moment when Argentina entered the world market as a significant exporter of foodstuffs.

For brevity's sake I cannot review the beginnings of protectionism, starting with the period of the 'Great Depression' of the late nineteenth century after an era of free trade – a brief interlude lasting no more than a few decades. This I have done elsewhere, arguing that before the end of the last century a significant break had already been introduced in the edifice of laissez-faire and in the international division of labour, which had granted overseas food producers (like Argentina) unlimited access to the markets of the advanced countries in Europe.[4]

Here I shall concentrate on the more recent period where events were underlined by the imbalances generated by the First World War but firmly based, all the same, on those far earlier events. In a first section I proceed to examine the crisis of the 1920s in world agriculture, and its effects on the United States and European importers. In the second section two specific additional shocks for Argentine agricultural exports are surveyed, that is, the threat of introduction of imperial preference by Great Britain and the adoption by the United States of a sanitary embargo against Argentine meat imports (and the imports of other countries affected by foot-and-mouth disease). A last section is devoted to an examination of Argentine commercial policy. This section ends with a discussion of commercial policies during the 1920s.

II

1. *Protectionism and the Post-war Agricultural Crisis*

By the end of the 1920s two-thirds of Argentine exports were made up of four products, wheat, maize, linseed and beef. In the world market for each of these products the position of Argentina was highly significant, definitely not marginal. Demand for these products was mainly concentrated in Great Britain and north-western continental Europe, to a varying degree in competition with domestic production of either those same products or close substitutes.

Furthermore, in the case of grain, the Argentine's most important export, the United States was also an important producer and, at least in one variety, an important producer in its own right. In the words of the Taylors the position of the four great exporting countries (United States, Canada, Argentina and Australia) with respect to trade policy was weak, inasmuch as they customarily bought less in the importing countries than they sold to them. In the specific case of Argentina, for instance, her wheat exports went mainly to the United Kingdom (34 per cent), Belgium (14 per cent) and the Netherlands (11 per cent). Only slightly more than one-quarter of her imports originated in these three countries. This last consideration applied also to the fourth export (beef), which was sold similarly to Great Britain (99 per cent of chilled and 54 per cent of frozen beef) and to a few other continental European countries.[5]

The vulnerability of Argentina's position became increasingly clear as the agricultural crisis unfolded. In the years preceding the First World War, supply and demand for wheat looked like having achieved some balance after decades of basic over-supply conditions. Although production continued to expand at a very fast rate, imports by countries in north-western Europe also increased dramatically. Not only was population growing but, as a consequence of prosperity, wheat was displacing other cereals and potatoes in the diet of the European population. In the 25 years from 1885–9 to 1910–14 world output went up by 44 per cent, but that of importing countries in Europe rose only by 11 per cent. Imports into Europe increased 5.4 million tons (almost two-thirds), and the amount was about the same as the increase in the sales of the four largest overseas exporters for the same period. Simultaneously, there were significant increases in exports by Russia and the Danubian basin countries.[6]

Wheat prices were on the increase from 1896 as a result of the exhaustion of the frontier in the US and the cultivation of new lands in Argentina, Canada, Australia and Siberia at increasing cost.[7] War brought severe problems for wheat production in Europe. Output fell by one-third between 1910–13 and 1914–18 in the importing and exporting countries of Europe taken together. Reduction in output and the disappearance of Russia as a major exporter led to a sharp increase in prices. The deficit was covered mainly by an increase of more than 10 million hectares in wheat cultivation in Canada and the United States, and of almost 5 million tons in exports by these same two countries. As a consequence both of shipping difficulties and of comparatively larger advantages in increasing livestock production, Argentina and Australia did not share equally in this boom.[8]

Geographical distribution of world wheat production had, therefore, suffered a significant transformation as a consequence of the war. But as the distribution was not the outcome of gradual change it was bound, at least partially, to be reversed once peace came. In addition to such forces behind supply, population was now lower in Europe, and some reduction in per capita consumption could be observed. For the moment we might concentrate on the United States.

2. *The 1920s Depression in United States Agriculture*

In the United States agricultural prices during the war increased faster than other prices. By 1918 the index of farm prices was almost 10 per cent ahead of an all-commodities index for the 1910–14 period. Farmers' incomes had increased from 7.5 billion in this quinquennium, on average, to 16.2 billion dollars in 1918. Land prices were up 29 per cent. Mortgage debt, however, had risen from 4.7 billion dollars to 10.2 billion dollars.[9] Farmers were expecting a drop in prices once the war was over. In fact prices, stimulated by world scarcity and United States credits to European purchasers, kept climbing till mid-1919. Thereafter the drop was sharp. By 1921 prices received by farmers were only 16 per cent above pre-war, while farmers paid 56 per cent more than before; rural wages were about double the pre-war level, and tight money conditions were making the burden of heavy debts contracted at past inflated prices even more unbearable.[10]

Early agitation by farmers against such a state of affairs led to the constitution of new organisations and the setting up of the powerful 'Farm Block', a bipartisan group in the US Senate which furnished the majority of the Agricultural Committee and enough votes to keep up pressure on both Congress and the Administration throughout the 1920s.[11]

As price declines coincided with monetary restraint it was not unusual for farmers' organisations to turn their attention mainly to financial remedies. Marketing organisation was also very much under scrutiny of those years, and proposals were discussed for setting up a generalised cooperative system for selling the US harvest. But tariffs were also revised, supposedly to help the farmer.[12]

The United States, especially from the Civil War period, was a high-tariff country. Tariffs were a very important political issue and more than one election turned on them. On the whole, the Republican party tended towards a protectionist policy while the Democrats preferred lower tariffs. Farmers both in the South and in the mid-West tended to support free trade and oppose protectionism. Duties, however, were imposed on some agricultural products 'in order to maintain the fiction that the agricultural population secured through them a share of the benefits of protection'.[13]

But with the election of Wilson as President late in 1912 public opinion expressed itself strongly against protection (vaguely connected in the public mind with monopoly power). Republicans split that year, and Democrats achieved a sizeable majority not only in the House of Representatives but also in the Senate – the body most prone to protectionism. Wilson lost no time and called for an extra session to discuss immediately tariff legislation. The new Tariff Act – the Underwood/Simmons Bill – was passed in October 1913. Not only did this act bring a general reduction in tariffs but, more specifically, it made wool and hides – for long the two most important exports from Argentina to the United States – free of duty. Wheat, maize and meat, as well as quebracho extract (another important agricultural product) were also made duty-free. Linseed, which would become Argentina's largest export to the United States, was taxed at the low level of 20 cents per bushel (56 lb).[14]

At the end of the First World War there was less justification than ever for a high tariff. The United States had become a creditor nation, and room had to be made for imports from foreign countries so that they could service their debts. A combination of circumstances, however, resulted in one of the highest tariffs ever legislated. The victory of the Republican party – first in 1918 and again in the 1920 elections – was no doubt one contributing factor. But another, perhaps the most important, factor behind the return to high protectionism, was the agricultural depression which had extended to a depression throughout the economy. In spite of the fact that for products like wheat, of which the United States had an export surplus, import duties could not possibly prevent price decline, pressure was brought to bear on Congress for protection to be applied to farm products. A Republican-dominated, lame-duck Congress immediately passed a protective bill which was vetoed by

President Wilson on his last day in office, early in January 1921. And in May of that year an 'Emergency' Tariff bill was passed, imposing high duties on agricultural products.[15]

The Emergency Tariff bill was to be 'understood by our [the United States] people [as] for the emergency only', and approved originally for six months. But as early as January 1921 the Ways and Means Committee of the House of Representatives started hearings for a new tariff bill. The Emergency Bill was re-enacted repeatedly until the new tariff legislation was approved in September 1922 (the Fordney-McCumber Act). If anything, duties on agricultural products were increased yet again. Linseed was now dutiable at 40 cents per bushel instead of 30 cents. Beef and veal duties were raised even further from two cents to three cents per pound. Moreover, in general the elimination of the restraining influence of farmers' opinion led to a widespread increase in duties. But, as Taussig explains for textiles, 'on the whole [they] showed no such marked accentuation of the protective policy as did the articles in which the agricultural West was interested. The difference was significant of the character of the Act and of the forces which led to its enactment.'[16]

There was no reason to suppose that import duties could help wheat prices and, as the Tariff Commission remarked in a later analysis, no relation could be detected between the enactment of the Tariff Acts and price movements. In fact, by making it more difficult for European importing countries to get hold of needed foreign exchange it reduced the market for American farm exports. Those duties were 'dust in the farmer's eyes', as Taussig remarked of a previous occasion. No wonder, then, that pressure from the mid-West on Congress did not subside after 1922, and that it turned its attention to more direct ways of supporting prices.[17]

Multiple initiatives were taken, of which the best known was that launched under the slogan of 'Equality for Agriculture'. In the analysis of George N. Peek and Hugh S. Johnson – two small, agricultural machinery manufacturers – 'the protective principle . . . operated in the benefit of industry to the detriment of agriculture'; crop prices were fixed by world prices, but industrial prices were raised under protection of the tariff. Their proposal, which in slightly changed form came to be known as the McNary–Haugen plan, envisaged purchases at a fixed 'ratio price' – redressing the fall from the pre-war levels in prices of farm products – and the sale of surpluses abroad at world market prices with losses borne by the farmers themselves. Several bills were submitted to Congress throughout the 1920s which incorporated such a plan. In two instances – in the years 1927 and 1928 – McNary–Haugen bills were passed by Congress but vetoed by President Coolidge. And early in 1929 a newly-elected Republican President (Hoover) called for a special session of Congress to consider a 'limited' revision of the tariff in support of the farmers' position. This initiative brought the enactment of the Hawley–Smoot Bill of 1930, which raised tariffs to an unprecedented level.[18]

I shall return later to an examination of the Hawley–Smoot Bill, as well as such other protective measures instituted by the US Government in the late 1920s which concerned agricultural products of particular interest for Argentine exporters. We shall now turn to Europe to analyse the impact of the postwar depression of agriculture on the commercial policy of the importing nations.

3. Protectionism among European Importers in the 1920s

The aftermath of the First World War in the agricultural market was characterised, as I have pointed out, by a marked redistribution of production among overseas countries and by reduced output levels, declining consumption, and a drop in prices. Agricultural protectionism in European importing countries responded to such a situation by some moderation in duties on foodstuffs, while in the United States, as we have seen, tariffs for almost all agricultural goods were raised.[19]

Leith-Ross singles out 1925, correctly, as the turning point for agriculture in the post-war period, more specifically for wheat, the all-important commodity. This was the first year that Europe's output (excluding Russia) rose above the average for the five-year period before the war. This was also the year when Germany recovered the freedom to formulate its own commercial policy, and when Mussolini launched the 'Battle for Wheat' in Italy. However, we shall see that signs of things to come were already very apparent in Europe beyond whatever the United States had already implemented.[20]

In France commercial policy in the post-war period (as soon as wartime prohibition was lifted) went through a phase characterised mainly by attempts to adjust duties – which were specific – to inflation so as to avoid any erosion of protection. A more systematic policy was inaugurated with the Tariff Revision of 1927, modified by the Treaty with Germany of the same year, by which the minimum tariffs negotiated with Germany were to be extended to all countries entitled to most-favoured-nation treatment by France. Agricultural duties, however, remained as prescribed in the tariff bill. To take some examples, wheat which was duty-free previous to this tariff became dutiable at about 20 per cent; beef duties were increased from 50 to 350 francs per 100 kg of fresh and chilled beef, and from 50 to 180 francs per 100 kg of frozen beef. It was estimated that the new tariff law, in combination with existing treaties, would yield an average rate of protection of 14.4 per cent (13.9 per cent in 1913), but that the corresponding figure solely for agricultural products was 23.8 per cent. 'As to agricultural protection, it has been placed by the new tariff in the very foreground', was the opinion of Delledonne, the author of one of the better-known books on European commercial policies in the 1920s. This opinion was definitely not shared by the Confédération Nationale des Associations Agricoles which demanded 'equality of treatment' and less emphasis on industrial development. In March 1928 agricultural duties were raised again, but without satisfying agricultural organisations.[21]

Germany, under the Treaty of Versailles, was deprived of sovereign rights as to tariff policies until 1925. Agriculture began to experience intense competition from abroad, which exerted a downward pressure on prices while costs were kept high. Even though opposed by the many left-wing economists, the 1925 Tariff reinstated von Bülow's highly protectionist system of 1902, with somewhat higher duties for livestock products increased in 1927.[22]

As a result of the 1925 Tariff Laws and the concessions granted to other nations under a series of commercial treaties signed during those years, it has been estimated that the general level of protection was 13.9 per cent (13.1 per cent before the war) but that it reached the level of 20.4 per cent for agricultural goods (18.3 per cent back in 1913).[23]

In addition to tariff measures, other more direct ways of supporting agriculture were put into practice. First, the import certificate system was reintroduced, which entailed a system of export subsidies for grain. Second, minimum prices for rye – much more important than wheat in Germany – were introduced in 1925, with the Government's direct intervention in purchases and sales after 1928. And, third, in July 1929 milling ratios prescribing a minimum of 30 per cent of domestic grain were enacted. All these measures would be reinforced after 1930 in Germany, and copied or invented again in most other countries.[24]

In Italy concern about the cereal deficit which emerged from the war was coupled with anxiety over a difficult balance of payments. Wheat imports, which at the time of Italian unification stood at 230,000 tons per year, had increased to 1.5 million tons in the years before the war and shot up to 2.5 million tons in the period 1921–4 as production lagged behind fast-rising demand. Wheat imports had come to represent more than half the deficit in the balance of trade in the early 1920s. Already in 1921 a highly protective Tariff Law was enacted, but duties of L 7.50 (gold) – equivalent to some $1.45 pre-1933 – were suspended. For the time being the Italian tariff disregarded agriculture. But in 1925, when the 'Battle for Grain' was launched, the duty on wheat was re-established. In 1928, additionally, the *bonifica integrale* programme (devised for land improvement) was put into action. Protection by 1926 was at the level of 14.2 per cent (12.7 per cent in 1913); for agricultural goods it stood at about 23 per cent (21.7 per cent).[25]

As for government intervention in agriculture in Britain, the decade was inaugurated with the Agricultural Act of 1920. Under this Act guaranteed minimum prices for wheat, oats and barley, which had been introduced during the war to encourage home expansion of the cultivated areas, were extended indefinitely into the future. But the next year, as prices collapsed in the post-war slump, the cost of this scheme was thought to be excessive; it was discontinued in an action described as a 'betrayal' of farmers. The only other break with laissez-faire in the 1920s was the subsidy for sugar-beet production. In manufacturing, although the Balfour Committee had recommended a general *ad valorem* tariff of 10 per cent at the end of the war, protection was limited to 'safeguarding' of 'key' industries and the persistence of the 'McKenna' duties introduced during the war on imports of 'luxury' goods (motorcars, amongst other things). The numerical significance of the 'safeguarding' duties was small; they covered only 0.1 per cent of the total imports of Great Britain in the 1921–5 period. But their existence and their renewal in 1926 – after the first five years of operation – revealed a changing attitude towards protection. Even more important in the present context is the actual beginning of 'Imperial Preference' – about which we shall say more hereafter – when rebates were granted on revenue duties imposed by the Finance Bill of 1919 and on the McKenna duties.[26]

After 1925, and long before the Wall Street crash, signs of over-production were observable in the markets of many agricultural products. A period of chronic decline in agricultural prices set in. In fact, according to Mandelbaum, real prices for wheat had been declining steadily since the early 1880s.[27] We shall now examine two powerful protectionist initiatives that dominated discussion in Argentina in the late 1920s.

84   The Political Economy of Argentina, 1880–1946

4. *Further Handicaps*

In the second half of the 1920s, in addition to the trend towards increasing protectionism that we have been surveying, some further dramatic shocks were added to the difficulties already faced by Argentina in markets for her staple export products. The first – with roots going back to the late nineteenth century – was the threat of the introduction by Great Britain of Imperial Preference. The second was the embargo imposed by the United States on sanitary grounds against fresh and refrigerated meat coming from Argentina.

5. *Imperial Preference and Argentine Exports to Great Britain*

The campaign for an Imperial 'Zollverein' had started in Great Britain as early as the 1870s, promoted by the Fair Trade League. The first Colonial Conference was held in 1887, and in 1902 the fourth Conference passed a resolution in favour of Imperial Preference.

The major obstacle was the need for free-trade Britain to introduce a tariff, and more specifically a tariff on foodstuffs, if it were to grant preferences on what were the main exports from the Empire to the home country. In fact in 1913, of total imports from the Empire into the United Kingdom, one-third was made up of food, drink and tobacco. The other leading items were raw materials – like Australian and New Zealand wool – the taxing of which was strongly opposed by British manufacturers.

Consequently, it is not surprising that Joseph Chamberlain's campaign, which was in full operation from 1903, met no early success. On the contrary, in the General Election of 1906 the Free Traders won a victory; free trade Liberals obtained a large majority precisely on the issue of tariffs. The campaign for 'Tariff Reform', however, did not stop there, and it kept winning adherents up to the beginning of the First World War.[28]

The First World War, by increasing awareness of the advantages of self-sufficiency, had quite an effect on this issue. The Imperial War Conference of 1917 passed resolutions favourable to the principle of Imperial Preference. But beyond those preferences which had already been granted on British products before the war by the Dominions, only minor concessions on Empire produce were introduced by Great Britain herself. Opposition to protectionism was still strong, and at the General Election of 1924 the Conservative Party, which had campaigned for

Imperial Preference on foodstuffs, was defeated. It took the Depression and the National Government of 1931 to overturn a policy of Free Trade inaugurated as far back as the 1840s.

Meanwhile, since the introduction of Imperial Preference, and consequently of restrictions on Argentine exports of foodstuffs to Great Britain, had now (by the early 1920s) become a distinct possibility, it was put to use by British interests in Argentina in their campaign (in full force after the first visit of the Prince of Wales in 1925) for preferential treatment.[29]

A second and most effective blow to the expansion of Argentine exports began in the United States, but it threatened to extend to Great Britain. Beginning in January 1927, the US Department of Agriculture prohibited imports of fresh or refrigerated meats from the Argentine Republic and from the 14 other countries in which foot-and-mouth disease was endemic.[30] The US market took only a tiny fraction of Argentine meat exports at the time; but it was one on which great hopes had been placed as domestic output lagged behind US consumption. More immediately serious, however, was the threat that almost the sole market for Argentine meat, Great Britain, could be closed down by foot-and-mouth disease. The US sanitary embargo had been prompted, in fact, by a British discovery that the foot-and-mouth virus remained alive for several weeks in the bone marrow and in some of the blood vessels of refrigerated carcasses. Acting on this knowledge the British government had prohibited – in June 1926 – imports of carcasses slaughtered in continental Europe. Almost simultaneously, conversations with the Argentine authorities were initiated that implied a tightening-up of sanitary measures so as to avoid export to the United Kingdom of infected carcasses.[31] It was made clear from the beginning that if the disease were discovered in a carcass arriving from Argentina it could become almost impossible for the British government to withstand pressure to shut down imports. Paradoxically, although the scientific discovery that the foot-and-mouth virus could remain present in refrigerated meat had originated in England, it was the United States that kept its market closed for Argentine exports. The British government contented itself with a few additional measures of sanitary control introduced by the Argentine government late in 1927 and early 1928.

It would take us far beyond the scope of this paper to substantiate such a statement in detail, but I am convinced that although originally the American sanitary embargo was prompted by a genuine fear of infection it gradually and increasingly became a protectionist device. I am also convinced that the British government stood firm against pressure from farming circles to stop importing Argentine beef, for fear of the impact on the cost of living.[32]

The fact remains that, apart from tariff increases, a new barrier had been raised against Argentine exports. It was the most severe of all possible blows, but it was not the last to be struck by the United States during the allegedly Free Trade era previous to the Wall Street crash. Disputes arose also on sanitary grounds for the export of Argentine grapes and, on technical grounds, of alfalfa seed. Linseed and corn exports were threatened with increases in duties as a consequence of cost investigations under section 315 of the Fordney–McCumber Tariff Act. These disputes were eventually sorted out, but they were followed by an even more serious event, a new, protectionist tariff bill, the Hawley–Smoot Act.

Although the Hawley–Smoot Act was finally approved in 1930, we have seen at the end of Section II.2 that the initiative for a new bill granting further protection to the farmer had been taken by President Hoover well before the Wall Street crash (in fact at the time of a stock market boom) when he inaugurated his term early in 1929. Hoover had called for a 'limited' revision, as had Harding in 1921. The revision came generally into force as early as May 1929, when it was passed by the House of Representatives.[33] By August 1929 reactions against the projected higher duties had been received in Washington from more than 24 countries, among them Argentina. In Buenos Aires the Sociedad Rural Argentina had convened a meeting of all institutions associated with agricultural production and trade, and the decision was taken to submit a letter to the President early in 1929. Opinions differed on the matter of either reducing duties for those countries which imported Argentine produce freely, or raising them – as the Unión Industrial Argentina suggested – against those that erected protectionist barriers. The idea behind all proposals was the same, i.e. that of 'reciprocity', about which I shall say more in the next section. No less than ten years, anyway, had been lost, and Argentina would be forced drastically to curtail imports under the impact of the the Depression. Even in 1929 Argentina remained a Free Trader.

III ARGENTINE COMMERCIAL POLICY

The basic law governing Argentina's customs' regime in the 1920s had been in force since the beginning of the century. Duties were nominally *ad valorem*, but they were calculated according to official fixed valuations as prescribed by a specific schedule.

1. Tariff Levels and Structure

The argument on Argentine tariff levels was largely inconclusive before 1931. Traditionally it had been widely accepted that the Argentine tariff was very low at least up to 1931 in response to the laissez-faire policies of that era. Both protectionists and free traders agreed on low tariffs, but they disagreed over the supposed advantages or disadvantages of such a tariff. In later years, however, some authors have revived (and in a way confirmed) the view that Argentine tariff levels were far from low if compared – without further qualification – with those prevalent in Europe, the United States and other countries in the so-called 'Regions of Recent Settlement'. The average Argentine tariff worked out at less than that of the United states, similar to that of protectionist Australia, and higher than those for Canada and Europe (except Spain). If such were indeed the case – it is argued – protectionist criticism of the Argentine tariff levels would be completely misplaced.[34]

A full discussion of this issue would take a degree of research rather beyond the scope of this paper. But in my opinion the pre-1931 Argentine tariff must be judged with care.

First, it is true that the Argentine tariff was much more encompassing than, say, that of the United States. Many raw materials and manufacturing inputs which were duty-free in already industrialised countries were dutiable in Argentina. Some authors took this fact as evidence enough of the revenue-raising character of the Argentine tariff. Others have suggested 'Protectionism in reverse' or, in modern parlance, 'negative effective protection' (that is, raw materials attracting duty at a higher rate than finished products).[35]

The larger coverage of the Argentine tariff meant that when attention is focused on dutiable items and a comparison is drawn, say, with the Australian tariff, the Argentine tariff appears to have been several points below the level of Australia's, and markedly inferior to that of the United States.[36] On the other hand, Díaz Alejandro's work on the all-important case of the textile industry has failed to confirm a generalised case of "negative effective protection". Except for silk products and tobacco, manufacturing raw-materials were normally taxed at rates lower than those for finished products.

The fact remains, however, that manufacturing raw materials in Argentina were in general actually dutiable, while they were almost always duty-free in industrialised countries and even in the United States. If rates on finished goods were comparable or even lower than, say, in the United States or Australia, taxation of raw materials in Argentina meant that rates of effective protection should have been lower.[37] In my opinion, therefore, there are grounds for believing that the level of effective protection of manufacturing was lower, in fact much lower, in Argentina than in other 'new' countries with what seemed to be a comparable level of tariff.

Second, it is unnecessary also to introduce some measure of downward correction in tariff levels if bias in exchange rates is also to be taken into account, because a uniform tariff rate applied on all and every imported article – which, as we have just seen, was much more the case for Argentina than for other countries – would be equivalent to a two-tier exchange rate system that made it more expensive to buy than to sell foreign exchange. Now, it may be presumed that such would be the correct policy to follow for a country the exports of which were derived from a sector whose productivity was higher and largely unconnected with that of the rest of the economy. Such is the case for present-day, oil-exporting countries, and it was so for an Argentina that freely depleted the top fertile layer of the pampa region in the era of the *agricultura-minera*. In such a situation the market exchange rate would tend to be below that which would be 'fair' for import-competing sectors. Consequently, in the absence of a two-tier exchange market which discriminated against traditional pampean exports – like the one introduced (but too mildly) in November 1933 – tariff levels would be playing only a compensatory role in terms of the exchange rate, and as such they cannot reasonably be compared to those of other countries without introducing some correction.[38]

In conclusion, reduced effective protection due to the existence of tariffs on raw materials in addition to exchange rate bias made for a much lower level of protection than indicated by unqualified comparisons.[39]

2. *Most-Favoured-Nation Clauses and Reciprocity in Argentine Commercial Policy*

Under article 74 of the 1905 Customs Law which remained in force throughout this period the President of the Argentine Republic was empowered to raise tariffs by up to 50 per cent in order to counteract discrimination by a foreign country, or to lower them by no more than 50 per cent in exchange for 'equivalent advantages'. Such an article was not new in Argentine tariff legislation. Throughout the 1890s clauses of this kind had been introduced in various tariff laws; their origin may be traced to French and United States commercial policy. In fact, under the Méline tariff of 1892 – which embodied an early form of agricultural protectionism – France had adopted a 'double-column' tariff which charged higher rates against countries that had negotiated treaties granting concessions of national interest. Two years before, in the United States, the McKinley tariff had included a provision for penalty duties – among which was one-and-a-half cents per pound on hides – to be applied to countries not giving preferential treatment to US exports. Reaction in Argentina had led to the passing of the 1892 Tariff Law which contained a penalty provision, like article 74 in the 1905 law.[40]

In the case of Argentina, however, provision for penalty duties was largely formal, as the country was tied up by most-favoured-nation (MFN) clauses in treaties signed with all important trading partners, and which, in the case of Great Britain and most European countries, were clearly of an unconditional character.[41] There was little possibility, therefore, for Argentina to discriminate against some foreign country's exports on the basis of provisions for penalty duties except in the case of the United States, although Argentina tended to adhere to the American conditional interpretation of the clause. As a consequence of such a limitation one may register, already from the 1890s, successive calls to denounce treaties of commerce containing MFN clauses so as to be free to follow a policy strictly based on reciprocity. In one such demand a preoccupation emerges which was to gain greater strength during the 1920s and to which we shall return later, i.e. the grant of special preferences to Great Britain in order to contain the threat of Imperial Preference.[42]

3. *Increased Protection in the 1920s*

As in all other countries, the post war crisis in Argentina and the difficulties of containing and preserving business unleashed a campaign for increased protection. The workings of the system of tariff valuations made for a drastically reduced real level of protection because of inflated import values. In July 1920, Law 11022 was passed which provided for a 20 per cent increase in official valuations markedly lower than the level of inflation.

Under the new President Alvear and at the initiative of his Minister of Finance, Herrera Vegas, a Commission was appointed to study the fiscal and customs system of the country; Alejandro Bunge was to head the Commission. Proposals for a rationalisation of the tariff included a subdivision of import products under four categories, from raw materials and machinery to those the importation of which was thought to be undesirable. Rates ranged from zero to 80 per cent. But the resignation of Herrera Vegas put an end to the work of the Commission. In November 1923 Congress passed a new law – Law 11281 – introducing a 60 per cent increase in official valuations, and raising specified duties by one-fourth. In the opinion of one foreign author 'these changes were primarily for the purpose of increasing customs revenue.' The renewed attempt to protect the development of Argentine manufacturing by tariff reform had failed.[43]

There was no change in the Argentine tariff regime for the rest of the 1920s, but pressure for change shifted to livestock producers as a result of the crisis of the early 1920s. In April 1926 the Sociedad Rural Argentina convened a Congress of Livestock Producers of the River Plate. At this Congress a resolution was passed calling for denunciation of all commercial treaties so as to be in a position to enter into reciprocity treaties and to grant special favours to neighbouring countries. The issue was taken up fervently by the Sociedad Rural leadership, both those ending their mandate in 1926 and the new headed by Duhau. Their enthusiasm, of course, was not completely unconnected with the imposition of the US sanitary embargo, and the renewed threats of Imperial Preference on the part of the United Kingdom. Beginning in January 1927, *Anales* – the periodical published by the Sociedad Rural – placed on all its issues the slogan 'Compra a quien nos Compra' (buy from those who buy from us) concocted by the British Ambassador. It only thinly disguised the purpose of the whole exercise of treaty denunciation, which was to grant preferences to Great Britain. President Alvear made reference to such a policy in his speech inaugurating Congress on 1 May 1927, and a whole stream of projects was submitted with the intention of enacting a preferential system.

There was no agreement in Argentina that such was the correct course of action. For instance, at the Segunda Conferencia Económica Nacional, attended by all representative and business trade organizations, a proposal to revise all commercial treaties with a view to denouncing – if found convenient – MFN clauses incorporated in their text, was not passed. In its stead a resolution was approved which called for the negotiation of commercial treaties on a basis of reciprocity, but only with neighbouring countries.[44]

In the meantime, the United States government, in pursuit of a policy inaugurated back in 1922, was trying to persuade the Argentine authorities to negotiate a new Treaty of Commerce which would include an unconditional MFN clause. As a result of their labours they received from President Alvear's administration only a note suggesting the addition of a denunciation clause to the existing 1853 Treaty between the two nations. Early in 1929, during the controversy unleashed by discussions of the Hawley–Smoot Act and under President Yrigoyen's administration, the US Chargé d'Affaires reported that having asked Dr Oyhanarte – Yrigoyen's Minister of Foreign Affairs – about the effects of the Sociedad Rural campaign, he had received the answer that 'the government thinks with its own head'. Only a few months afterwards the Argentine government was signing the D'Abernon agreement and other measures which gave preference to Great Britain.[45]

IV CONCLUSION

Reacting against discussion of the highly protectionist Hawley–Smoot Act in the United States, *La Nación* – a leading Argentine newspaper – depicted, very synthetically, the situation I have been examining in this paper. In a leading article under the title 'La excepción argentina', it declared that world conditions had undergone a complete transformation over the last years. All countries had tried to industrialise; they had attempted to limit their purchases abroad and to rely exclusively on themselves. But there was one exception, and that was the Argentine Republic.[46]

In fact we have seen that while the whole world, with the partial exception of a reluctant Great Britain, had turned towards protectionism, Argentina did little to change its commercial policy. Moreover, if there was a strong campaign favouring *some* changes it was only one that advocated special concessions for Great Britain, rather than greater self-sufficiency or greater diversification within the economy. Argentina in the 1920s was both a primary producer and, unilaterally, a free trader.[47]

NOTES

1. Alejandro Bunge, 'La nueva política económica argentina', *La Economía Argentina*, vol. III (Buenos Aires, 1928) ch. 1. This was the text of a paper delivered by Bunge in 1921.
2. See Confederación Argentina del Comercio, de la Industria y de la Producción, *Primera Conferencia Económica Nacional* (Buenos Aires, 1919), and the Proceedings of the Second Conference of 1924.
3. See Guido di Tella and Manuel Zymmelman, *Las etapas del desarrollo económico argentino* (Buenos Aires, 1967) ch. 1.
4. See my 'Free Trade in One (Primary Producing) Country: the Case of

Argentina in the 1920s', Working Paper (Instituto Torcuato di Tella. Buenos Aires, 1983).
5. See H. C. Taylor and A. D. Taylor, *World Trade in Agricultural Products* (New York, 1943) p. 110. For figures on the destination of Argentina's principal exports see Carlos F. Díaz Alejandro, *Essays on the Economic History of the Argentine Republic* (New Haven, Conn., 1970) p. 20.
6. See Banco Central, 'Tendencias de la producción agropecuaria', *Revista Económica*, n.s. I (1937).
7. See Société des Nations, Comité Economique, *La crise agricole* (Geneva, 1931) p. 50.
8. See Banco Central, 'Tendencias', tables 40, 41.
9. See Murray R. Benedict, *Farm Policies in the United States, 1790–1950* (New York, 1953) p. 168.
10. See Société des Nations, *La crise agricole*, p. 9, and Benedict, *Farm Policies*, p. 173 fn. 1.
11. Benedict, *Farm Policies*, ch. 9.
12. Ibid.
13. F. W. Taussig, *The Tariff History of the United States* (New York, 1923 edn) p. 249.
14. Ibid., chs 5–9, and Benedict, *Farm Policies*, p. 204, fn 93.
15. Taussig, *Tariff History*, ch. 10.
16. Harding's Message to Congress, 12 April 1921, and Taussig, *Tariff History*, p. 467.
17. W. B. Kelly, Jr (ed.), *Studies in US Commercial Policy* (Chapel Hill, N.C., 1963) p. 10, and Lynn Ramsay Edminster, *The Cattle Industry and the Tariff* (New York, 1926) p. 198.
18. The whole story of the 'Equality for Agriculture' movement is in Benedict, *Farm Policies*, ch. 10.
19. See above for US commercial policy in the early 1920s and Société des Nations, *Considérations relatives a l'évolution actuelle du protectionisme agricole* (Geneva, 20 May 1935) Annex II.
20. See Société des Nations, *Considérations*, Annex I; 'Le protectionisme agricole en Europe pendant la période d'après guerre', p. 16.
21. See O. Delledone, *European Tariff Policies* (New York, 1928) ch. 3; M. Tracy. *Agriculture in Western Europe: Challenge and Response, 1880–1980* (London, 1982 edn) ch. 8. and Société des Nations. *Considérations*. Annex I.
22. See Tracy, *Agriculture in Western Europe*, pp. 96–100.
23. See Delledone, *European Tariff Policies*, ch. 4.
24. See Tracy, *Agriculture in Western Europe*, pp. 102–3 and ch. 9.
25. See Delledone, *European Tariff Policies*, ch. 5, and M. Tracy, 'Fifty Years of Agricultural Policy', *Journal of Agricultural Economics*, XXVII (September 1976).
26. See J. Henry Richardson, *British Foreign Economic Policy* (London, 1936) ch. 4, and Tracy, *Agriculture in Western Europe*, ch. 7.
27. See Vladimir P. Timoshenko, 'World Agriculture and the Depression', *Michigan Business Studies*, V, no. 5 (1933). W. Mandelbaum's calculations are included in his book *The World Wheat Economy* (Cambridge, Mass., 1953) fig. 9, p. 106.
28. Delledone, *European Tariff Policies*, ch. 2.

29. For post-First World War imperial preference policies see Delledone, *European Tariff Policies*, and Richardson, *British Foreign Economic Policy*. For the British campaign in Argentina and the use of the imperial preference threat to extract concessions, see Jorge Fodor and Arturo O'Connell, 'Argentina y la economía atlántica en la primera mitad del siglo XX', *Desarrollo Económico*, 13 (April/June 1973). See also 'The British Campaign against American Trade and Capital in the Argentine' (29 May 1929) in US National Archives and Record Service, Dept. of State, Record Group 59.
30. For the text of the order see Bureau of Animal Industry (BAI), Order 298, in Service and Regulatory Announcements, BAI, 1926, pp. 72–3.
31. For a letter incorporating recommendations agreed with an Argentine representative in London, see Public Record Office (London), Foreign Office, file 371 (General Correspondence) no. 11954 (1926).
32. See A. O'Connell, 'La fiebre aftosa, el embargo sanitario norteamericano contra las importaciones de carne y el triángulo Argentina–Gran Bretaña–Estados Unido en el período entre las dos guerras mundiales', *Jornadas de Historia Económica Argentina* (San Juan, 1983).
33. See US National Archives, Dept. of State, Record Group 59, 611.355 (Corn and Linseed), and D. B. Riefler, *Trade Relations of the United States with Argentina* (New York, 1929), as well as Argentine Foreign Ministry, Despatches of the Argentine Embassy in Washington, *Memoria* (for 1926 and 1927). For the Hawley–Smoot Act see also Kelly, *Studies in U.S. Commercial Policy*, pp. 11–14, and PRO (London), memorandum in Washington, despatch 8 March 1929, FO 118 + 620, file A1976/139/45.
34. Díaz Alejandro, *Essays*, ch. 5, and George J. Eder, 'Current Trends in the International Trade of Argentina', *International Conciliation*, 271 (June 1931), and the opinion he quotes of Professor Jones as well as his own. For international comparison see Société des Nations, *Taux indices des tarifs* (Geneva, 1927).
35. See Díaz Alejandro, *Essays*, and also, for instance, Julio Irazusta, *Balance de siglo y medio* (Buenos Aires, 1960) where one specific case of 'protection in reverse' is illustrated.
36. Díaz Alejandro, *Essays*, p. 286.
37. Ibid., tables 5:3, 5:4 and 5:5 (duty-free imports consisted largely of railway supplies).
38. Such a correction would be different from one which took into account only variations in time of the exchange rate. As part of this work I have myself corrected Díaz Alejandro's series for the combined effect of the exchange rate and the tariff level on 'protection' as it existed in 1914 (Díaz Alejandro, *Essays*, Tables 5:1 and 5:7). Instead of using cost of living indices to estimate 'real' devaluation against the dollar and the pound sterling I have made use of the wholesale price indices which I believe to be a better procedure. On such a basis, real devaluation is much lower than that estimated by Díaz Alejandro; real devaluation at the end of the 1920s, for example, compared with 1914, is only slghtly above 10 per cent instead of being around 30 per cent.
39. As a consequence of my own figures for the 'real' exchange rate, the 'combined effect' of the variations in time of average tariff levels and the

'real' exchange rate shows an increase, between 1914 and 1929, of the order of 10 to 15 per cent lower than the figure of 30 per cent given by Díaz Alejandro.
40. See art. 14 of the 1892 tariff law and discussions in the Chamber of Deputies, 18 July and 4 November 1892: *Diario de Sesiones* (Buenos Aires, 1892).
41. Benjamin H. Williams, *Economic Foreign Policy of the United States* (New York, 1929) ch. 14.
42. See a bill from Senator Igarzábal calling for the elimination of all MFN clauses from international trade treaties, or for the outright denunciation of such treaties if elimination of MFN clauses proved impossible, 18 July 1892: *Diario de Sesiones*.
43. See Vernon Phelps, *The International Economic Position of Argentina*
44. See Confederación Argentina del Comercio, de la Industria y de la Producción, *Segunda Conferencia* (Buenos Aires, 1924) p. 165.
45. For Oyhanarte's pronouncement see US National Archives, Dept. of State, Record Group 59, file 611.353, B.A. despatch 497, 14 March 1929. For the whole 'Compra a quién nos compra' campaign and the 1929 Anglo-Argentine agreements see Fodor and O'Connell, 'Argentina y la economía atlántica'.
46. *La Nación*, 26 January 1929 (my translation).
47. Bunge, 'La nueva política económica argentina', p. 61.

6 The Economic Formulae of the 1930s: a Reassessment

PETER ALHADEFF

Generally speaking, the literature has distinguished two approaches to the State management of the Argentine economy during the 1930s, one before and the other after Federico Pinedo took over the Finance Ministry in 1933. Javier Villanueva, in particular, has given countenance to this view.[1]

This paper attempts to show that the difference between these two approaches to economic management have been overemphasised, and their common features underplayed. There was a far greater continuity of views and policy than has been suggested so far, and this will be illustrated in the first part of the paper. The second part establishes the contribution of the economic measures of 1931–3 to the policies adopted by Federico Pinedo after the second half of 1933 – what Villanueva has chosen to call the 'new formulae' of the 1930s.

I ECONOMIC POLICY OVERVIEWED

Throughout the Depression and during the rest of the 1930s the public sector was inclined to practise cautious economic management by balancing the budget, by keeping a good credit name in the Republic and abroad, and, as far as was possible in the 1930s, by preventing the currency from sharply depreciating. This behaviour of the Argentine authorities has on occasion been explained by the powerful influence of an inherited body of economic thought. The early 1930s are especially favoured by analysts to illustrate the point. Villanueva, for example, has said that much of economic policy-making between 1929 and 1931 consisted of nothing more than a series of ad hoc responses dictated by traditions.² Ferrer goes one step further: the initial response to the Depression, biased by orthodoxy, was to put into practice a neoclassical prescription.³

Ultimately, however, there was little room for dogma in decisions affecting government finance, and practical considerations were paramount in any given course of action.

1. *Balancing the Budget*

The Argentine Government's concern with a balanced budget in the early 1930s had more to do with the disarray that the Depression had left in State accounts than with any ideological adherence to current economic dogma. The Provisional Government took office at a time when the total receipts collected by the State could not pay for the expenses of its own administration.⁴ Import dues by 1932 were roughly 30 per cent below the levels of 1929, and their contribution to national revenue sank from 54 per cent in 1930 to 39 per cent in 1934.⁵

The machinery by which revenue could be mobilised domestically at short notice was undeveloped in the early 1930s, so that the limit to what could be achieved in revenue raising was set by the international context, with its depressing effect on Argentina's foreign trade. Thus, when the balancing of the budget was declared by General Uriburu to be a fundamental aim of the revolution of September 1930, and Finance Minister E. Uriburu announced a policy of budgetary equilibrium to be the cornerstone of government economic strategy,⁶ the emphasis could not perforce be as strong on increasing revenues as on decreasing expenditures.

Between 1930 and 1932 total expenditure cuts amounted to 242 million pesos (Table 6.1) at a time when the two new taxes on income and transactions yielded only 76.5 million,⁷ so that as much as 68 per cent of the reduction in expenditure was net; the likely conclusion is that the Government adjusted its balances by an effective reduction of its outlays. Moreover, 1932 was the year after 1930 when real expenditure was at its lowest (Table 6.1): for administrations pledged to practise budgetary economies since the September revolution, this result would be the expected one if allowance were made for a time lag to make those policies work.

The State's administrative costs were the most expensive item in the accounts of the public section and it was there that the government looked for savings. Between 1931 and 1932, in the midst of the

TABLE 6.1 *Real expenditure, 1928-39*

	Total expenditure (in millions of pesos)	Wholesale price index (base 1926 = 100)	Real expenditure
1928	919.0	98.5	9.3
1929	988.2	96.4	10.3
1930	1 091.8	92.2	11.8
1931	908.4	89.0	10.2
1932	849.9	89.5	9.5
1933	880.4	85.6	10.3
1934	954.2	98.2	9.7
1935	980.9	97.0	10.1
1936	1 051.8	99.2	10.6
1937	1 221.1	112.6	10.8
1938	1 278.2	105.5	12.1
1939	1 460.4	108.2	13.5

SOURCES Comité National de Geografía, *Anuario Geográfico 1941* (Buenos Aires, 1942) pp. 369 and 406.

Depression, expenditure and general administration took an average 73 per cent of annual revenue, but by 1934 that figure had fallen to 54 per cent. In the second half of the decade costs of general administration averaged annually 56 per cent of total revenue, and by 1939 only 52 per cent of the revenue was needed to pay for the State's bureaucracy. This was a marked improvement on 1930, not itself the worst year of the Depression, when administrative costs swallowed 83 per cent of total receipts. On the other hand, the weight of general administrative expenditure in export value showed a declining tendency in the 1930s, and though there was a rise in 1938, by then the percentages of exports to gross domestic product had fallen compared to the figures of the early 1930s;[8] in any case, the State relied more on the domestic economy to raise the revenue it needed.

Deficit spending was not fashionable in government circles during the 1930s. The weight of budget deficits in the value of Argentina's total production fell from 6.5 per cent in 1929-30 to 1.3 per cent during the Depression years of 1931-34, itself a remarkable achievement. As the international and the domestic situation improved towards the mid-1930s, it became easier for the government to make ends meet and small budget surpluses were obtained between 1935 and 1937. Again, as a proportion of production value, the budget deficits of the later 1930s (1938–40: 2.7 per cent) were considerably smaller than the deficits of the late 1920s (1928–30: 4.4 per cent) (Table 6.2).

Beveraggi Allende suggests that General Uriburu put into practice fiscal policies that were anti-deflationary and that compensated for the fall in aggregate demand before Keynesianism became an established body of economic thought.[9] Budget deficits did occur in the early 1930s, but to ignore the efforts to control expenditure and deficit spending is misleading and entirely misrepresents the character of the Provisional Government. Lascano maintains the opposite view, that is that there was a rigid adherence to economic orthodoxy in the early 1930s which, he adds, led to the divorce of economic policy from practical reality.[10] In so far as budgetary policy is concerned, the view that the administration of the early 1930s responded to the Depression in an orthodox manner is closer to the truth. However, the point that the adoption of a traditional course of action was not suited to reality not only needs to be proven, but is at odds with the trend of economic policies in other nations. In the USA, the reduction of the federal budget deficit of 1931 was of the utmost concern to President Hoover (1929–31), who believed that the duty of government was to spend within its means; Roosevelt himself was outspoken in his opposition to the budget deficit during the presidential campaign of 1932, and blamed Hoover for controlling expenditures loosely.[11] Great Britain did not resort in the 1930s to a policy of budgetary deficits to promote internal recovery, even when before 1932 it was difficult to maintain a balanced budget and simultaneously avoid a price deflation.[12] Australia was prepared to enforce stricter expenditure controls than the Argentine during the Depression years,[13] and it appears that in Brazil, as well as in other Latin American countries, the authorities remain on the whole committed to fiscal orthodoxy in the early 1930s.[14]

Villanueva argues that the heterodox economic policies practised in other countries to promote internal recovery (e.g. the New Deal in the USA) made Argentine policy-makers doubt the efficacy of their traditional remedies, and as a result the Argentine authorities became incipiently Keynesian in their outlook after 1933.[15] In his later work,[16] Villanueva detects the presence of new formulae in government economic policy which led to a 'new economic orientation' for Argentina after 1933. Here it should be pointed out that deficit spending did not enjoy the favour of the Argentine Government even after 1933, and that there was no doubt in the minds of policy-makers in the 1930s that a policy of budgetary equilibrium served the interests of the

TABLE 6.2 Public expenditure and budgetary results as a proportion of total production, 1928–39

	Value of national production (in millions of pesos)		Budgetary deficits (−) and surpluses (+) (in millions of pesos)	Public expenditure (in millions of pesos)	Deficits or superavits as a percentage of production		Public expenditure as a percentage of production	
	Bunge	1960 prices			Bunge	1960 prices	Bunge	1960 prices
1928	6 320	4 216	− 2.7	918.9	0.000	0.0006	0.15	0.22
1929	6 290	4 405	− 214.9	988.2	0.03	0.05	0.16	0.22
1930	5 210	4 424	− 357.0	1 091.8	0.07	0.08	0.21	0.26
1931	4 540	3 928	− 131.4	908.5	0.03	0.03	0.20	0.23
1932	4 490	3 805	− 41.4	849.9	0.01	0.01	0.19	0.22
1933	4 380	3 978	− 23.6	880.4	0.01	0.01	0.20	0.22
1934	4 930	4 928	− 9.6	934.2	0.002	0.002	0.19	0.22
1935	5 340	4 527	+ 24.9	980.9	+0.005	+0.01	0.18	0.22
1936	5 610	4 585	+ 0.6	1 051.8	+0.0001	+0.0001	0.19	0.23
1937	6 650	4 950	+ 13.5	1 221.1	+0.002	+0.003	0.18	0.25
1938	5 630	5 017	− 196.1	1 278.2	0.03	0.04	0.23	0.25
1939	-	5 094	− 60.5	1 460.4	-	0.01	-	0.29

SOURCES Bunge's estimates for production value from Comité Nacional de Geografía, *Anuario Geográfico 1941*, p. 198; production values at 1960 prices from Fundación Banco de Boston, *Argentina Evolución Económica, 1915–1976* (Buenos Aires, 1978), pp. 15 and 57; budgetary results from *Anuario Geográfico 1941*, p. 406.

economy best: Argentina could still be portrayed in 1938 as being the sole remaining country to adhere to the principles of classical finance.[17]

The economic measures of November and December 1933 implemented by Pinedo, the Finance Minister generally regarded as having engineered Argentina's recovery from the Depression, did not rely on the running of budget deficits;[18] much the reverse, since the 'new formulae' of the 1930s relied on the old formula of a balanced budget. Pinedo, moreover, acknowledged that he was continuing the policy of his predecessor of maintaining an equilibrium between revenue and expenditure, and he confirmed that no recourse was had during his administration to spending over and above receipts.[19] As a result of the world slump of 1937 and gloomy prospects for world peace, prudence and caution in the management of government finance became catchwords in the late 1930s. Sr. Groppo repeated them time and again at his inaugural address as Finance Minister in 1938, and emphasised the continuity of his policies with those of earlier administrations.[20] In fact, Argentine Finance Ministers were never inclined to advocate deficit spending as a means of boosting aggregate demand in the 1930s. This applied equally to the management of the central bank: the maintenance of a balanced budget, it was felt, was of vital importance for the soundness of Argentina's monetary system.[21]

2. *Debt Service*

The favourable record of the Argentine government as a borrower was well known overseas. Argentina, it was reported in 1931, was in a financially superior position to any other South American republic, and compared very well even with older countries in Europe;[22] she was described in 1934 as being the only South American borrower to meet 100 per cent of her external debt service throughout the Depression, promptly, unquestioningly, and with good grace.[23] A handful of provinces and municipalities suspended either interest or sinking fund payments in the early 1930s, but the Argentine Government continued to meet its foreign debt obligations in full.[24]

The annual service of the public debt weighed less heavily in the expenditure column of the budget than the costs of the public sector's administrative services. Between 1930 and 1932, the annual service of the public debt averaged 16 per cent of export value, and consumed 31 per cent of total revenue (Table 6.3). But these were relatively small figures compared with the State's administrative costs which averaged

TABLE 6.3 *Annual debt service as a proportion of export value, public expenditure and revenue, 1929–36*

	Export value	Public expenditure	National revenue
1929	8	18	24
1930	14	18	30
1931	14	22	30
1932	19	29	34
1933	22	28	33
1934	15	23	29
1935	12	21	24
1936	11	19	23

SOURCES Comité Nacional de Geografía, *Anuario Geográfico 1941*, pp. 434–5 and Ministerio de Hacienda, *El Ajuste de los Resultados Financieros 1928–36* (Buenos Aires, 1938) p. 146.

nearly 40 per cent of export value and swallowed 73 per cent of total revenue.[25]

Even if the size of the public debt service were not big, the necessary exchange cover to pay foreign creditors had to be found. In the early 1930s many governments attempted to solve this problem by setting up exchange controls to prevent a drain on foreign reserves.

Indeed, according to Beveraggi Allende, the Argentine exchange control system of the 1930s was originally intended to check the increase in the cost of the external debt service brought about by the outflow of foreign exchange.[26] The second consideration was, of course, that the service of the public debt pointed to the government's capacity to meet its obligations with the private sector; if the government met its debt service punctually it could expect to raise finance when needed, but not otherwise.

In the early 1930s, the punctual payment of debts by the State guaranteed domestic interest in national bonds and a continued supply of domestic finance at a time when the international money markets were closed to Argentina.

The most pressing financial problem for the State between 1929 and 1932 was the payment of its floating debt, that is the liability the government incurred when it borrowed short-term to meet its fluctuating needs for cash. Successive budget deficits since 1929 increased the absolute size of the floating debt (in 1931 it was 62 per cent above the

1929 value) and its relative weight in the total public debt (between 1929 and 1932 the annual average increase was 32 per cent).[27]

To raise the necessary funds abroad to pay for the floating debt was out of the question in 1932, as an Argentine government loan could not expect to be floated with much success at the time. However, the government enjoyed a sound reputation as a debtor among the bondholders of Argentine government stock in the Republic, and it could use this good credit to its own advantage by tempting private savings to come forward and then channelling them back in payment to creditors in the public and private sectors.

It is clear from the issue of (and subsequent subscription to) the Patriotic Loan in May of 1932 that the good standing of national credit was of benefit to the State and to the private sector. The object of the issue was to provide the necessary finance to sink or fund the government's unwieldy floating debt. The 150 million pesos subscribed by the general public, together with 170 million pesos in cash advanced by the Conversion Office in exchange for an equivalent deposit of Patriotic Loan bonds, allowed the government, at least for the time being, to bring salary payments up to date and meet its obligations with suppliers.[28] In fact, it was reaping the rewards for having paid its bondholders punctually in the past. Argentina's producers obviously welcomed the Patriotic Loan, as part of the proceeds were to be used to pay the debt of the government in the private sector. Representatives of the so-called *fuerzas vivas*, among them the Rural Society, the Unión Industrial, the Bolsa de Comercio, and the Argentine Confederation of Commerce, Industry and Production, gave their unanimous approval to the Patriotic Loan law and asked for its quick implemenation.[29]

The floating debt was built up, of course, by deficits in the budget, so that a sound budgetary policy as well was needed if this liability were to be cancelled altogether. As a sound budgetary policy was in fact effected during the early 1930s, by the mid-1930s the floating debt was virtually eliminated: it was reduced from 1200 million pesos early in 1932 to 100 million pesos in 1935,[30] and its weight within the total public debt fell from 38 per cent in 1931 to an insignificant 3 per cent in 1935.[31]

Furthermore, Argentina had to cope, of course, with the annual service of her longer maturing obligations. Figures available for the years between 1930 and 1937 show that the service of the domestic debt cost more than the service of the foreign debt in every year except 1934 (when interest charges paid by the government on its domestic debt were brought down considerably as a result of the first operations to convert the public debt at lower interest rates; see Table 6.4).

TABLE 6.4 *Domestic and foreign composition of the annual service of the public debt, 1929–37 (in millions of pesos)*

	Domestic	Foreign	Total	Domestic/Total %
1929	98.3	91.2	189.5	52
1930	97.5	92.5	190.0	51
1931	105.5	91.3	196.8	54
1932	120.0	93.6	213.6	56
1933	135.6	88.1	223.7	61
1934	103.6	170.2	210.8	49
1935	106.1	92.7	198.8	53
1936	140.1	91.8	213.9	60
1937	114.9	76.6	191.5	60

SOURCES League of Nations, *Public Finance 1928–37*, vol. XXV (Geneva, 1938) pp. 16–17.

In 1938 Phelps had already observed that the Argentine government was relying more and more on the local capital market to raise finance, since most of the increase in the public debt between 1914 and the early 1930s had come from domestic sources.[32] Indeed, the continued service of the public debt in the 1930s appear to have been more a matter of defending the national interests in the economy than of rewarding the foreign bondholder.

3. *The Supply of Money*

To a great extent, the conservative attitude of policy makers in Argentina in the 1930s was influenced by the monetary disturbances that shook the world in the late 1920s. Out of the 36 countries that broke away from the gold standard between April 1929 and April 1933, Argentina was the second country to do so after Uruguay: in December of 1929 the Conversion Office was closed and it was only for the service of the public debt that gold exports were allowed.[3] A year after the closure of the Conversion Office, the Argentine peso fell 25 per cent below its parity value,[34] and by 1934 it had lost as much as 60 per cent.[35]

The monetary policies of the 1930s were indeed partly designed to bring about a return to normal. Raúl Prebisch, second man under the Finance Minister in the Provisional Government, has made it clear that the large quantities of gold exported in payment for the service of the foreign debt between 1930 and 1931 were meant to safeguard the value of the peso.[36] The government believed that gold exports were necessary when the Conversion Office was closed to maintain confidence in the peso and prevent it from plummeting; in the event Argentina lost about half of her gold reserves in the space of two years, while the gold guarantee of the currency fell from 77 per cent in 1930 to 47 per cent in 1931.[37]

The government's first interventions in the exchange market in March and October 1931 were intended simply to prevent a further depreciation of the perso;[38] at the beginning of October, when the Exchange Control Commission was created, panic was reportedly breeding more panic and the peso was sinking rapidly under the weight of so-called psychological influences.[39] In March 1931 it was reported in the City of London that the Argentine government aimed at a very gradual improvement, a slight appreciation of the peso to allow commerce, both exporters and importers, to arrange its finances without any fear of the disorganising influence which a violent monetary readjustment would cause.[40] In fact a number of authors have insisted on the over-valuation of the Argentine peso between 1931 and 1933,[41] and though it is difficult to know what exactly the natural equilibrium rate was, it may safely be concluded that a key objective of the Exchange Control Commission was to prevent any additional fall in the value of the peso.[42]

It is true that the measures taken by the Pinedo team late in November of 1933 relied on depreciating the peso. However, a number of points should be made. First, the Buenos Aires quotation for sterling had pegged the Argentine peso at a high level, and by general agreement the depreciation was long overdue.[43] Second, the dollar had devalued by 17 per cent six months before the November measures were taken (during four weeks in April and May)[44], and no adjustment was made for this in the value of the Argentine currency. Third, the depreciation of the peso followed the conclusion of the Roca funding loan and the virtual completion of arrangements for the funding of dollar blockages:[45] both schemes gave the Government a chance to release foreign exchange by the concession of a long-term loan. Finally, it must be remembered that before the November measures were put into practice, the authorities put aside the exchange resulting from the blocked funds and then prevented current demand pressures from building up by introducing prior exchange permits: without this control, in Minister Duhau's own admission, the depreciation of the peso would have been greater.[46]

The next significant peso devaluation after November 1933 came in November 1938, and this time a system of quantitative restrictions on imports was introduced by the government at the same time as devaluation to check any excess demand on the exchange available. As Prados Arrarte[47] and Salera[48] have observed, the devaluation of November 1938 was the result of the government's failure to stick to an over-valued selling rate for the peso, and in this the devaluation of November 1938 was not different to the devaluation of November 1933.

Increasing the supply of money in circulation (i.e. the supply of notes and coins held by the public and by the banks to meet their daily cash requirements) was not a policy favoured in government circles during the early 1930s or, for that matter, during the rest of the decade. Between 1930 and 1935, the supply of money in circulation continued to fall in every year except 1932, when the Government discharged its obligations to suppliers, private banks, and the *Banco de la Nación* by the issue of a Patriotic Loan. Between 1936 and 1939, once the price deflation was over and Argentina's production recovered, the supply of money in circulation expanded, yet even then the annual figures were below 1928. And it appears that the money supply was lower in the late 1930s than in the early 1930s when figures of money in circulation are corrected for price changes (Table 6.5). Means of payment, defined as the sum of the money supply in circulation, bank deposits, and bank gold holdings, were also below the levels of 1928 and 1929 for practically the whole of the 1930s. Deflating the figures once again by a price index, the real aggregate declines towards the end of the 1930s, below the levels of the early 1930s and the late 1920s (Table 6.5).

The administrations of the early 1930s did not support expansionist monetary policies since it was felt that this would add to the disturbances in the local money market at a time when the automatic link between gold and paper had been severed by the closure of the Conversion Office. Prices were falling in any case, so that even if no new money were printed the amount of currency in circulation bought more and more goods produced locally. In other words, the real money supply was growing in the absence of any government action to increase the nominal money supply.

This may cast some light on why, in a deflationary environment, an inflation of the means of payment was feared inside and outside government circles. During the debates in Congress on the Plan of Economic Action 1934, Pinedo and Duhau (the Minister of Agriculture) had to reply to the charges of Enrique Dickmann of the Socialist Party that the devaluation of November 1933 was inflationary,[49] and in 1935 the government's financial project for the creation of a central bank was still being fought bitterly in the Chamber of Deputies by the Socialist

TABLE 6.5 Money in circulation and means of payment, 1929–40

	Money in circulation (in millions of pesos)	Means of payment (in millions of pesos)	Wholesale price index (1926 = 100)	Money in circulation ÷ Wholesale prices	Means of payment ÷ Wholesale prices
1929	1 246.7	5 243.6	96.4	12.93	54.39
1930	1 260.7	5 238.8	92.2	13.67	56.82
1931	1 245.1	4 769.7	89.0	13.99	53.59
1932	1 338.8	4 868.9	89.5	14.96	54.40
1933	1 213.9	4 685.3	85.6	14.18	54.73
1934	1 171.5	4 600.8	98.2	11.93	46.85
1935	1 177.9	4 555.6	97.0	12.14	46.76
1936	1 301.5	4 971.7	99.2	13.12	50.12
1937	1 359.6	5 240.7	112.6	12.07	46.54
1938	1 327.6	5 118.9	105.5	12.58	48.52
1939	1 401.5	5 314.9	108.2	12.95	49.12
1940	1 413.0	5 353.9	123.4	11.45	43.39

SOURCES Money in circulation: *Anuario Geográfico 1941*, p. 425; means of payment: ibid., p. 425; Wholesale price index: ibid., p. 369.

and Progressive Democratic blocs on the grounds that it paved the way for inflation.[50] In 1938 the Central Bank criticised a policy of expanding artificially the volume of the means of payment with a view to encourage internal economic activity, on the grounds that, in a country like Argentina where the external sector was so important to the economy, it would bring about a rise in imports which would have to be paid for out of the gold reserves of the banking system.[51] The Central Bank believed that, in Argentina, the 'ancient principle which lays down that redundant media of payment . . . tend to force monetary reserves out of the country' was still valid.[52]

To suggest that there was a shift in monetary policy after 1933 based on 'new formulae' of management would be a mistake. The Conservative governments sought to protect the internal and external purchasing power of the Argentine peso during the whole of the decade. Minister Pinedo was known to follow the financial and monetary polices laid down by his predecessors,[53] and admitted to that himself.[54] Ferrer has said that monetary policy was undeniably expansionary after the mid-1930s,[55] but this does not seem to have been the case. The Central

Bank was simply a new device in the hands of the government that gave it the power to suit the currency needs of the economy to the trade cycle; the emphasis on sound monetary management, however, did not change. Ernesto Malaccorto, the director of the Income Tax Administration created in 1931, aptly described the polices pursued by Raúl Prebisch as general manager of the Central Bank between 1935 and 1943 as what the 'desarrollista' school would now call monetarist and orthodox.[56]

II THE CONSTITUENTS OF THE 'NEW FORMULAE'

The measures implemented by the Pinedo team after 1933 owed a lot to the earlier financial policies under ministers Perez, Uriburu, and Hueyo. This point has been under-emphasised by much of the literature, since Argentine analysts have given overriding importance to the changes which took place in the domestic and the international economy in 1933, with 1933 as a natural dividing line.

There was a close link between the policies of 1931–3 and the 'new formulae' of the 1930s. The connection will be examined in the remainder of the paper.

1. *The Budgetary Reforms of 1931 and 1932*

Government finance before 1930 depended mainly on the collection of import dues at the Argentine customs house. Over three-fifths of the government's total revenue was made up of customs duties and harbour dues of one sort or another in the late 1920s. Between January 1929 and September 1930, import and export dues collected at the port of Buenos Aires fell by 10 per cent and 45 per cent respectively, while other items of revenue were hard hit by the recession and these included purely internal sources of income such as land, licence and stamp taxes.[57]

The Argentine Government reacted to the drop in State revenue in two ways. On the one hand, expenditure was reduced in an effort to balance State accounts. But at the same time the Argentine authorities sought to find alternative sources of revenue to compensate for the decline in custom duties. In April of 1931, the Provisional Government introduced various revenue-producing charges: internal post and telegraphic charges were doubled, and so was the five cent post rate to countries of the Pan American Union, while certain formerly duty-free articles were to pay tariffs of 5 to 25 per cent and they included fuel oil, printed books, machinery and spare parts, certain heavy chemicals, special industrial sewing machines, eggs, dried beans and pulse, and pleasure boats.[58] A general 10 per cent increase in import tariffs followed in September 1931. In an unprecedented step, a tax on income was announced by the government early in 1931 and introduced in 1932. A new tax on business transactions was put into effect in 1931 and, a year later, petrol was taxed for the first time.

All of these taxes compensated in time for the fall in customs revenue. Receipts under the system of taxation in existence before 1931 would in fact have been insufficient to balance the financial year of 1932.[59] President Justo reported that without the new taxes on business transactions, petrol, and income, it would not have been possible to arrive at a financial equilibrium between 1931 and 1934:[60] the income tax almost counterbalanced the fall in customs dues in 1934, and between 1932 and 1936 the combined receipts of the sales and petrol taxes almost made up for the fall in customs revenue.[61]

In the early 1930s the Argentine authorities took the first step towards severing government revenue from the hazards of the import trade. To give flexibility to government finance it was necessary to pave the way for a switch from indirect to direct methods of collecting tax. This was indeed the contribution of the Provisional Government. Argentina's simple and traditional tax system was reformed in the early years of the Depression, and these changes could only benefit the economy later.

The tax reforms of the early 1930s went hand-in-hand with an improvement in the method of budgeting. By making a point of publicising periodically the state of the accounts in the federal budget, and by breaking down expenditure outlays to show clearly the use to which funds were put, the Provisional Government managed to place the whole process of Argentine budgeting on a sounder footing. For *La Prensa*, the budgetary reforms initiated under the rule of General Uriburu were the starting point of a more realistically-minded management of government finance.[62] The budget reforms of the early 1930s were in fact to lay the foundations of the perfection of Argentina's budget during Justo's presidency.

Expenditure accounts in the 1930s were simplified, and hidden sources of past deficits were incorporated explicitly in the budget. Examples were the expenditure for Social Assistance and for the National Council of Education, and the accounts of the Autonomous Departments, all of which were included in the federal budget to give a more accurate representation of the state of government finance.[63] The concern of the Conservative administrations in the 1930s with the production of statistics is also noteworthy and can be gauged by the wealth of statistical material now available.

The tax and budgetary reforms of the early 1930s were part of what Villanueva has described as the ad hoc economic policies with which the government in Argentina responded to the Depression before 1933.[64] But Villanueva's suggestion is that these were piecemeal, and that a broader economic strategy would have been preferable to combat the Depression. Villanueva in fact minimises the importance of the tax and budgetary reforms in the early 1930s, even when the solid financial position of the Argentine government towards the mid-1930s was largely a consequence of those reforms. He identifies an economic strategy for the administration of the Argentine economy as coming into existence only once Pinedo took office in 1933. It is fair to point out that the so-called ad hoc economic policies before 1933 made that strategy possible.

2. The Conversion of the Public Debt

During Pinedo's term in office between 1933 and 1935 the cost of the public sector's internal and external obligations was lowered. Proposals were put forward to reduce the incidence of the debt service in the government's expenditure outlays, and they were carried out. This was achieved by resorting to 'conversion' operations that lowered the interest paid by the public sector on its debt; the conversion proposals extended the duration and the cost of the loans but resulted in smaller annual debt services that brought immediate relief to the government and to the private sector at the expense, of course, of the bondholder.

Initial sacrifices were required from local bondholders. The government estimated that by converting its internal debt it could save 56 million pesos in the first year only, and it was stated that this figure would eliminate the need for further tax increases and assure a balanced budget for 1933.[65] Total government expenditure in 1933 stood at 880 million pesos, so that with the internal conversion operations the government expected to economise over 6 per cent of its total expenditure outlays.[66] Debt service payments in 1933 were nearly 250 million pesos, which meant that savings in that item of expenditure could be as much as 22 per cent.[67] The sacrifices initially required of internal bondholders were later extended to foreign bondholders. In 1934, the internal and external conversion operations yielded savings of 36 million pesos,[68] a figure equivalent to 5 per cent of cash expenditure by the government,[69] which fell just short of the demands of Congress to the Cabinet in 1933 for economies of 40 million pesos in debt payments.[70]

The conversion operations allowed the government sizeable savings in the service of the public debt. The scheme was successful, however, because bondholders were prepared to accept a lower return on their bonds when a present date was taken as the basis for amortisation payments. The Government gave bondholders the choice of exchanging their bonds for new updated issues. It imposed no obligation on them to accept the scheme. As creditors of the State, bondholders could have asked if they wished for full compensation for their capital.

Yet bondholders responded well to the government's conversion offer. Only 5 per cent of the amount tendered initially was rejected: 930 million pesos worth of government stock (about £62 million) were exchanged by bondholders even when the conversion reduced the interest rate on government bonds from 6 to 5 per cent.[71] By the time the internal debt had been fully converted, 3 billion pesos (£200 million) worth of bonds had been negotiated by the government.[72] Even though the State held one of the 3 billion in bonds in its coffers, the success of the operation was undeniable. The size of the figures involved, moreover, was of the first magnitude. President Justo did not hesitate to describe the conversion of the public debt as the biggest financial operation ever attempted in the Argentine.[73]

The timing of the conversion scheme was good. The prospects for trade and finance in Argentina looked uncertain until the middle of 1933. The government could not expect bondholders to subscribe. But the launching of the conversion operations late in 1933 was a success because the timing of the measures was right. Confidence about future economic prospects in Argentina was slowly improving, and bondholders could expect the credit of the State to be sound. Argentina had already secured a market for its export trade by signing the Roca–Runciman agreement. The treaty also made possible the negotiation of a loan to free blocked funds without destabilising the peso. The conversion operations would probably have failed without these efforts to stabilise the Argentine peso as they maintained the confidence of the investor in Argentine bonds.

The conversion of the public debt brought about a general fall in interest rates and alleviated the burden on debtors throughout the country. It reduced the likelihood of more taxation as it brought down government expenditure by cutting on debt service payments. It also made productive investment more attractive relative to bondholding. As a result, the conversion of the public debt had a reflationary effect on economic activity in general. In the language of Villanueva, this was a 'new formula' of economic policy.

It is true that Federico Pinedo was responsible for the operation. But the contribution to its successful implementation of the financial policies practised between 1931 and 1933 cannot be in question. Surveying Argentina's economic and financial recovery from the Depression, Pinedo reminded Congress in 1935 that if earlier governments had chosen to suspend interest and sinking fund payments on their securities, or if they had pursued a policy of printing money to meet debt payments regardless of the consequences, the credit of the Argentine nation would have received a hard blow, and, in that event, bondholders would not have been as obliging with conversion operations as they were.[74]

Federico Pinedo knew for a fact that he was working on the foundations laid down by his predecessors at the Finance Ministry. Pinedo, when he took over the Finance Ministry, inherited a sound financial legacy. Without it, the conversion operations would have been doomed to failure. Pinedo was lucky also in that during his term in office the time was ripe to put forward conversion proposals to the bondholders of government stock. Any Finance Minister who sucessfully carried out the conversion of the public debt was bound to increase his popularity, since his policy benefited the private sector as well as the government. Pinedo's forerunners at the Finance Ministry knew this, but there was little they could do short of coercing bondholders into accepting the offer of conversion.

3. *The Monetary and Banking Reforms*

In fact, the monetary and banking reforms that were carried out by Federico Pinedo in 1935 would not have been readily accepted by the public or, indeed, by the private banks that became shareholders of the new Central Bank, without the efforts of ministers Perez, Uriburu and Hueyo to restore confidence in the paper peso and to allay suspicion on the state of local banking. In the climate of uncertainty of the early 1930s it was, of course, vitally important to restore confidence in the future before economic recovery might set in.

The administrations of the early 1930s knew that innovative economic measures added another element of uncertainty to what was already a bleak situation. A sweeping financial reform was thus delayed, and a conservative approach to economic policy was preferred because it could be widely trusted. The balancing of the budget, the prompt payment of the State's floating and other debts, and the closure of the

Conversion Office to protect gold holdings, might not have been a daring set of measures to combat the Depression, but under the circumstances they were expeditious, they avoided making matters worse for the peso, and, because the policies were traditional in character, they could be understood and relied upon by the general public.

Projects to create a central bank and to sanction the first legislation for the regulation of banking activity in Argentina were put forward before Pinedo took office in 1933. In January 1931, the Provisional Government declared itself openly in favour of creating a central bank, and a project was put forward under Minister Perez. A few months later, Minister Uriburu presented a new banking scheme based on the revaluation of Argentina's gold holdings. Minister Hueyo abandoned this idea, and prepared instead a law regulating banking activity and rediscount operations. In 1932 the government asked Sir Otto Niemeyer for advice, and early in 1933 he submitted his plans for a central bank and a banking law.[75] Economic recovery, however, became apparent only towards 1934. It was after that date that the financial reforms were eventually made into law.

At the heart of the financial reform of the mid-1930s was the revaluation of Argentina's gold stocks. The government revalued its gold holdings at a profit to coincide with the opening of the Central Bank in 1935. The profit was distributed in a number of ways. On the one hand, it was used to pay one-third of the Central Bank's capital and all the capital of the Institute for Mobilizing Frozen Bank Investments. The function of this Institute was to bolster up confidence in a number of banks that held investments in assets that could not be made liquid at short notice. These banks could find themselves in trouble in the future and put other banks at risk, a fact that the Institute sought to prevent by gradually acquiring the immobilised investments. On the other hand, the profit was used to repay the remaining debt of the government with the Banco de la Nación, to transfer back to private banks deposits that had been taken over by the government, and, finally, to repay Treasury Bills held by private banks.

The revaluation of Argentina's gold stocks strengthened the position of the banking sector. Moreover, the government's floating debt in 1935 was mainly with the private banks so that this obligation was all but eliminated with the proceeds of the gold revaluation. Thus, immediately before the sanction of the important reforms of 1935, government finance was placed on a firm footing and the liquid reserves of private banks were propped up. This cleansing of Argentine finances with the profits resulting from the revaluation of Argentina's gold holdings made possible the significant changes in monetary management and practice of 1935.

There was little doubt that a revaluation of gold stocks was practicable in 1935. 1934 had been heralded as the 'year of recovery' by the *Review of the River Plate*,[76] and this it turned out to be. The peso was becoming stronger and stronger, the budgetary deficit of the government had been practically eliminated, and for the first time since the Depression, there was an atmosphere of confidence in the future.

Argentina could have revalued her gold holdings before 1935, but there was at least one good reason why she did not. Gold, after all, was a unique commodity throughout the Depression, almost the only one for which demand increased and the price advanced. However, a revaluation of gold holdings during the Depression years was not to be recommended, since one of the essential problems that the governments of the early 1930s had to contend with was the devaluation of the peso. A revaluation of gold stocks was tantamount to a fall in the gold value of the Argentine currency, which was precisely what the administrations of the early 1930s had wanted to prevent.

Federico Pinedo may ultimately have been responsible for carrying out the financial reforms of 1935, and for this he deserves credit. But as Raúl Prebisch recognised, it was necessary to regularise the local monetary situation before the creation of the Central Bank, the bedrock of the monetary and banking reforms. Prebisch added that this was done between 1931 and 1935 by curtailing State expenditure, devising a new system of taxation, converting the public debt, and paying off the heavy floating debt.[77] According to the Ministry of Finance, the basis of the programme of monetary regularisation put into practice between 1931 and 1935 was the elimination of budgetary deficits and the reduction of the floating debt.[78] Again, this suggests that the debt Pinedo owed to earlier administrations cannot be brushed aside lightly.

4. *The Minimum Price Guarantee for Farmers*

Probably the best known feature in the 'new formulae' of economic policy attributed to Federico Pinedo was the stimulus given by the State to production, in particular agricultural production. Starting in November 1933, minimum prices were guaranteed by the government for wheat, maize and linseed at a time when the international quotations for these staples were depressed.

The minimum price guarantee afforded relief to agricultural

producers badly hit by the Depression and by an over-valued exchange rate, and, given the importance of agricultural production in the national economy, it led to a general improvement in the returns of commerce and trade. The funds to subsidise cereal prices were obtained by modifying the system of exchange controls to yield a profit. This profit was derived from the difference between the rate at which the State bought foreign exchange and the rate at which it sold. The minimum price guarantee was announced as a temporary measure, and when the recovery in international grain prices rendered it useless towards the end of 1936, it was abandoned.

It is of interest here to discuss the background to this economic measure. Before the exchange system was modified to aid agricultural producers, it was necessary to secure foreign funding loans to release blocked funds in Argentina. A large and constantly increasing mass of funds, representing the cost of imported merchandise and the profits of foreign-owned companies, could not be remitted abroad between 1931 and 1933 because of the scarcity of foreign exchange. As long as this mass of funds was awaiting transfer, the future of the Argentine peso was uncertain. The foreign funding loans were necessary because, without them, the sudden release of blocked remittances would have brought about a drastic devaluation of the peso.

Negotiations to secure a funding loan to release blocked remittances began before Pinedo took office in August 1933. He announced his new economic measures only after the conclusion of negotiations for a funding loan in pounds sterling and the virtual completion of arrangements for funding blockages of Swiss francs and US dollars.

The most important of these funding operations was procured by the so-called Roca Funding Loan. The weight of the Roca Funding Loan in the sum total of the funding operations was very considerable. In December of 1933, the subscription of the bonds for the Roca Funding Loan stood at 167.7 million pesos (£11.2 million) and this compared with 53.7 million pesos (£3.6 million) for bonds of the dollar funding loan and 51.6 million pesos (£3.4 million) for the bonds of the funding loan in Swiss francs; by May 1934, the subscription of the Roca Funding Loan was 167.8 million pesos (£11.2 million), compared to 75.9 million pesos (£5.1 million) for the funding loan in Swiss francs, 59.0 million pesos (£3.9 million) for the dollar funding loan, and 16.8 million pesos (£1.1 million) for a supplementary loan in pounds sterling.[79]

The issue of Roca bonds was stipulated by the Roca–Runciman agreement signed in London in May of 1933. Ever since the start of the

Roca negotiations it was clear that British commerce and banking, as well as railways and other British companies in Argentina, attached great importance to the question of freeing British frozen credits; a solution was vital to further progress.[80]

Following a visit of Dr Roca to Mr Evelyn Baring on 24 February, it was announced that the problem of the release of blocked funds was on the point of being resolved on the basis of a loan of about £10 million sterling. According to the data gathered in London by the Board of Trade, the banking operation which would permit mobilising British credits would affect approximately 20,000 British creditors whose funds were blocked in Argentina by the Exchange Control Commission.[81] Towards the end of March, a telegram arrived in London from Buenos Aires in which it was stated that Finance Minister Alberto Hueyo had expressed confidence in the final success of the negotiations in London on the frozen credits. The Minister hoped that the loan could be arranged for a period of 20 years at an interest rate of 4 per cent.[81]

The negotiations over the proposed £10 million sterling loan proved to be one of the last stumbling blocks to completing the Roca agreement. The terms of the loan were finally agreed early in April and confirmed later that month, and the Roca treaty was signed immediately afterwards.[83] It was agreed that the Roca bonds would be issued at par, would carry an interest rate of 4 per cent p.a., and would be repaid within 20 years (repayment beginning after five years). The exchange rate at which the Roca bonds were to be converted and other conditions of the bonds were to be agreed in future between the Argentine government and a committee representative of holders of the balance concerned (Article Two, paragraph four, of the Roca treaty).[84]

The interest rate of 4 per cent on the Roca bonds was an attractive offer for the Argentine government. Alberto Hueyo explained much later (in 1943) that the terms of the Roca Funding Loan were the most advantageous ever to be negotiated abroad.[85] Compared with the interest rates at which the Argentine government bonds had been issued in the past in European markets, the rate of the Roca bonds was lower by one to two percentage points. Undoubtedly, at a time when the foreign credit of many other nations had collapsed, this was a reward for the careful financial management of the administrations of the early 1930s.

The Roca agreement was signed while Alberto Hueyo was at the head of the Finance Ministry. He was responsible ultimately for the bulk of the negotiations for the Roca Funding Loan. Federico Pinedo inherited the Roca agreement with the undertaking to put into effect the issue of the Roca bonds. Under Pinedo, agreement was reached by October 1933 on the exchange rate at which the bonds were to be converted, and on the conditions under which the bonds were to be marketed. These were finishing touches stipulated in the Roca agreement and signed under an earlier administration.

Pinedo disclosed that changes in the system of exchange control in November 1933 were announced only after the government had obtained the necessary funding loans to release the blocked foreign funds in Argentina. He added that a sharp devaluation of the peso would have ensued if the blocked remittances had been released before the funding loans were secured.[86] As the Roca Funding Loan accounted for by far the biggest share of the blocked remittances that were released, the inevitable conclusion must be that the Roca Funding Loan made possible the changes in the system of exchange controls, and that without the Roca Loan the State might not have been in a position to guarantee minimum prices for wheat, maize and linseed.

Villanueva has not allowed for the contribution of the Roca Funding Loan to the modification of the system of exchange control, which in turn made possible the financing of minimum grain prices for farmers. As a result, the very direct link between the Roca Treaty and this 'new formula' of economic policy is not explored. Yet, at a general level, Villaneuva acknowledges that the Roca agreement constituted the point of departure for the Pinedo team.[87] This was indeed the case, and when the connection between the Roca Treaty and the reform in the system of exchange control is recognised explicitly, the contribution of the earlier administrations of the 1930s to Pinedo's 'new formulae' of economic policy cannot be in doubt.

III

It is argued, then, that the financial policies of Ministers Perez, Uriburu and Hueyo made possible the confident implementation of expansionary measures late in 1933. It is further suggested that the differences in views and actions before and after 1933 need not be exaggerated. The relation between the administrations of the early 1930s and Pinedo was, in point of fact, one of complementarity; the 'new economic reorientation for Argentina', which supposedly came about with the Pinedo team, was less a starting point than a result of earlier policies.

NOTES

1. J. Villanueva, 'Economic Development', in M. Falcoff and R. H. Dolkart (eds), *Prologue to Perón: Argentina in Depression and War, 1930–1945* (Berkeley, Calif., 1975) pp. 57–82.
2. Ibid., p. 62.
3. A. Ferrer, *Crisis y Alternativas de la Política Económica Argentina* (Buenos Aires, 1977) p. 58.
4. S. G. Irving, 'Economic Conditions in the Argentine Republic', report to the *UK Dept. of Overseas Trade* (31 Oct. 1931) p. 19.
5. República Argentina, *Memoria del Departamento de Hacienda 1934*, vol. I (Buenos Aires, 1935) p. 70.
6. *Revista de Economía Argentina*, XXVII (Sept. 1931) p. 156.
7. República Argentina, *Memoria del Departamento de Hacienda 1934*, vol. I, p. 70.
8. Costs of general administration as a percentage of national revenue and export value, 1930–9, were calculated from Comité Nacional de Geografía, *Anuario Geográfico 1941* (Buenos Aires, 1942) pp. 374, 402–3, 406 and 434–5.
9. W. Beveraggi Allende, *El Servicio del Capital Extranjero y el Control de Cambios* (México, 1954) pp. 163–4.
10. M. R. Lascano, *Presupuestos y Dinero* (Buenos Aires, 1972) pp. 131–2.
11. V. Vázquez Presedo, *Crisis y Retraso: Argentina y la Economía Internacional Entre las Dos Guerras* (Buenos Aires, 1978) pp. 81–2.
12. H. W. Arndt, *The Economic Lessons of the 1930s* (London, 1944) p. 125.
13. *Review of the River Plate*, 24 Aug. 1934, pp. 16–17.
14. C. F. Díaz Alejandro, 'Latin America in Depression, 1929–39' (unpublished paper, Yale University, 1980) p. 16.
15. J. Villanueva, 'Aspectos de la Industrialización Argentina', in T. di Tella and T. Halperín (eds), *Los Fragmentos del Poder* (Buenos Aires, 1969) p. 337.
16. J. Villanueva, 'Economic Development', p. 72.
17. *Anglo-Argentine Review*, vol. I (June 1938) p. 12.
18. Cf. C. F. Díaz Alejandro, *Ensayos Sobre la Historia Económica Argentina* (Buenos Aires, 1975) p. 102.
19. Interview given by F. Pinedo to *Esto Es*, 27 July 1954 (in Instituto Torcuato di Tella, *Trabajo de Historia Oral*, Buenos Aires, 1971).
20. Ministerio de Hacienda, *Comunicado*, 21 Feb. 1938.
21. Banco Central de la República Argentina, *La Creación del Banco Central y la Experiencia Monetaria Argentina entre 1935–1943* (hereafter: *La Creación del BCRA*) vol. I (Buenos Aires, 1972) pp. 58 and 166.
22. Bank of London and South America, *Monthly Review*, XIII (London, Sept. 1931) p. 386.
23. *Economist*, 28 Apr. 1934, p. 933.
24. The Province of Santa Fe and the City of Rosario suspended sinking fund payments but not interest payments; the Municipality of Tucumán, the Municipality of Córdoba, and the Province of Córdoba defaulted on

coupon payments: Public Record Office (London), FO 371/15799 and 16543, and *Argentine Report 1932*, p. 20.
25. For costs of general administration as a percentage of national revenue and export value, see note 8.
26. Beveraggi Allende, *Servicio del Capital Extranjero*, p. 167.
27. Floating debt and public debt totals, 1929–36, were taken from Ministerio de Hacienda, *El Ajuste de los Resultados Financieros de 1928 a 1936* (Buenos Aires, 1938) p. 151.
28. A. Hueyo, 'Mirando al Pasado', *La Prensa*, 1 Sept. 1943, p. 9:5.
29. *La Nación*, 31 Aug. 1932, p. 6:1.
30. *South American Journal*, 6 July 1935 (from the newspaper cuttings of the Corporation of Foreign Bondholders, Guildhall Library, London, hereafter CFB).
31. For floating debt and public debt totals, see note 27.
32. V. L. Phelps, *The International Economic Position of Argentina* (Philadelphia, Pa., 1938) p. 118.
33. *Whitaker's Almanack* (1936) p. 525.
34. V. Salera, *Exchange Control and the Argentine Market* (New York, 1941) p. 49.
35. R. Prebisch, 'La Inflacion Escolástica y la Moneda Argentina', *La Nación*, 2 July 1934, p. 4:6.
36. *La Creación del BCRA*, I, pp. 280–1.
37. Comité Nacional de Geografia, *Anuario Geográfico 1941*, p. 424.
38. Banco de la Nación, *Economic Review*, V (Feb.–Mar. 1932) p. 42.
39. Ibid.
40. *The Bankers Magazine*, CXXX (Mar. 1931) p. 32.
41. See H. E. Peters, *The Foreign Debt of the Argentine Republic* (Baltimore, Md., 1934) p. 175; Phelps, *International Economic Position*, p. 65; J. Prados Arrarte, *El Control de Cambios: Parte I del Intervencionismo de Estado en la Argentina* (Buenos Aires, 1944) p. 80; and Salera, *Exchange Control*, p. 63.
42. See also Beveraggi Allende, *Servicio del Capital Extranjero*, p. 167.
43. *Economist*, 1 Apr. 1933, p. 693.
44. Arndt, *Economic Lessons*, p. 67.
45. See section II.4.
46. Ministerio de Hacienda, *El Plan de Acción Económica National* (hereafter *El Plan de Acción*) (Buenos Aires, 1934) pp. 125–6.
47. Prados Arrarte, *Control de Cambios*, pp. 142–3.
48. Salera, *Exchange Control*, pp. 201–2.
49. Ministerio de Hacienda, *El Plan de Acción ante el Congreso Nacional* (Buenos Aires, 1934) p. 127.
50. *New York Times*, 2 Mar. 1935, p. 23:4.
51. Banco Central, *Annual Report: 1938*, p. 9.
52. Ibid.
53. *The Times*, 28 Aug. 1933, p. 16b.
54. F. Pinedo in *Esto Es*, 27 July 1954 (see note 19).
55. Ferrer, *Crisis y Alternativas*, p. 59.
56. Instituto Torcuato di Tella, *Trabajo de Historia Oral* (Buenos Aires, 1972).
57. Irving, 'Economic Conditions in the Argentine Republic', report to the *UK Dept. of Overseas Trade*, 31 Oct. 1931, p. 19.

58. *Economist*, 4 Apr. 1931, p. 730.
59. República Argentina, *Poder Ejecutivo Nacional 1932–38*, vol. I (hereafter *Poder Ejecutivo Nacional 1932–38*) (Buenos Aires, 1938) ch. IV (n.p.).
60. Ibid., I, ch. IV (n.p.).
61. *Memoria de Hacienda 1934*, I, p. 70.
62. *La Prensa*, 4 Oct. 1933, p. 8:1.
63. *Poder Ejecutivo Nacional 1932–38*, I, ch. IV.
64. Villanueva, 'Economic Development', p. 62.
65. *The Times*, 14 Dec. 1932.
66. Ministerio de Hacienda, *El Ajuste de los Resultados Financieros*, p. 146.
67. Ibid.
68. *Crítica Social*, XII, no. 164 (1936) p. 18.
69. Ministerio de Hacienda, *El Ajuste de los Resultados Financieros*, p. 146.
70. *New York Times*, 29 Sept. 1933, p. 35:7.
71. F. Pinedo, 16 Nov. 1933, quoted in *El Plan de Acción*, pp. 10–14.
72. *Poder Ejecutivo Nacional 1932–38*, I, ch. III.
73. Ibid., I, ch. III.
74. *Crítica Social*, XII, no. 164 (1936) p. 18.
75. *La Creación del BCRA*, I, p. 266.
76. *Review of the River Plate*, LXXVI, 23 Feb. 1934, p. 9.
77. *La Creación del BCRA*, I, p. 264.
78. *Memoria de Hacienda 1934*, p. 15.
79. F. Pinedo, *En Tiempos de la República*, vol. IV (Buenos Aires, 1944) p. 247.
80. *South American Journal*, 25 Feb. 1933, p. 202.
81. Ibid., 4 Mar. 1933, p. 230.
82. Ibid., 25 Mar. 1933, p. 298.
83. Ibid., 29 Apr. 1933, p. 418.
84. Ibid., 6 May 1933, p. 456.
85. A. Hueyo, 'Mirando al Pasado', *La Prensa*, 1 Sept. 1943, p. 9:7.
86. *El Plan de Acción*, p. 84.
87. Villanueva, 'Economic Development', p. 66.

7 Economic Controversies in Argentina from the 1920s to the 1940s

GUIDO DI TELLA

This paper will deal with economic controversy rather than performance for the Argentine economy from the 1920s. It covers a period when Argentina, after the great turn-of-the-century expansion, began to *close* its economy. One can see how an increasing ambiguity crept into the principal policies of the inter-war period, particularly when compared with the confident assumptions before the First World War. However, it was not until the end of the Second World War that a conscious inward-looking strategy was pursued, and this was a phenomenon which continued in practice until the 1960s. From then on, doubts began to mount; even if reluctantly, the country began to try more open strategies.

In Argentina there have been times when policy changes have accompanied economic changes, with significant lags; at other times one can detect a certain discrepancy between what can be seen today as the main economic problems of the period and contemporary diagnosis. The analysis of these policy changes, and the kind of appraisals successively made of the main issues from the end of the First World War until the preoccupation with internal development, is the main subject of this paper.

Before we start, it may be worth remembering that conventional economic theory considers growth as a rather abnormal and transitory phenomenon, a fact intimately connected with the existence of non-normal profits. The Marshallian normal competitive profits are not an adequate basis for the process of accumulation. We have to look at non-normal profits to find an adequate and realistic source of accumulation and growth.[1]

There have been two principal sources of non-normal profits to which Argentina has had access. The first was the rent from natural resources – something compatible with a competitive situation and the cause of the first significant period of growth at the turn of the century. But the country had access to the rent not only of a fixed stock of natural resources, but of a growing stock which accelerated even further the rate of accumulation and growth. The other sources have been related to the existence of oligopolistic quasi-rents originating in collusive practices rather than technological innovation. Collusive quasi-rents were generally the consequence of scarcity rights, that is tariffs, quotas, special permits, etc., granted by governments to certain firms or sectors, which had created a sub-optimal situation. Even at a cost a source of non-normal profits had appeared – not a good one, but better than none. Argentina was unable to obtain access to significant quasi-rents originating in technological innovation (a much healthier and more permanent basis for accumulation). These are the consequence of initial reductions in costs or increase in value of the products, and give rise to a transitory oligopolistic situation which will last only for a short while until the technology becomes common knowledge to the industry. The Schumpeterian view – which is much more realistic than the Marshallian – is that only continuous techological innovation will provide the economy with a permanent and dynamic basis for growth. Argentina has gone through one stage of growth based on rents, and another on collusive quasi-rents resulting from protected industrial growth. But the Republic is finding it difficult to reach a stage of growth based on innovative quasi-rents.

Many of the economic discussions which have taken place in Argentina over the last half-century have related to the changing basis of the process of accumulation and growth. At the beginning of my period, around the First World War, the situation was strongly affected by the extraordinary expansion that had taken place in the previous four decades based on the continuous incorporation of new lands. During this period the country expanded its economic frontier, built railways at an extraordinary pace (more than 1000 kilometres per year), and incorporated more than 100 million hectares into the economy; immigration increased the population more than fourfold, all in less than 40 years. The Argentine economy could be viewed as an Edgeworth box, or better still, a cube, in which the three axes increased every year but not in the same proportion. Land was not a constant factor; rather it increased faster relatively than any other, and in doing so increased the country's specialisation and comparative advantage in land-using activities. This expansion meant that for the purpose of accumulation, the country not only realised additional profits, but also important additional rents. Accumulation was based on the latter, and on foreign capital which was entering into the country in order to take advantage of the new level of rents. Economic growth exceeded more than 6 per cent per annum at the turn of century, being practically unmatched at the time anywhere else in the world. This was seen wrongly as a permanent feature of the economy – a mistake that was at the root of what today can be seen as wild expectations, even if shared by some of the outstanding and sober personalities of the day: Carlos Pellegrini declared, a decade before the First World War, that:

> Our national ideal is to be tomorrow what the US is today, and to occupy in the world some day the position which that country occupies already. We have to examine the ways and means in which that country has been able to reach its present position and see the distance which still separates us.[2]

Unfortunately the expansionary process had to come to an end, the stock of free land (or, if not free, of easily available land) would eventually be exhausted. This is precisely the meaning of the concept of the closing of the frontier, something which happened soon after the First World War. The war did not in itself have any specific bearing on this process; it just coincided with the end of the incorporation of new lands a few years earlier.

The rate of growth of the economy, after the closing of the frontier, averaged about 3 per cent per year in the inter-war period, and about the same from the Second World War. But when the actual development is compared with the pre-1914 performance, or even more so with the expectations nurtured at the beginning of the century, Argentine performance looks dismal. It is this false comparison between a wrongly-based projection and the actual performance that has contributed to the sense of failure which permeates the Argentines' view of themselves as a Nation.

The end of the expansion over new areas meant a drastic qualitative change in the process of growth, a fact that was not perceived at the time. After the First World War the official policy was a return to 'normalcy', which was understood as a return to the pre-war policies which had been so successful – a strategy that ignored the fact that no easily-available, new lands were left. In other countries after the war the return to 'normalcy', defined in this manner, might have been a mistake; in Argentina it was a serious one.

For a while, however, these policies seemed to bear fruit. In the ten years after 1919 the rate of growth, which had collapsed during the war, went up again to about 6 per cent per year, a fraction less than that prevailing in the ten, pre-war years. However, this expansion was qualitatively different from pre-war – the outcome of the coincidence of several short term developments that could not be expected to continue for long.

I am referring in particular to the persistent improvement in the terms of trade from 1918 to 1929 (with the small setback of 1926–7), to the exceptional climatic conditions over the last years of the 1920s (a typical Argentine weather cycle which gave rise to exceptional harvests not exceeded for many years), and finally to the last bulge of railway expansion cut short by the war. None of these factors could continue, but they contributed to the impression that the country had again found the same old road to growth.

It is very significant that already in this period some of the highest per capita figures in cultivated land, railways, and agricultural exports were reached. These were the first indication that a reversal in factor proportions was taking place, and that a shift in the growth strategy was therefore required from land-using to more capital-based activities. Comparative advantage was moving from extensive agriculture towards intensive agriculture and industry. This does not mean that agriculture was less optimal, but that more and more of the new investments had to incline towards industry rather than agriculture. While previously investments were directed towards the incorporation of new lands into the economy, investors now had to choose between intensifying agricultural production (more capital), or starting new (capital-intensive) industrial activities. While a certain scope existed for the first alternative, labour expelled from the agricultural sector plus population growth made industrial expansion necessary and optimal. Despite the general complacency of the 1920s some people saw very clearly what was going on. Very soon after the war, in 1922, Alejandro Bunge pointed out that:

> the breeding of cattle, the development of agriculture and railroads have already reached their highest level and very little can be expected from them in the future as factors contributing to growth.
>
> Now, the industrial and the building stages have to start. A great

opportunity will be opened up for these lines of endeavour in the next 50 years, in the same way that [it was] for other activities 50 years ago.[3]

A distinguished visitor, a philosopher, not an economist, José Ortega y Gasset, writing in 1936, gave one of the best descriptions of what was happening to the country:

> Argentines, hurry up. Times go by and the life of colonial times is finishing and with it a way of living *ex-abundantia*. The land begins to be filled with people. Population becomes dense. There is no longer as much free land. When there is excess the history of land cannot begin, it is still the time of geography, which is the same as saying that it is pre-history.
>
> It is like paradise, it is the life of the land and of the people who live in it as a small accident. Colonial life has some extremely pleasant and bucolic traits; it is land, abundant, surrounding few people. But now history, in the full meaning of the word will begin. Adam comes out of paradise and begins his pilgrimage. Good luck Argentines, in this history that for you only now begins.[4]

Bunge and Ortega were right; they had detected the end of one stage and the beginning of another (much more difficult).

It is one thing to found expansion on an increasing stock of natural resources, and another to base it on industry of the Schumpeterian kind, continuously introducing new technologies, new products, and new cost-reducing procedures. Industry is inherently 'innovative-intensive' (as one might call it); it requires a different set of abilities and a different attitude towards organisation and risk-taking. No wonder that at this juncture the temptation was to try to develop industry based on some form of collusion between the business sector and the government. The basic dividing line, crossed in the first half of the century, had been precisely this change from growth founded on the continuous addition of land to another based no longer on natural resources.

It was not the 1930 world crisis that was the dividing line, although it has been described as such.[5] All that can be said is that it prompted some decisions that would have had to be taken sooner or later. Argentina found its way out of the Depression, but it never again discovered new geographical areas of expansion.

An analysis of the other factor, labour, is complementary. Population, or the lack of it, was the main preoccupation of Alberdi and his generation.

Population is the end and the means... it is the essence around which all basic economic and social phenomena take place... A million people in a territory which can easily accommodate more than 50 million, how else can this be said to be other than miserable?[6]

The rate of increase of population until the First World War was smaller than the rate of increase of usable land, while later the reverse was true. Immigration, which had been so significant before 1914 – when it nearly trebled the natural growth rate of Argentina's population – continued at a significant pace even after the closing of the frontier. This increase, combined with developing mechanisation in agriculture, created a certain amount of excess labour which found neither a sufficiency of new opportunities in the agricultural sector nor an outlet in the small, though growing, industrial sector: pressure was thus put on the service sector and on the State to provide new jobs. This pattern was already observable during the 1920s; and it was partially acknowledged by the Radical governments – indeed it was part of their political appeal. The problem was not critical during the decade, although unemployment, which had peaked at from 18 to 20 per cent during the war, was reduced (but only to 7 or 8 per cent). But, in the 1930s, all of a sudden unemployment became a very serious problem, reaching a level of about 28 per cent of the workforce, by far exceeding the reduction in the national product.[7] Really what happened was that the growing and unavoidable fall in the demand for labour was compounded by shorter-term problems, and while at first unemployment was mainly attributed to these, as time went by a certain awareness of the long-term problems developed. It became increasingly evident that the agricultural sector could not provide full employment for the whole of the population, and for the first time it was possible to detect concern that the increase in population could be excessive in relation to the opportunities opened up by the exploitation of natural resources. Industry was at last seen as a possible solution to the problem of a potential surplus of population. As a leading contemporary industrialist put it somewhat later, it was thought that

> the development of manufacturing solves the employment problem when land-intensive activities are no longer able to absorb the natural growth of the population, a situation which can already be observed. This points out the paradox that for Argentina, in the absence of industry, emigration would be the alternative, logical solution.[8]

At the time, the arguments in favour of industry did not put much emphasis on the level of efficiency required for its industrial development – it was thought sufficient that it should contribute to the reduction of unemployment (admittedly a particularly serious case of inefficiency).

The case of the businessmen's association, the Unión Industrial Argentina (UIA), is a typical example of this 'second best' attitude in defence of industry. In several instances the UIA let it be understood that it never suggested that industry should become as important and as essential a sector as agriculture. This is somewhat curious, since the appearance of structural unemployment was sufficient evidence of a change in comparative advantage; industrial activity had become optimal and not just second best.

This structural problem has in some ways persisted even when industry became a major employer;[9] for a short while after the war, the increase in employment exceeded the natural growth of population. This situation, which was reversed from 1960 onwards, has been reflected in relatively low wages, little growth, and a faltering distribution of income.

The 1930 crisis put an end to the preceding era of prosperity. By so doing it has given the superficial impression that it was the end of a stage, an interpretation which is still maintained by some of the economic historians writing on Argentina. However, it can be seen today that it was a relatively short affair, more an interruption in the growth process than a turning point. The crisis lasted for less than a decade, while the international disruption of trade lasted for less than 20 years, being able, after the war, to resume its growth at an even greater pace. The world was no longer the same as it had been in the 1920s. It is clear today that the optimism, the expansion, the new levels of world investment and the volume of trade prevalent in the 1960s meant in some ways a resumption of the pace and the spirit of the 1920s, to the point that some people speak today of the 'roaring 60s' much as their predecessors used to refer to the earlier period as the 'roaring 20s'.

While the 1930 crisis had a strong impact on employment, its effect on production was rather benign. The drop in GNP of about 11 per cent from 1929 to 1932 was reversed thereafter to the point that growth from 1929 to 1939 progressed at an annual rate of 1.5 per cent. Industry started its recuperation earlier and was able to grow in the same period at more than 3 per cent per year, helped paradoxically by the deterioration of the terms of trade, which shifted resources out of agriculture into industry.

There is little doubt that this good performance was due in part to the management of the economy during the decade. A substantial updating was accomplished, to a great extent under the influence and leadership of Federico Pinedo (twice Minister of the Treasury) and by an outstanding team, Raul Prebisch, Guillermo W. Klein and Ernesto Malaccorto among them, many of whom had had recent links with the Socialist Party. A whole set of far-reaching measures was introduced, such as the creation of the Central Bank, the National Income Tax Agency, and the State purchasing agencies (among which were the very influential grain and meat boards).

The emphasis was clearly placed on lack of demand as one of the basic causes of the crisis, and on the need to reactivate it at all costs in order to get out of the depression. A strong emphasis was put also on the need for State intervention, and on the desirability of some kind of technocratic planning. Particularly towards the end of the decade, some non-orthodox views could also be detected for the issue of money, and a renewed emphasis was placed on the need to implement measures like personal income tax and public housing. No wonder that some of these measures, and the group that carried them out, were looked upon with some suspicion by the more traditional sectors.

On the other hand the fact that these measures were taken under a right-wing government that originated in the military coup of 1930 and remained in power on the basis of electoral fraud, and the circumstance that the economic team had links with vested interests, have prejudiced subsequent analysis and tended to dismiss the experience somewhat lightly. A perfectly legitimate view is that this experience in Argentina was a limited reform scheme, like Keynesianism and the New Deal elsewhere, intended to avoid more drastic revolutionary changes. But in most instances reform is the most that can be achieved and has to be identified as such, even when it operates in an apparently contradictory environment.

The somewhat mild effect of the crisis and Argentina's relatively rapid recovery were helped by significant technological developments that had been taking place since the 1920s, and not only in Argentina. I am referrring to the important introduction of new kinds of consumption goods and services such as automobiles, domestic electricity, plastics, synthetic fibres, etc. While railway building was losing its momentum, the expansion of automobiles was gaining its own. This meant the installation of important assembly plants, the development of national dealer organisations, and a network of petrol stations; more significantly, it meant the launching (towards the end of the period) of an important road building programme. In other cases, such as electricity, there was a substantial increase in generating capacity, in the number of houses wired for electricity, which in turn gave rise to a demand for, and eventual production of, electrical, durable goods. This technological revolution created new demands and new investments, and it contributed to the struggle to take Argentina out of the crisis and to change the face of the country and its habits.

During the 1920s the country maintained its free trade policies in the face of increasing restrictions in world trade. The 1930 crisis cannot be ignored. It brought drastic change, to the point that it can be considered as a dividing line between free trade and protection in the country. But this was still a matter of expediency; it was considered to be a transitory state rather than a change in basic philosophy. The significant change took place only after the Second World War, when there was a real choice as to whether to open the economy again or to continue and intensify the predilection for internal, self-sustaining development.

British influence can hardly be said to have diminished during the 1930s. On the contrary, Argentina was thrown into a panic by the thought that if the British market were lost, disaster would follow. The consequence was that Argentina realigned itself with Great Britain during the 1930s to the extent of negotiating the Roca–Runciman treaty. Argentina was one of the few countries in Latin America where British influence not only failed to diminish, but actually increased. The shift from British to American influence was delayed and took place as a consequence of the Second World War and not of the economic crisis. The problem was finally settled less because of internal development than as a result of the relative decline of Britain in the world.

During the last years of the decade and during the war, a very important discussion took place, not so much as to whether the country should continue its industrial development but as to which industries should be expanded and which discontinued. Various groups and institutions made significant proposals in what today can be seen as an outpouring of new ideas prompted by the war and by new conditions. The first proposal put forward by the official sector, and indeed one of the most elaborate, was the 'Plan de Reactivación' sent to Congress in 1940 by the Minister of the Treasury, Federico Pinedo; it was prepared with the help of Raúl Prebisch, who was at the Central Bank at the time. In a way this proposal was a follow-up of a number of measures taken during the preceding decade. The programme envisaged, quite typically, a strong need to reactivate demand. This was to be achieved especially by State purchase of agricultural surpluses, by the launching of a programme of low-cost housing, and by what was a real novelty, the promotion of industry. The 'Plan de Reactivación' combined some short-term, anti-cyclical measures with an attempt to bring about structural change. The financing that was envisaged implied substantial new issues of money; these were to be reabsorbed as a consequence of the reactivation of the economy when monetary surpluses were to be built up (an idea rather similar to the balancing of a budget over the whole cycle rather than in any one particular year).

The promotion of industry was clearly never intended to be a short term strategy. With permanence in mind it emphasised the need to stimulate not all industries indiscriminately but those only that had a reasonable chance of developing efficiently and at a low cost. The programme envisaged in particular the development of the so called 'natural industries', that is, those that processed the agricultural raw materials which Argentina produced so cheaply. They were supposed to have a good chance of reproducing in processing the advantage enjoyed by Argentine raw materials, something which could have been true only if they were not excessively capital-intensive.

The programme stressed also the fact that the industries that were to be developed should to a large extent be able substantially to export not only to other countries in the area – the proposed Unión Aduanera del Sud – but also to the large American market. It was thought that 'there [was] no logical reason why [Argentine] industry should not be in a position to take advantage of such a market.'[10]

The programme was too far reaching for the era; it was said to share some of the characteristics of the New Deal. It was rejected by Congress not only because of its economic stance but largely because of the uproar produced by a similarly far-reaching programme that the Minister had tried to agree with the head of the Radical opposition, former President Marcelo T. de Alvear (a reconciliation between government and the opposition).

The main lines of the Pinedo programme were not taken up by other groups. War had removed the fears of the crisis, and the Argentine economy, unlike its experience in 1914–18, was able to withstand the disruption of trade. Industry developed significantly, at a rate of more than 4 per cent per year from 1933 to 1945, and actually increased its share of GNP.

One of the few proposals which followed the tradition of the Pinedo line was the report prepared by the Armour Research Foundation for the Corporación para la Promoción del Intercambio, a private but State-funded organisation. Its report is exemplary for its clear economic guidelines, quite modern at the time. It stood for a selective industrialisation programme that put stress on efficiency, and was geared not only to the local market but also to the foreign. It made some extremely interesting points about the role of oligopolies, economies of scale, external economies, and the effects on production of changes in the distribution of income. Exports were considered to be necessary to overcome the small size of Argentina's local market, which in many respects inhibited the full exploitation of economies of scale. However, the report, dating from 1944, seems to have paid no attention to the problems that the end of the war might bring to the economy, a subject which by that time had moved to the centre of the economic debate.

The Unión Industrial Argentina, and more particularly its recently created Instituto de Estudios y Conferencias Industriales (IECI), very soon became one of the most important forums for the discussion of the future of the industry. The capacity to create employment, which had formed an important part of the discussions of the 1930s, was resurrected, but it was not as central as it had been. The new focus of attention was the criteria for selecting those industries to be saved and those to be sacrificed. It was felt that the end of the war would expose industry to world-wide competition; not all would survive. However, as the discussion proceeded, the list of industries that were to be saved became longer and longer. The UIA also discussed industries processing raw materials, but by now they had in mind iron, petroleum and aluminium. They thought of industries derived from these and of other industries such as sulphuric acid and plastics. It was the wider range of industries that distinguished the UIA from the Pinedo-Armour line, rather than differences in theoretical approach.

The case of the steel industry is a very special one, not only because of its repercussions on the rest of the economy and on the metallurgical industry in particular, but also because of the interest shown in it by the recently created Fabricaciones Militares. Its first President, General Manuel Savio, one of the most influential figures of the decade, strongly defended the industry despite the fact that he recognised that the conditions in which it might have been made did not exist. His main argument was that

> the basic reason for the establishment of mineral processing industries has nothing to do with whether they produce more cheaply compared to imported goods; the basic reason for their existence is that they, and only they, are capable of supplying us in difficult times. Therefore nothing needs to be added to show that they are clearly and decisively economically necessary.[11]

This reasoning led him to keep some restraint on the size of the industry to be developed: according to him, it should not attempt to reach self-sufficiency. It was enough that it should reach a sufficient size to avoid a national collapse in time of war, and to permit a stronger negotiating position with steel suppliers in times of peace. He also thought that steel should be sold to local industry at something like the international price, coining the slogan 'cheap steel for a cheap [low cost] industry' even if to do this the State had to pay the difference.

Within the same pro-industrial line, another group that had a marked influence towards the end of the war was one that was gathering around the Revista de Economía Argentina and which, at the death of its founder Alejandro Bunge, organised an institute that bore his name. We have seen that Bunge, since the First World War, had drawn attention to the need to accelerate industrial development, convinced that any scheme based on the expansion of the frontier was already somewhat out of date, and that industry was absolutely necessary in order to acquire a certain degree of autonomy *vis-à-vis* traditional trading partners, Great Britain in particular. The protectionist, Bunge line was much influenced by continental authors whom he knew very well, like List and Thünen. As time went on, and particularly under the influence of Bunge's followers, the group became very anti-liberal. This attitude was extended to political aspects as well, leading to a certain mistrust of the so called liberal-capitalist system, an attitude very typical of Catholic groups. In an interesting piece published in the review of 1945, the group developed its strong preference for a semi-autarchic industry and especially heavy industry. It took slight account of efficiency, while it stressed the importance of the internal market. It is interesting to note that Bunge and his group devoted a great deal of attention to population and lately to social and labour problems. This group was influential in the new military government, particularly in its initial stages. But this was not so very much beyond 1948, even if it influenced the initial constitution of the Consejo Nacional de Postguerra, an institution that was to acquire great significance immediately after the war.

The Consejo was created by the military government and consisted of leading industrialists and military men who had been active in the industrialisation debate. One of the more important characteristics of the work of the Consejo was, within the importance it attached to rapid industrialisation, its perceptive combination of industrial development with a strong programme in favour of the labour sector, stressing the need to integrate social with economic policies. The Consejo's reports seem to have been writtten on a different wavelength from those presented until then: in some respects, they were clear forerunners of the possibility of an industrial-labour alliance with military support, an idea that reappears in the Argentine political scene even to our own day. Whatever the consequences, the opportunity to carry out some of the ideas of the Consejo came with the advent of the Perón Government, from 1946.

NOTES

1. J. Hicks, 'Growth and Anti-growth', *Oxford Economic Papers*, Nov. 1966.
2. Carlos Pellegrini, 'North American Letters, 1904', in Rivero Astengo (ed.), *Carlos Pellegrini* (Buenos Aires, 1941).
3. Alejandro Bunge's contribution to the Dartmouth Conference, 8 Nov. 1922, reprinted in the *Revista de Economía Argentina* (Oct./Nov. 1922).
4. J. Ortega y Gasset, *Meditación del pueblo joven* (Buenos Aires, 1958).
5. By Aldo Ferrer, *La economía argentina, las etapas de su desarrollo y problemas actuales* (México, 1963), and Carlos Díaz Alejandro, *Essays on the Economic History of the Argentine Republic* (New Haven, Conn., 1970).
6. J. B. Alberdi, *Bases y puntos de partida para la organización política de la República Argentina* (Buenos Aires, 1876).
7. Guido di Tella and M. Zymmelman, *Los ciclos económicos Argentinos 1876-1952* (Buenos Aires, 1973).
8. Torcuato di Tella, 'El futuro de la industria', reported in *La Prensa* (1943), as delivered to the Instituto Popular de Conferencias.
9. O. Baccino, R. Bajraj and Guido di Tella, 'Eficiencia y ocupación en la Argentina', *Económica* (May/Aug. 1970).
10. The 'Plan de Reactivación', presented to the Senate, Nov. 1940, by Frederico Pinedo, Minister of Hacienda, was prepared with the assistance of Raúl Prebisch, Ernesto Malaccorto and Guillermo W. Klein.
11. Manuel Savio's remarks were published in vol. I of the *Proceedings of the Instituto de Estudios y Conferencias Industriales* (Buenos Aires, 1943).

8 Argentine Economic Policies since the 1930s: Recollections
RAÚL PREBISCH

I find it very difficult to delve into the past when I have so many worries about the present and the future; but having done it, I do not regret it, as this was an extremely interesting period in Argentine history.*

The starting point of the chosen period is 80 years ago, thus coinciding with another, more personal span which I would rather not have mentioned. But if I do refer to my 80th birthday it is because I see myself as a witness to four great international crises: the First World War, the Great Depression, the Second World War and the Great Inflation. These four crises have posed problems that surpass conventional theories; indeed, the latter have been more of a hindrance since they have not allowed us to see a reality which exceeded the assumptions on which such theories were grounded. How were we, young economists in the 1930s, to face up to the Great Depression? Confronted with this question, I am reminded of Antonio Machado's words, 'Caminante, no hay camino, se hace camino al andar.'

The doubts reflected in the papers given at this conference as to whether or not an orthodox policy was followed in those years can be explained by the bewilderment brought about by the Great Depression. At first we sought to come to terms with this serious situation by applying an orthodox policy; I take a major responsibility for this since Dr Pinedo was not active at the time. I personally convinced those in government of the need to apply an orthodox policy, the only path I

---

* This is the taped and transcribed version of Raúl Prebisch's talk, delivered on 3 July 1981. It is followed by a transcription of most of the discussion that took place afterwards. Adolfo Gurrieri is to be thanked for editing this chapter, and Celia Szusterman for its translation.

knew in those days. I do not think it was mistaken, given the need to stop inflation and check the fiscal deficit before they became uncontrollable. What did this orthodox economic policy, for which I was totally responsible, consist of? In the first place, it took the form of a considerable fall in public expenditure, including a 10 per cent cut in public sector wages; these were brutal measures that allowed for a drastic reduction. In the second place, it meant an increase in taxation; in this area we decided to seek new paths by introducing an income tax.

I persuaded the President of the Republic of the need to introduce an income tax, a step previous governments had not considered – in 1916 Hipólito Yrigoyen had put forward a bill which Congress did not pass. During the crisis we took the opportunity to carry out a proper tax reform which became the basis for an income tax. Not all was orthodox. Other, heterodox measures were also adopted, such as the rise in customs both for fiscal and protectionist reasons. But I must confess that in those days we took great care not to speak about an industrialisation policy, since the doctrine of the international division of labour was still prevalent not just among landowners but within the political parties themselves. Even the Socialist Party accepted the doctrine of the international division of labour, a theory Juan B. Justo supported throughout his life. Any industrialisation that required a subsidy, a protectionist tariff, was condemned outright. The Socialist Party, the agrarian interests, newspapers like *La Prensa* and *La Nación* – albeit the latter in a more lukewarm fashion – in short, all public opinion was against industrialisation.

Guido di Tella has referred to Alejandro Bunge's standpoint; Bunge had shown high regard for me when I was one of his students at the university and yet, since I too had been drilled in the neoclassical theory of the international division of labour, I parted with Bunge when he persisted in favouring tariff barriers. Nevertheless, faced with a crisis of such proportions and the inability of the country to pay for its imports, we thought it essential to start, or rather accentuate, the process of industrialisation already under way. High customs duties were imposed without stating that their purpose was to encourage industrialisation; the group of young men who were behind these steps were very careful not to make any reference to industrialisation.

Who were these young men? They were a small group of economists trained in Buenos Aires who had been with me since the creation of the Economic Research Unit at the Banco de la Nación Argentina in 1928. Part of the group which I led ended up fortuitously working in the Provisional Government and launching those mostly orthodox ideas.

The reasons for that orthodoxy lay not only in what they had studied and what I in particular had taught at the university, but also in the belief that we were facing a normal economic cycle, and thus experiencing the effects of a process typical of the central countries, which had to be endured until events developed bringing about a recovery. At the beginning of 1931 practically all reputable newspapers and publications were maintaining that recovery was around the corner. Our policy was to keep going as best we could, avoiding inflation, until the situation showed signs of a change for the better. But it did not turn out like this.

The first blow was the fall in sterling, which sent shock waves through Buenos Aires and was an added factor in the contraction of the economy. We realised that it was necessary to establish exchange controls, partly because exporters – faced with the possibility of the devaluation of sterling – held on to their foreign exchange, but also because the contraction in exports meant that the previous level of imports could not be maintained. In fact, there was an unfavourable combination of an external contraction and an internal expansion which led us to act in both areas: on the one hand, to check internal expansion by means of a balanced budget, and on the other, to intervene in the export sector. Exchange controls were an additional, selective instrument which enabled us to define what had to be reduced in order to import what was deemed essential. That was the start of the theory of exchange controls, seen as an emergency measure. Thus one can trace the way in which (from the beginning of our period – the end of the 1920s – until the devaluation of sterling which forced the establishment of exchange controls) a certain development took place which could not be described as neoclassical: import substitution was encouraged, while simultaneously the outflow of foreign exchange, which the country badly needed, was controlled.

After a time we realised that, far from improving, the international situation was worsening. Furthermore, the first signs of unemployment began to appear, mainly in Buenos Aires. Soup kitchens were put up in Puerto Nuevo to feed the people, and this made a deep impression – so much so that the need for a change was felt, even though it was not a fundamental change in budgetary policy (which remained restricted) but in the need to take some steps to encourage economic activity. That was the substantial task that Pinedo undertook.

I would like to add that our group, which at first had no links with Pinedo, welcomed his arrival in the administration, given his considerable attributes: a clear and incisive intelligence, a great sense of action, an enormous personal integrity, and the ability to excite the loyalty of those who worked with him. All this was coupled with an emormous stamina and a strong feeling for the national interest. I state this without hesitation or reservation of any sort since I believe that this outstanding man has not been adequately appreciated in our country because of political passions, but his significance grows with time. It is my belief that under a more favourable political constellation he could have been one of the great presidents in the history of Argentina. This conviction was strengthened as time went by; had I said this in 1935 it would have been the result of the close association between our group and Pinedo. But today, with the benefit of hindsight and after having met countless men both within and without Argentina, the full significance of Pinedo for my country is borne upon me.

Pinedo had favoured free trade and held solidly orthodox ideas. These same ideas are held today and not only in Argentina, although they lack Pinedo's brilliance, depth and intellectual authority. It is as well to make a distinction among those who share this point of view. The Great Depression – just like the great World Inflation of the present day – posed new problems, and those men who had a similar theoretical background were split. On the one hand there were those capable of rejecting dogma, willing to seek new paths; on the other, there were those who dogmatically persisted in solutions which made matters worse. Such is the basic distinction that has to be made, and it refers to the manner in which both the internal and the external problems were tackled. Frequently the latter are not taken into account, and the attempt is made to carry out measures as if the rest of the the world were living in great stability. Pinedo was one of those men who refused to be restricted by dogma, and I recall an occasion that will help to illustrate this.

Since the internal situation worsened after we had established exchange controls, Minister Enrique Uriburu decided to put into effect an old banking rediscount law which had been passed at the start of the First World War. Naturally, in a country acutely aware since 1890 of the dangers of inflation, the slightest sign or threat of inflation produced considerable reaction. When the news was published, Dr Pinedo came to see me to warn me that we were going to unleash a galloping inflation. I explained our reasons for enforcing that old piece of legislation. He was very impressed by the fact that the Banco de la Nación, in control of the clearing operations, held an amount of money which was less than the clearing deposits – that is to say, it did not have enough money in case of an emergency. I also described to him the way in which the fiscal deficit was being adjusted, and told him about further steps I was trying to implement, such as taxing profits. We talked at length and I finally asked him what he would do if he were in charge of the Exchequer. He replied, 'I would do what you are doing....'

On realising the gravity of events, from that day onwards this man (who was then in the opposition) underwent a remarkable transformation that showed his aptitude to grasp reality. Dr Pinedo was not acquainted with the government officials in charge of economic policy, so I introduced them to him. A dialogue was thus opened which made it possible for Pinedo to share, if not the actual responsibility of government, at least our diagnosis of the situation.

When the Provisional Government came to an end, Dr Hueyo took over the Finance Ministry; either because he belonged to a different generation, or because of his own disposition, he regarded any heterodox measure with considerable wariness. He checked the budget deficit, launched the Empréstito Patriótico (Patriotic Loan) and, all in all, his management of the economy was adequate, if undistinguished. But the times required imagination and a sense of innovation which Hueyo lacked. There was a ministerial reshuffle and Pinedo was offered Finance, while Agriculture went to Luís Duhau, another worthy man who has not been fully appreciated. They started working closely together and I played the role of adviser to both, thereby providing a degree of consistency to economic policy-making.

Which were the main decisions taken during that period? In my view, they were those aimed at overcoming the serious problems of unemployment and of the disastrous effects of the drop in world prices on agricultural output. I shall first take up the latter issue. We had learnt through the branches of the Banco de la Nación that people in the countryside were becoming so despondent that the land was not being tilled. What was the point in tilling the land if prices did not cover minimum costs? It goes without saying that had the land not been sown, the consequences for the country would have been catastrophic.

The measures adopted could not be labelled as 'orthodox': minimum prices were set for wheat, maize and linseed – I believe these were the three main crops – so that at least production costs would be met. How were we to pay such minimum prices if world prices were lower? – by means of a devaluation of the peso to adjust it to the new price situation. The increase was not immediately transferred to exports but instead, the extra earnings resulting from the new exchange rate (at the time it was called 'exchange margin') were kept to subsidise exports and compensate for the difference between the fixed minimum internal prices and export prices.

We debated at length about the need for such an interventionist measure which we felt was unavoidable. Not all the benefits from the devaluation went to make up those funds; some had a positive effect on prices and encouraged other exports facing a very difficult world market. The rise in the exchange rate stimulated industry which had already seen a massive and rather improvised stepping up in protectionist tariffs. Therefore the sale abroad of grains was promoted while simultaneously encouraging industrial expansion – already initiated as a result of the increase in customs duties. These measures favouring industrialisation had to be adopted without spelling out their aim. Fortunately the deficit in the balance of payments prevented the development of a theory of industrialisation that, in those days, would have sparked off considerable opposition both in the political parties and in the press.

Many people who have read the documents of that period are under the impression that we had not thought about industrialisation since we did not mention it. The first time we began to be slightly more explicit was around 1940 in the annual reports of the Central Bank, where we resolutely maintained that it was necessary to embark on an active process of industrialisation. As far as I was concerned, it took some time before I wholly embraced this conclusion. When Perón dismissed me from the Central Bank and I had a few years to reflect, I concluded that industrialisation, condemned by the theory of international division of labour, was not so much a *deviation* from sound economic theories as a *requirement* for developing countries.

I sought to show – first, teaching at the university and then at the Economic Commission for Latin America – that industrialisation with moderate protectionism was an economic solution to those problems of unemployment and of internal supply which could not be satisfied by exports. It was not an anti-exports policy but one that would allow us to do, particularly given the plight of the world economy, what exports could not. If one pictures the situation in the 1930s, in which protectionism was advancing throughout the world, in which the behaviour of the main capitalist centre (the United States) led to a great world depression, to the breaking-up of the economy, to bilateralism, was it conceivable that Argentina would hoist up the banner of free trade when she painfully needed to set about establishing new import-substitution industries? The only viable industry at the time was import-substitution, and many years would pass before one could even think in terms of exporting manufactures.

Then came the crisis unfolded by the Second World War, during which the sale of commodities to Europe was substantially reduced.

Once again there was a deficit in the balance of payments at a time when the Argentine economy had recovered; once again there was unemployment and the threat of a growing contraction in foreign trade. It was under those circumstances that Dr Pinedo returned to the government, and the famous Plan de Reactivación Económica (Economic Recovery Plan) was put into effect. It included expansionary measures aimed at increasing demand and stimulating the growth of industrial output so as to attenuate – if not eliminate – the trend towards unemployment. One of the chief elements in the general expansion of demand was the construction of public housing. But the question was how to face up to the impact this policy would have on imports, since it is a well known fact that when growth speeds up, and when the aim is to maintain a given rate of growth while exports fall, the result is a disequilibrium in the external sector.

It was at that time that the decision was taken to stress a selective imports policy, and simultaneously to seek abroad new public sources of finance so as to be able to apply this policy without too many restrictions. I was entrusted with the task of negotiating loans in the United States from the Export–Import Bank and from the Treasury, and as a result we obtained loans for 110 million dollars under very favourable conditions. Unfortunately, while I was undertaking these negotiations in the United States, Dr Pinedo left the government and this policy could not be carried out.

After some time, it became possible to export to Europe once more and thus the urgent need for an expansionary policy was largely removed. The Argentine economy began to function again during the war albeit with great difficulties that had to be overcome. I must insist then on this point: confronted with new problems we had to find our own path without relying on solutions offered in textbooks; we had to use our imagination and good sense to decide what to do, for instance, in the case of an anti-inflationary policy. Thus it happened that when the economy and exports recovered their rhythm, we were faced with the problem that since it was not possible to import all that was required, foreign exchange would accumulate and give rise to international expansionary effects. To avoid the latter the Central Bank followed an anti-cyclical policy releasing its considerable holdings in bonds to pick up that money and neutralize it, thereby reducing the inflationary impact of the accumulation of foreign currency. Subsequently we have heard people say that inflation cannot be controlled if there is an accumulation of foreign exchange; in fact, it can be controlled if there is a well-organised Central Bank that has learnt to operate in such matters.

The above shows that having started with a relatively orthodox policy, international circumstances led to the combination of fiscal orthodoxy – which was essential – with measures to strengthen the economy and to control foreign trade; that is to say, with deviations from orthodoxy. Those who have said that we took off with orthodox policies were right, but such policies did not prevent the enforcement of a series of very important measures which orthodoxy would not have advised. I would like to stress that I consider it essential that in all economic and social systems, and in all situations, the budget should be balanced, except perhaps in a period of contraction when an expansionary policy could be temporarily strengthened through the budget. But generally, if the purpose is to follow an expansionary policy, it must be done by other means: construction, the encouragement of new investment in industry, etc., but not through a fiscal deficit (which, moreover, implies an enormous wastage of human resources). Besides, it is necessary to single out those occasions that demand a fiscal policy from those that require a monetary policy. If a government lacks the aptitude, ability, or political means itself to reduce the fiscal deficit, it cannot fight inflation by restricting credit to private enterprise; it is counter-productive.

Taking a considerable step forward in time I would now like to refer to the 1955 Emergency Plan. The Plan has been the object of the most fanciful and nonsensical interpretations; for instance, that its purpose was to destroy industry. It was based essentially on the fact that Argentine industry was in great difficulty because there was no foreign exchange to pay for imports of intermediate and capital goods. As a result the key problem was to bolster once more agricultural exports so that the country should acquire the foreign exchange necessary to industrialise. Since this would take some time – abrupt changes cannot be achieved in this area – it was decided to borrow abroad. This caused an uproar. It was unthinkable that Argentina should get into debt abroad!

I was to find out later that my serious mistake had been to talk of borrowing abroad just as one would talk of public works or taxation, since it had led people to think that I was pointing to only *one* source of borrowing: the United States. But this was not the case, since I was thinking in a generic sense. Nor was I referring to private foreign investment which was not necessary at the time. I meant public funds that would encourage industrialisation and agricultural productivity. Unfortunately that Plan was misunderstood; if there was something I was known for in Latin America it was for my defence of industrialisation within ECLA. So it came to pass that in my own country I was labelled as an 'anti-industrialist'; in fact there was no such contradiction, even though I should have perhaps taken greater care in the language I used and insisted more on the complementarity between primary exports and industrialisation.

In addition I put forward and struggled for the creation of the Instituto Nacional de Tecnología Agropecuaria (National Institute of Agricultural Technology) because it was necessary to encourage the development of new technology in Argentina. The results of such an endeavour have not been swift but they have been positive. In all these matters I believe I was right, but I was wrong as far as devaluation was concerned. Repeatedly I have been asked whether I would again advise that 1955 devaluation in Argentina. If I had known then what I know now, what I have learnt after having come a long way and having been the subject of much criticism which I felt deeply, I would not have offered such advice. What would I have advised instead? That there is no chance of fighting an inflation such as that of Argentina with monetary or fiscal policies. There is no other solution but to transform the system. This is my present and categorical conclusion.

I have arrived at the conclusion that when in the course of structural changes in the economy – typical of the development process – the political and trades union power of the masses unfolds (and this is to be welcomed to counteract the power of appropriation of the surplus by the higher strata in society), the result is a type of social inflation that cannot be curbed with traditional methods. It cannot be either in Argentina or in the United States, where the situation is alarming; as yet I cannot see a real solution to the problem.

I would have liked to talk about the transformation of the system that I envisage, but I suspect that Professor Platt and Dr di Tella have not invited me to proclaim a theory of transformation but to talk about the past. Moreover, the book where I expound my view of the crisis of capitalism on the periphery, and put forward a series of measures to bring about such transformation, has just been published in Mexico, and it would not be appropriate to repeat here what I have already said.

DISCUSSION*

O'Connell: You have not referred in favourable terms to the role played by foreign capital in developing countries. Yet in 1928 you helped draft

---
* Questioners were identified wherever possible.

the Sociedad Rural's report on the meat-packing pool.

Prebisch: It was in my own handwriting.

O'Connell. None the less, when you were in government in 1930 and the Roca–Runciman agreement was signed, you accepted the British Government's freezing of the pool system which had been confirmed in that agreement. Moreover, you also mentioned the importance of raising tariffs to encourage industrialisation, and yet in that same agreement a series of preferential tariffs was granted for those products which were of relevance to the British economy, some of them in competition with industries which were achieving considerable magnitude in Argentina, like the textile industry. I am aware of the discrimination the United States was practising against the Argentine economy, but don't you think that at that time Argentina and you yourselves could have had a stronger bargaining position *vis-à-vis* Britain? And if you did not have it, what were the pressures against it?

Prebisch: I shall reply with other questions. Which were the industries that suffered as a result of that agreement? Did textile output drop, did factories close down, or did textile output continue to increase?

O'Connell: Output continued to increase.

Prebisch: So? The scope of certain consequences of that agreement has been greatly exaggerated. It should be examined in the light of the exchange control mechanism which we had in our hands. Concessions were made but at the same time the exchange mechanism was being controlled to prevent any adverse outcome for Argentine industry. I believe that all those who have referred to this matter did not find even *one* case of damage being caused. Damage was caused by other reductions in duties which were subsequently granted in times I would rather not remember, but not in our time. I recall that while in London I suggested some finishing touches, but in the belief that the proposed rebates would have no effect other than to encourage some competitiveness.

As far as the first point was concerned, indeed I showed that there existed a pool or cartel among meat-packing plants which, since they had to load their ships in a fixed period of time given the quality of chilled meat (it could be no longer that 15 or 17 days), shared out amongst themselves the purchases in the market. This gave them considerable power to set a margin between local prices and those at Smithfield. In the light of my research I discussed the matter with Sir Frederick Leith Ross, the chief British expert in economic and financial policy, a man with a very sharp mind, who commented ironically that it seemed there was an incremental factor on the margin when the Equator was crossed, that accounted for the difference between the price paid by meat-packing plants in Argentina and the price they obtained at Smithfield market. The Argentine government and the cattle-breeders maintained that it would be possible to fix an export quota to control the meat-packing plants, but the British followed the same reasoning in believing that they could impose an import quota. An agreement had to be reached. All we succeeded in obtaining was for an international auditing firm to examine the problem; that is to say, practically nothing. In those years British capitalism had the power of the purchaser: the power to fix quotas, and the threat it posed to Argentina's interests was very serious. Meat producers were very agitated at that time. Many people believe that the agreement protected the cattle-breeding oligarchy, but it was this same oligarchy that bred the cows that produced Argentina's foreign exchange. I would not have opposed the substitution of this oligarchy, but the fact of the matter remained that we were interested in exporting meat and preventing local production from suffering cuts in favour of Australian production. What else could we have done under those circumstances? Nothing, except to complain and keep complaining. In the nineteenth century the British had a very persuasive way of protecting opium exports to China: the use of force. We could not use force against Great Britain.

In the same way, it was impossible to force the United States to allow linseed or meat imports. That was the situation in the world, and it still remains so. One should take advantage of commercial gaps, of the continuing industrial complementarity between Latin American countries, of trading opportunities with the rest of the world. In so far as we are faced with the barriers set by the centre countries to exports from the periphery, there are no other solutions.

Fodor: I am rather surprised by the emphasis you place on the danger of inflation in the early 1930s when prices were falling, and your further emphasis later, in the 1940s, on the setting up of a very dangerous mechanism, the arrangement with Britain. You explained very well the safeguards taken by the Central Bank in the clearing operations with Germany. So why didn't you do with Britain what the United States did, demand 'cash-and-carry', or for that matter do what Canada did, demand dollars? Or even other countries such as Sweden, who in the clearing agreement limited the amount of sterling it was prepared to accumulate? I believe that in fact the Central Bank missed many opportunities. You may not have been aware of this, but there were many situations in which Britain was ready to pay in dollars, and yet you continued to grant credit facilities. The Central Bank had a sizeable debtor in Britain, and as you have explained, the debtor has considerable clout. Keynes used to say 'If you owe your bank a thousand pounds you're in its hands. If you owe it a million, it is in yours.' The Central Bank placed itself in a position that worsened after 1943, but the mechanism had started operating earlier. Britain bought meat in Argentina for the United States. The United States paid Britain in dollars. Britain paid Argentina in sterling; she was quite ready to pay in dollars. A similar case occurred with foreign investments. Morgenthau said 'I want the stuff and I want it now' when he negotiated the repatriation of British investments in the United States, and he forced the sale of a very large firm in one week. The situation was very different on the Argentine side. The Central Bank had a much weaker attitude than the South African Central Bank, much weaker than the Canadian Central Bank, all of which must bewilder us. All those Central Banks were established at about the same time, and comparing the behaviour of the Argentine Central Bank, the number of missed opportunities cannot but amaze.

It is true that after the fall of Belgium and Holland the British position became stronger because Argentina had no other buyers. For instance, the Central Bank obtained the guarantee of the value of the sterling it held – an important achievement – but in October 1940 Britain transformed this gold set-aside clause into a straightforward exchange guarantee. The consequences were serious for Argentina since she was struck off the list of priorities for British exports. Until 1940, while the Central Bank was demanding gold – even though it had to be resold in Britain – it was important for Britain to export to Argentina; the latter country was in the same list as Canada, the United States and Sweden. After 1940 Argentina was struck off that list; there was no interest in exporting to Argentina. Britain had to increase her production of armaments, therefore she did not find it convenient to sacrifice productive forces with the purpose of exporting to countries willing to grant her credit facilities. The situation got worse in 1942–43 and subsequently it became calamitous; but the mechanisms that worsened later were already functioning.

Prebisch: It may be that you are right and I accept that mistakes may have been made; I am anxious to see your work, as it will allow me to analyse the problem more adequately. In any case, you should not forget that these negotiations were undertaken by the Central Bank acting on behalf of the Argentine government. What would the British do, could have done, or were thinking of doing? Until yesterday I was unaware that Keynes was involved in the negotiations with Argentina. Should you be proved right, I shall be the first to acknowledge it.

Fodor: But the danger of inflation was not a secret and in the same Central Bank report you were aware of what was going on and said so. But other countries were able to check this danger. . . .

Prebisch: It would have been necessary to export less. . . .

Fodor: Not necessarily, because Britain, if she had had to export gold, would have preferred to export goods instead. . . .

Prebisch: I wonder whether in the middle of the war Britain would have been able to export the goods Argentina needed. What I can tell you is that in the Central Bank we had to administer the system of need permits that the United States imposed, and we were forced to study all demands very carefully since both stock and production restrictions were considerable. I am inclined to think that difficulties were even greater in Britain, which was undergoing the Nazi bombardment that disrupted her industry. Perhaps Britain was able to export those goods and Argentina missed the opportunity; maybe it was like that, but I think it highly unlikely.

Fodor: Britain had a list of priorities and there were three or four shifting categories. Argentina was in category 1 but after October 1940 she was transferred to category 3 and thereafter Britain, which had few goods to export, sent them to other countries. . . .

Prebisch: What countries remained in category 1?

Fodor: Canada, the United States, Sweden.

Prebisch: Transport conditions were different. Transportation from Britain to South America had to go in convoys and more than one ship was lost on the way. What I can tell you is that in the Central Bank we followed such matters with the keenest interest. But it is quite possible that we were wrong and I would be the first one to admit it if thus proved. proved.

Question: How did the progressive sectors in Argentina envisage the future after the events of the 1930s?

Prebisch: I shall not refer to what was in the collective conscience, if it can so be called, but to what I myself expected. I thought that the industrialisation process and the experience we were acquiring in a relatively rational handling of the economy would lead the country through a regular process of development. I had hoped that if the country continued to grow, not at an extraordinary but at a moderate rate, since population growth was also moderate, in a few years' time Argentina would be self-sufficient in financial resources, as long as she followed an intelligent foreign trade policy. But this did not take place. It could have, but it did not. Furthermore, there was a serious political problem that cannot be overlooked and which had originated in the 1930 coup that paved the way to electoral fraud and all **those regrettable** subsequent events. The country could not come out of that. General Justo was much abused, but his aim was to ensure a political way out for the country on the basis of the majority party: Alvear as president or perhaps Ortíz – as in fact happened – but you know what unfortunately occurred. He was eager for such a solution because he realised the country could not continue like that. But political interests led to the Patrón Costa solution which the country could not accept and turned out to be a further irritating element. Let us not forget – and this has not been mentioned at the present conference – the Nazi influence in our country. I have seen it; I experienced it myself while in the Central Bank. The penetration of Nazism in the army, in certain newspapers, aided by considerable resourcefulness from the German Embassy, was a highly disturbing element in Argentina. All this contributed to the arrival of Peronism.

Question: How do you perceive the role of the United States during the Second World War in terms of your economic and commercial strategies before 1943, in terms of the failure of the Pinedo Plan, and perhaps in terms of the rise of Peronism?

Prebisch: I do not admit the role of the United States at that time. Neither before nor after. First of all, US economic policy was quite detrimental to the interests of Argentina and to their own long-term interests. I have explained that one of the problems that greatly concerned us was the growing trade disequilibrium with the United States. We were getting exchange from the British to pay for imports from the United States. I can assure you that no constructive measure was taken by the United States to put this right. And when I went to Washington I had to discuss some of these problems about the trade very confidentially. I discovered that they thought that our attempt to divert trade imports from the United States to other countries in the non-liberated areas invaded by the Germans, was the result of the preachings of Dr Schacht toward bilateralism. They confessed that to me. And it was nonsense. But they thought that what we were doing in Argentina was the result of a deliberate doctrine of foreign trade. But it was a distortion of the facts. We had an arrangement with the Germans similar to the one we had with the British, with the difference that Argentina was the only country in the world that accepted a bilateral trade treaty with the Germans – the only country that said, 'We shall export to Germany in so far as they will send us exports'. It was a very primitive way of striking a balance, but it was the only way that Argentina could avoid what had happened to other countries that had accumulated huge balances. This was the result in the last instance of the credit contraction in the United States in the 1930s and of their protectionist policy. And indeed, they would not see what were their own long-term interests. There was ill-feeling in Argentina in the 1920s in relation to trade, but Roosevelt saw the difficulty; he had a different way of dealing with the problems. Later on there were no great differences between Democratic and Republican governments, except in the short time of Kennedy. Kennedy was the real hope: he was a man with whom it was possible to discuss on the basis of mutual, long-term interests.

Question: Earlier in your talk you spoke very briefly of an occasion in which you said you went personally to President Uriburu and persuaded him of the efficacy of an exchange control and income tax policy. Thereafter the historical part of the talk referred to the relationship between what we might call the political action of the Government itself and the action of the group of progressive technocrats, and I wonder if you might just briefly go back and reflect for a moment on the relationship that you and your group had with what after all was a succession of régimes during a 12-year period; historians have identified differences between them. It would seem that at least superficially there were some important differences between Uriburu, Justo and Ortíz and then, Castillo, and you worked intimately with all of them. Yet you gave us insight into the direct contact only with one. Were they all the same? Were they all open to you? Did you find them politically the same? How did they receive your ideas?

Prebisch: It was not always the same. Perhaps our greatest difficulty was with Hueyo. I could not stand him. I resigned. I went back to the Banco de la Nación which was my main post, so it was not a great heroic act on my part. But even so, I think that Dr Klein [one of the participants at the Conference] will agree with me, Hueyo was a different type of man. While Pinedo was extremely intelligent, would grasp matters immediately and understand them quickly, and had a tremendous capacity for action, Hueyo was a very hesitant, very suspicious man. He never inspired fire in us. This was one difference. There were others in between. But undoubtedly with Pinedo it was possible to work harmoniously, and with a great sense of devotion.

Question: But were these only personality differences? Were there no ideological differences? What about later, when Ortíz was president, or when Castillo became acting president? Surely there must have been some fundamental shifts of policy at the top which affected you and those working with you.

Prebisch: I consider that Ortíz, when he was in good health, at the head of the Ministry of Finance, continued this policy. He understood it and he did not break with what Pinedo did, on the contrary, he deeply respected what Pinedo had done. At that time, the Central Bank was functioning, the big institutions had their own dynamic, so it was not so difficult as at first. But – and this was an accident, or perhaps a design of God – he became sick. We never knew how serious his illness was. So when the risk of the Second World War was more and more evident, I had a long talk with the Minister of Finance, Groppo, who was a medical doctor, quite an intelligent man, a good friend of Pinedo, a man of good sense, and I served him. In 1940 the banking system was under an extraordinary pressure: bank deposits were withdrawn, public bonds were withdrawn, public bonds went down, there was great instability. I think that we had to be prepared for this emergency. And there were resources. Why don't we put together (I thought then) all the resources of public institutions? At that time we had the power to put them together and give money – outside rediscount operations – to the banks, or to intervene in the Stock Exchange and buy bonds in order to contain the adverse effects of a possible emergency. The Minister said he agreed with me and suggested we went to see the President. We went to see him. I explained the matter to him. He said, 'Don't worry. If there is such an emergency, I will send the troops to police the city.' This intelligent man, this man of commonsense, was absolutely lost.

And then came Castillo, the Vice-President, who was a good man but a sheer mediocrity; it was impossible to deal with him. He was from a little province, from the deep interior, without any view of the world; he was an honourable man, but one who would go to the Central Bank and sit there for hours to ask for a small post for a relative or a friend. Our relations with the Ministers were not the same. But as I told you before, the Central Bank was already organised, it had some capacity for action and we were able to carry out many things.

Question: An excessively concise question: were Perón and Peronism an historical accident or an unavoidable occurrence?

Prebisch: To be able to answer that question I would have to take the matter up with the Divine Providence, and as yet I have not acquired this talent. And yet I am inclined to think that in great part it was an historical accident, but only partly so, because there was an enormous incompetence in the dominant forces in the country prior to Perón's access to power. A certain style in the running of the economy – or rather, lack of it – turned out to be fatal for our country. The export data during the Peronist period cannot be explained solely by a change in the composition of exports, but by erroneous policy. The neglect of agriculture, the ignorance of the rest of the world's technological advances, the over-valuation of the peso, these measures were all highly adverse to the economy of the country.

Question: I would like to ask you two questions. You were critical of certain aspects of economic policy during Perón's government between 1945 and 1955 but I would like to know your opinion about trade unions; the matter is very relevant to your theory on the transformation of the system and, as is well known, Peronism played a significant role in the consolidation of the power of the unions in Argentina. Beginning with the Peronist government the unions became an important element within the power structure of the country and if one compares that situation with the one existing in other Latin American countries, I think there was a qualitative change which was one of Peronism's historic achievements. The second question is on a different matter but also relevant: what was the role of the armed forces throughout this period?

Prebisch: Perón did not create the unions; they existed in Argentina and they were quite healthy, with capable leaders and not at all corrupt. I think that the labour movement has been pushed off course, corrupted and distorted, but I maintain as well that the power of the unions is indispensable to counteract the appropriation of the results of technical progress by the higher echelons of society. But such counteraction leads to social inflation, which is not an answer; neither is it to suppress political and trade union power.

Question: You have pointed out that today you would consider the question of the 1955 devaluation in a different light. Could you expand on this matter?

Prebisch: Certainly. The Argentine economy was decapitalised as a result of all the errors committed during the Peronist years. Agricultural production had been discouraged and industrial production was hindered because there were not enough capital goods. The railways were totally destroyed. Large investments were required, and it could not be expected that all the effort should be made with international resources, because we would not have been able to obtain those resources. Argentina had to make the effort internally. The idea of devaluation – the correction of an excessive overvaluation – was based on the principle that the resulting rise in the price of exports or in the price of imports would in turn mean that the economic surplus (a term which was not then used, but which is crucial to my present theory) would be re-established. In our present system, the continuation or acceleration in the rate of growth is dependent on the increase in the economic surplus. This is unavoidable, since the greatest part of resources for capital accumulation stem from the economic surplus. At the same time, those resources that allow for the imitation of the consumption patterns of the Centre countries also stem from that surplus. That is to say, the surplus is a dynamic element and, simultaneously, an element on which the privileged consumer society is based. But under the régime we live in there is no other solution. This I perceive today very clearly, but I did not at that time, thus I followed the advice that good theory provided in similar conditions. Why wouldn't I recommend the same step now? For a very simple reason from both an economic and a moral standpoint: to re-establish the dynamics of the economic surplus it would be necessary to restrain real wages, stop them from rising to allow for the creation of that margin that will allow those who appropriate the surplus to increase their accumulation. This is why I would not be prepared to recommend today what I recommended then; now I understand fully the problem because I have tried to understand the essential mechanisms of the system.

My self-criticism is not connected with the issue of industrialisation; rather with the mechanism used to transfer resources from the popular to the higher strata with the aim of accumulating more, both in the countryside and in the cities. In those days it seemed a commonplace, but I no longer think so.

Question: You said that the 1955 Plan was misunderstood and that you regret only the devaluation; I wonder whether it was convenient to stimulate agriculture to capitalise the country given the conditions in the world market which were not at all favourable to Argentine agricultural exports. Was there an alternative to capitalise the country? Was that a viable alternative?

Prebisch: We have all agreed that there was a 30 years' technological lag in Argentine agriculture. Recovering the lost time demanded capital accumulation. Furthermore, as far as meat exports were concerned, two adverse factors contributed to their fall; in the first place, the EEC's restrictive policy, and in the second, internal consumption. With the growth in population and incomes, an increasingly large part of the meat supply was consumed domestically. It made no difference to the producers whether the meat-packing plants sold the meat internally or abroad; they received their share in either case, so they could not see any problem. The problem existed from the point of view of the country, since the rise in internal consumption was at the expense of exports. If there had been an intelligent technological policy, livestock output could have expanded in different ways, as was pointed out at the time in an ECLA report; but many years had passed without any action being taken. This meant that capital accumulation had to be increased. The mistake of that policy was to restrict wages so that others could accumulate; I would never again recommend such a course of action.

Question: I would like to ask a question about the technological lag in agriculture as a result of which in the 1930s and notwithstanding the policies directly geared to achieve a series of improvements in the countryside, it was not possible to get the agricultural producer to introduce the innovations which he should have done, at least in theory, in response to the incentives he was offered. Moreover, why was it necessary to await the arrival of the 1960s for such responses, given that all through those years quite favourable policies had been implemented in respect of agriculture?

Prebisch: Leaving aside questions relating to the land tenure system, such innovations in agricultural technology advance slowly. It was necessary to organise research, train people, send them abroad, bring experts from abroad. Once certain breakthroughs that take years are achieved – for example, a hybrid – one must ensure their dissemination, a task that also demands time and resources.

Question: But ought one not to look at the rationality of the system of agricultural accumulation itself to find the reasons for the incorporation of certain types of innovations and the rejection of others, or even of the opportunity for certain innovations . . . ?

Prebisch: On this I have come across two conflicting opinions. Some say that the great landowner has been very open and has made good use of those innovations; others say just the opposite; I do not know which is the correct interpretation.

Question: When you refer to the transformation of the system in relation to the fight against inflation, and thus to the possibility of solving the contradictions of the system, to what do you specifically refer? Do you refer to the transformation of the ways in which the economic surplus is produced and so to the relations of production, or do you refer to the distribution of the surplus?

Prebisch: Naturally in any economic and social system the surplus must grow since it is that portion of the increase in productivity which is not transferred to the labour force in the form of larger incomes. There is a surplus in every economic and social system; what matters is what it is used for. I favour what I call the social utilisation of the economic surplus in such a way that part of the increase is devoted to expand accumulation, another to outright redistribution, and still another to public expenditure. That is to say, I am for the introduction of a principle of rationality in the utilisation of the economic surplus.

Traditional economists boast about the rationality of the system they advocate; certain aspects are rational, but not all. To put it simply, I believe it is necessary to arrive at a great synthesis between Socialism and Liberalism. Socialism as far as the distribution of the surplus is concerned, in the way I have pointed out (accumulation, redistribution, public expenditure), is a process which must be the subject of collective decisions that do not require the transfer of the means of production to the State, fundamentally for a political, and not merely economic, reason – so as not to give the party in government, the sole party, unbridled power. Socialism then, inasmuch as the utilisation of the economic surplus cannot be decided by the laws of the market, and economic liberalism inasmuch as once those problems are solved, the market can be left to play a role which is both economically and politically important. Do not let us blame the market for the unequal distribution of income which has continued to prevail in almost all Latin American countries; the market has nothing to do with this. This pattern of income distribution is the result of the increasingly disturbing interplay of power relationships between different social groups. If this were somehow to be corrected, if there were a certain equality and rationality in the distribution of income and in the accumulation of capital, then the market would have a role to play.

Nor has the market guaranteed the productive resources effectively. Has it been able to solve the ecological problem, the problem of the irresponsible use of natural resources? What has been the efficacy of the market as far as oil and pollution are concerned? This does not mean to say that every individual has to be told how to use oil, or how to deal with the problem of pollution, but collective action is needed for the market to operate rationally.

Now it is true to say that Friedman maintains that the oil crisis could have been avoided if the pricing system had been used; but it happens that the pricing system is not dependent on the spontaneous interplay of economic forces. A deliberate increase in the price of oil would have been necessary to guarantee its correct use, and not the outcome of the interplay of market forces. I mention ecology because it is another crucial problem that shows the aberration of insisting that great collective economic problems can be solved by the interplay of market forces.

The essential thing is for incomes to be correctly distributed. Neoclassical economists maintained – and they still do – that the interplay of economic forces not only leads to a rational allocation of productive resources, but that it unavoidably leads to a situation of equilibrium in the system in which the remuneration received by the different productive factors corresponds to their specific contribution to the productive process. Consequently, the same economists maintain that the interference of the labour force – with its political and trade union power – prevents the system from reaching its equilibrium point. This is not so; rather, it is the only means the labour force has to achieve its share of the surplus. Thus one cannot demand from the market what it cannot give. Rationality has to result from collective decisions as far as accumulation, distribution, foreign trade, and ecology are concerned.

9 The Origin of Argentina's Sterling Balances, 1939–43

JORGE FODOR

I

Sterling balances have played an extremely important role in the determination of the postwar course of Argentine economic policy. In particular they strongly influenced the external economic policy of the first Perón government and contributed to the diffidence felt in influential quarters in Argentina towards further integration into the world economy. In some extreme moments it was felt even that there was not much difference between exporting to Britain for sterling and dumping products into the sea.[1]

Hence sterling balances poisoned relations between Britain and Argentina in the immediate postwar period. Argentina asked for very modest concessions in this field, such as a 2.5 per cent rate of interest on her credits with Britain, at a moment when international inflation was very high. Seen from Britain, however, such demands were totally unacceptable, not because of their intrinsic cost, but because of similar demands that they would inevitably have encouraged from other, much larger holders of sterling.

For Argentina the study of the question of sterling balances is of importance not only for the light it throws on some controversial decisions in economic policy for 1946–8, but also for many problems raised by the war itself. Many aspects will be touched upon and I hope to be able to contribute to a better understanding of the problems that the evolution of the war posed for policy makers in Argentina.

The solution chosen was very peculiar; political neutrality combined with extreme generosity to Britain in financial questions. It is more accurate to say that this path, which is probably the worst that Argentina could have followed, was not chosen by anybody, but was the result of innumerable factors. The outcome was that Argentina was considered, especially in the US, as following a pro-Nazi policy when in fact she was giving very substantial help to Britain.

Argentina, an independent country, accumulated sterling without setting any limits; in doing so she created much less trouble for Britain than some of the Dominions, like Canada and South Africa, and than other neutrals, like the US, that demanded payment in dollars or gold until Britain had exhausted her reserves. But why was Argentina willing to accept the currency of another country – furthermore, a currency that was twice devalued in 1931 and again in 1939? Seen from this angle, the question touches one of the most important questions of international monetary economics in this century: the gold exchange standard.

My paper deals with the origins of the sterling balances up to the military coup of June 1943. During this period the Banco Central was run by the same group of people, under the leadership of Raúl Prebisch, and there was continuity of policy, although naturally the course of events produced modifications. After the coup there were abrupt changes, and although foreign debt repatriation was accelerated, balances increased at a much more rapid pace. In some respects this second period may be seen as a caricature of the first, combining perversely even greater political isolation from the Allies with even more economic concessions to Britain. It is however another period, and it will not be discussed here.

II

By 1941 economists working at the War Cabinet Office estimated that British production of weapons was similar to that of her enemies, an astonishing achievement if one takes into account the delays in British rearmament and the fact that Greater Germany alone had 79.5 million inhabitants while Great Britain had 45.5 million.[2] Germany, however, was still employing about 27 per cent of her working population in agriculture, compared with less than 5 per cent for Britain. These figures are still very far from giving us an adequate picture: while Germany could count on the resources of almost the whole of continental Europe, Britain had the benefit of the resources of a vast Empire and of those of many other countries. For instance, she could obtain oil with very little effort from the rich fields of distant regions; Germany had to invest much instead in building plants that produced synthetic oil.

However, there were complications. If for each man abroad producing goods for Britain a British worker had to produce exports, the only benefits that would have emerged would have been those arising from international specialisation. A much more significant advantage could be achieved if a method could be found that did not require imports to be matched by exports. In this case workers could be taken from the different sectors of the economy and transferred to the production of armaments or to the fighting services, while imports continued to flow in. This was the aim, and it brought war finance into the centre of the war effort. If imports were not to be paid for by exports, they could be had only by one (or by a combination) of the following alternatives: (1) running down reserves; (2) selling foreign investments; (3) credits from abroad; (4) gifts from abroad.

The running down of reserves was in any case inevitable, and by the autumn of 1940 Britain had almost exhausted her gold and dollar reserves. Foreign investments were sold, but this was far from easy, and it was done with the utmost reluctance as it weakened Britain's external position after the war. Gifts were important, especially the 1942 Canadian 1,000,000,000 dollar gift and the crucial element of unilateral transfer contained in Lend Lease. But all this was not enough, and loans were needed. They could not be obtained in the US because of American aversion to Payment Agreements and because the Johnson Act of 1934 prohibited loans to countries that had defaulted on their debts to the US. But with other countries things were not as difficult.

With the outbreak of war in September 1939, Britain was faced with one main problem in its relations with Argentina; this was how to pay for all the foodstuffs she was buying. As exports to Argentina were bound to diminish with the transformation of the British economy into a war economy, these purchases could be paid for in gold or dollars (the least desirable method for Britain), Argentine pesos or sterling. Paying in pesos posed difficulties, as it was not clear how to get enough of them. A peso loan would have been necessary, and this had drawbacks. Paying interest and getting into debt in a foreign currency were two obvious problems, but there were also others. First of all it would have implied making the issue a matter of public debate in Argentina, as the Banco Central was not authorised by its charter to lend pesos to foreign governments. Secondly, a peso credit would have had a ceiling and a date of redemption. In the third place, its size would probably have been conditioned by the limited capacity of the Argentine money market and of the Argentine government to raise the necessary amounts. Payment in sterling was the best of all options: no interest would probably be required, and in the meantime there would be time to discuss other related matters, like the repatriation of Argentine securities held in Britain.

The problem arose directly on 4 September 1939, the day after the declaration of war. Britain wanted to buy 1 million tons of wheat and 500,000 tons of maize, but Argentina had asked for payment in pesos. This is not surprising, as the pound was in the middle of a downward slide in New York. On 24 August the Exchange Equalisation Account had withdrawn support for the pound, with the result that the dollar exchange fell from 4.68 to 4.04 (at which point it was stabilised in mid September).[3]

The alternatives posed by Argentina's request were summarised by the Treasury in a letter to the Food Defence Plans Department: (1) accept; (2) negotiate credit; (3) pay in pounds.[4] Matters dragged on until the pound was stabilised; shortly afterwards, while the Argentine Minister of Agriculture was saying to the British Commercial Secretary that Argentina preferred payment in pesos, the Banco Central had agreed to accept sterling, but demanded that balances in its favour should be in dollars or used to buy bonds.

'You will see that the last cable contemplates payment in sterling and we are very anxious to close with this rapidly', wrote Niemeyer on 28 September. Two days later an offer was made to the Banco Central: purchases would be paid (in sterling) into an account at the Bank of England in the name of the Banco Central. From this account Argentina could pay for her commercial purchases and financial services in the UK. Balances would be converted into pesos at the rate of 13.50 to the pound and settled with 5 year UK bonds in pesos; an interest of 4 per cent was suggested.

The reply of the Central Bank accepted payment in sterling and the centralisation of payments, but it did not take up the idea of a peso bond. Instead it made clear a very important objective: 'Our government wishes to devote sterling surpluses, above a working balance mutually agreed upon, to the purchase in Great Britain of Argentine securities.' But it was stressed that the government could buy only according to its means. The question of the use of accumulated balances if they exceeded the amount which the Argentine government could devote to the purchase of securities was left for further discussion. As there was no peso loan, an exchange guarantee was requested.

In a preceding communication the Bank of England had offered only to discuss matters if sterling depreciated in terms of the dollar by more than 10 per cent. Now, the Bank of England agreed to guarantee for three months the value of sterling accumulated above 1 million pounds by converting it into gold set aside for the purpose, to be reconverted into sterling at the rate prevailing at the end of the agreement.

In Niemeyer's words, the agreement 'is provisional for three months, to get something started; and leaves the major questions over for discussion at greater leisure and, I think, via Meynell' (Niemeyer to Waley, 10 October 1939). Meynell was a partner in a Buenos Aires firm that had very close links with Barings'; he was also Treasury and Bank of England representative in Buenos Aires. And Barings' were financial advisers to the Argentine government.

From the British point of view, this state of affairs was satisfactory; nothing dangerous had been conceded, and the gold could be had back. The fact that Argentina wanted to buy back her own securities was reassuring; that she did not say explicitly that she was interested in her National Government bonds most satisfactory. In a period that was to start only a few months later, one of the main objectives of Britain in her negotiations with Argentina was to convince Argentina to buy back her railways and not her own National external debt.

The hope that future negotiations would be effected through Meynell can be better understood from a telegram that Meynell sent to the Treasury on 13 October 1939, showing his very peculiar status in the Banco Central: 'Central Bank undertakes to show me all telegrams received and has asked me to collaborate with them in framing their replies. I will telegraph to you through Embassy on all points affecting negotiations.' Meynell's position was of the greatest use for Britain; he could give advance notice of what was being thought at the Banco Central; time and again he was asked from London whether it was necessary to grant certain concessions to Argentina; he was usually able to find out that it was unnecessary. He could discuss how much could be demanded from Argentina without overstretching the limit. His help in framing *Argentine* replies could be invaluable in a situation where a single word could make a big difference in a crucial telegram.

The Banco Central, since its birth, had had close contacts with the Bank of England. Its charter followed very closely a project drafted by Sir Otto Niemeyer; Powell, also from the Bank of England, had spent a considerable period working at the Banco Central before the war. At the Bank of England there was therefore a very precise knowledge of the workings of the Banco Central, of the personalities involved, and of their abilities and weaknesses. This was not a peculiarity of the Banco Central; close contacts with other Central Banks were a long standing preoccupation of Montagu Norman's.[5]

A question that was left in the air was Argentina's right to convert a part of her sterling into dollars or gold in order to pay a part of her external debt in third countries. Since the 1936 Agreement, this sum had been reduced to £1.5 million, and up to October 1939 the question had not been raised in negotiations on the Payments Agreement. Niemeyer did not think Britain would be willing under exchange control to release resources, from the Argentine surplus for American debt payments, and Argentina had not asked for it: 'Let's hope they won't.'[6] When a few days later Argentina did ask for the £1.5 million, a Treasury official annotated on the telegram 'I suppose we must agree.' The matter was left there; some months later, when the inter-bank agreement was renewed, Argentina was given its £1.5 million but in exchange it accepted sterling from Eire.

It was thought that Britain would have a big deficit with Argentina (Hall-Patch to Monick at the French Embassy, 27 October 1939), but the question of what Argentina would do with its sterling was left unresolved:

> The suggestion has been made that the Argentines should purchase the equities of the railways, but this has not been received very enthusiastically. The agreement has therefore been made temporary for three months from the middle of October and this question will have to be settled in the meantime. (Hall-Patch to N. Young, at the British Embassy in Paris, 27 October 1939)

The question was not to be resolved so easily and in the end took years; as a Treasury official commented much later, 'C'est ne que le provisoire qui dure'. In the meantime, from the British point of view, things were quite satisfactory. In the words of the *Official History*:

> On 27 October 1939, the British government made a very encouraging payments agreement with Argentina, a country which had great importance as a supplier of food.... Its broad effect was to enable the British government to continue importing without making immediate payment.... The neutral Argentinians had thus shown themselves ready, like the members of the sterling area, to lend their resources to the belligerent British: or to state the situation in reverse – the British had succeeded in softening a currency which they had originally reckoned as 'hard'.[7]

Britain had traditionally used her importance as a market to extract concessions from primary producing countries. It is not surprising, therefore, that Leith Ross proposed to use purchases in Argentina and other South American countries to get some advantages. He suggested asking for a favourable rate of exchange for remittances of public utilities, and in this way hit at least two birds with one stone.

> I need hardly point out to you that not only would any improvement in their condition reduce the strain on the exchange and give you increased income tax to use, but would lead to an increase in their capital value if ultimately you have to sell or pledge securities to the governments concerned.[8]

Britain needed the food, but it seemed to him worth trying. At the Treasury this proposal was not received with favour:

> It seems to me that it is very difficult to get any commercial concessions when we are talking about methods of payment, for it is we who are, in a sense, asking favours in trying to borrow what we can and to avoid paying in dollars. (Waley to Cobbold, 21 November 1939, commenting on Leith Ross's proposal)

There was no definite progress in the negotiations on the subject of what was to be done with Argentina's sterling balances, and the interbank agreement was renewed twice for three months and once for six months. But by the time of its expiry in October 1940, many things had changed.

III

The fall of France was bound to have an impact on Anglo–Argentine negotiations. For some time the idea of obtaining concessions from Argentina against a very big purchase of agricultural products was put forward tentatively. Had Britain bought only what she needed anyway, her bargaining position would have been weak. But if she had guaranteed purchase of big amounts of Argentine produce, even if she could not be sure of shipping them, she could have demanded substantial concessions. It should be remembered that with some Dominions this had been done, and that Australia and New Zealand had been assured of a market for the whole of their wool clip at favourable prices at the beginning of the war.

In the case of Argentina, Britain hoped to use the carrot of purchases to obtain financial concessions. A good vantage point is that offered by an exchange of correspondence towards the end of June, between the Treasury, the Bank of England and the Ministry of Food. On 24 June Waley of the Treasury asked for Niemeyer's opinon on a 'comprehensive arrangement' that was conveniently divided in two parts: part A, 'What we want' and part B, 'What we offer'.

Two things were wanted from Argentina: a long term peso credit for purchases of cereals during the war, and a favourable peso rate for meat imports. What was offered was the purchase of all available canned meat and a certain amount of maize (possibly 1 million tons). Of one of these last two items it must be said that it was not much of a concession, since it was Britain that urgently needed the canned meat to store while the German air raids were menacing her communications. On this question the pressure came from Britain. What makes Waley's letter particularly interesting is that on the most important issue it was intellectually confused. The issue was the effect on the Argentine economy of a credit to Britain. Was it good or bad? Buying agricultural produce that would otherwise remain without a market was clearly favourable to Argentine producers; not to have to provide financial resources to help producers was also attractive to the Argentine Treasury. But the effect of a credit without raising taxation was clearly inflationary. Purchasing power would be given to agricultural producers, but no goods would be obtained through imports. In the short run, there was a danger that the net effect on the Argentine economy would not be very different from buying the goods from agricultural producers and throwing them into the sea.

Waley did not grasp the problem clearly, arguing simultaneously that it would help Argentina and that it would damage her. After saying that one object of the whole exercise was 'to avert Argentine bankruptcy giving a handle to Hitler', he added: 'I recognise that a big credit to us means inflation and unsound finance for the Argentine. But is it not a time for desperate remedies?'[9] Times were indeed desperate for Britain with Germany near total victory, and during this period there are frequent hints to the effect that financial obligations would not matter much if the war were lost: 'If we lose the war we will not be in a mood to worry about the Argentine debt' was how Mather Jackson concluded a long minute on the whole affair.[10]

On the same day that Waley wrote his letter, Niemeyer wrote a sharp reply (the Ministry of Food also managed to reply the same day, an indication of the efficiency of the government machine during the war). Niemeyer mercilessly exposed Waley's confusion:

The Argentines are at present giving us credit of £6.25 million (their balance here under our present Agreement) and if it is correct to speak of 'Argentine bankruptcy', which I should have thought exaggerated, they would hardly be attracted; nor indeed would it divert that bankruptcy for them to give us a further peso credit (long-term at that) for an unspecified amount and period.

Niemeyer had a very clear idea of what policy was desired from Argentina, but did not feel it necessary to spell it out in detail. It was left to Hutton from the Ministry of Food to have the pleasure of giving a lesson in clear thinking in the field of finance to a senior Treasury official,

If you think that additional means of payment will have to be found, then perhaps we can help you to find the means of persuading or bribing the Argentine to give us the necessary financial help. I should think that anything we can do to assist Argentina's fiscal position would be important in this direction, since it is clear that the problem is one of internal finance rather than of transfer. This inevitably means, I would argue, that our policy must be directed towards the encouragement of inflationary finance in Argentina plus a depreciation (in time) of the Argentine peso on the pound. This will be a slow business and one of great difficulty.

It is clearly useful to take the problem in two parts, one of internal finance and another of transfer. The whole discussion on German reparations, which had attracted so much attention among economists in the inter-war period, had been clarified by such a distinction. The German government could raise sufficient internal resources from its taxpayers to pay reparations, but unless other countries were willing to allow Germany to have a big surplus in the other items of her balance of payments, she could not find the necessary foreign exchange to effect the transfer.[12] Clearly the problem for Argentina was exactly the opposite: she had the goods and Britain wanted them. But the internal budgetary problem was completely unsolved. Unless financial resources were extracted from consumers, exports on credit to Britain would mean inflation in Argentina.

The question remains why it should have been convenient to Britain for Argentina to pursue an inflationary policy. At first sight it could be thought that the opposite was the case, since inflation would mean, unless accompanied by devaluation, higher sterling prices for Britain.

The reality was that inflationary finance in Argentina was convenient to Britain because it was less visible than taxes, and therefore less likely to provoke discussions in Argentina about the Payments Agreement between the two Central Banks. Also in its financial negotiations with other countries, Britain claimed officially that these countries should accept inflation as a by-product of their exports to the UK. In the case of Canada, this problem threatened to become serious, and it is recorded in the official history of war finance. Canada was reluctant to give too many Canadian dollars to the UK if she could not obtain a similar amount from the public either through taxation or sale of securities. Inflation would have resolved the conflict between consumption levels and war effort, and after a period Canadians implied that they were unwilling further to reduce consumption levels; exports to Great Britain would have to suffer: 'London had strong views to the contrary: Canada should face some inflation and acknowledge the need for war supplies as the determinant factor.'[13]

IV

Keynes moved to the Treasury in June 1940, and his impact was felt immediately in discussions concerning Argentina. He soon started propounding a paradoxical but brilliant idea: the fall of France had increased Britain's bargaining power with those neutral countries that produced primary products:

There has been a great increase recently in the strength of our bargaining power, of which so far we have failed to take advantage. There is no longer the possibility of scarcity of supply and high prices in the international markets. On the contrary, in commodity after commodity there is the prospect of a hideous unsold surplus and a market collapse. Reasons of internal politics and internal economy will turn most overseas countries, when they have fully tumbled to the new situation, into suppliants for our custom, passionately anxious to find a market on almost any terms for their overwhelmingly burdensome domestic surplus.[14]

His ideas were received with interest but also with reserve. When explaining to the Bank of England Keynes's ideas, Waley took care to make clear that these ideas did not belong to him:

He [Keynes] has just put to me the view that, now the French are no longer purchasing in South America, we are in a very strong negotiating position, and ought as soon as we can to revise our policy of promising the South American countries a guarantee in the form of gold, and bully them into using their sterling to buy up their own securities. (Waley to Cobbold, 11 July 1940)

At the time Keynes's position was considered extreme even by his friends. 'Maynard thinks we are in an almost infinitely strong bargaining position, and can force what terms we like on the South American countries', wrote Playfair in a draft letter to Richard Kahn (T.160. 1143. F.16707/3).

A few months earlier it was thought that, as Britain was paying with blocked sterling, the offer to buy cereals could not be presented as a favour. After the fall of France this was no longer true, and the offer to buy, even with blocked sterling, was an important asset. Faith in sterling was not unshakable even in the highest ranks of the Foreign Office, as can be seen by the following entry in the diary of A. Cadogan, the Permanent Under-Secretary (31 May 1940) – 'Went with Theo to choose rugs. Just as well to give away Treasury notes, which will be worth nothing, for goods of value.'[15]

But even so, countries threatened with unsaleable surpluses were faced with a grim choice: either accept sterling, which in the case of Argentina could at least be used to repatriate the foreign debt, or let the harvest rot. In this last case, if no help were given to farmers there would be no inflation, but the whole sector could have been ruined; if help were to be given, then it was better to risk accepting sterling of doubtful value than just to put into practice inflationary finance. If farmers were helped, inflation was the outcome in any case. Given this situation, selling for blocked sterling was unattractive but better than not selling at all. Furthermore, during the second half of 1940 it was impossible to foresee the future evolution of the balance of payments between Argentina and Britain. From week to week there were enormous changes in British intentions, as their purchasing plans had to take into account changes in shipping, the effect of German bombings on harbours, etc. Although the Argentine side knew only a part of these oscillations, what it saw was more than enough to establish that the future was most uncertain; for some time even a deficit with the Sterling Area looked likely.

Argentina had lost her markets in France, Belgium and Holland; all exports to continental Europe were subject to the British blockade. In the perceptive words of an official at the Ministry of Food: 'the Ministry of Economic Warfare is, of course, concerned with the major economic and political question of starving Europe on the one hand and thereby building up unmarketable surpluses in producing countries on the other.'[16] Argentina was faced with an enormous maize harvest which was unsaleable. Maize exports accounted for over 20 per cent of total exports before the war, and notwithstanding an exceptionally good harvest in both 1940 and 1941, maize exports by 1941 accounted for less than 1 per cent of exports. The result was a collapse in the price of maize.

The Argentine government intervened with various measures to help farmers: already in April 1940 credits were granted through the Banco de la Nación, in May a limit was set to maximum daily changes in the price of maize, and in August Congress allowed the government to purchase the whole harvest.[17] Thus the crucial decision was taken; given that it was, it was understandable that the Banco Central was keen to accept sterling if the harvest could be sold.

From mid 1940 up to the first months of 1941 there were long negotiations between the two countries, where all aspects of their economic relationship were discussed. During this period, Argentina's main worry was the need to increase sales of cereals, while Britain was trying desperately to save as much gold and dollars as possible for the purchase in the United States of vital weapons and raw materials. With the intensification of the struggle, financial prudence had disappeared and all resources were thrown into the battle. French orders for weapons in the United States were taken over, and gold and dollar reserves dwindled at an alarming pace. It soon became obvious that financial help from the United States would be necessary if the struggle were to continue. As early as May 1940 Churchill had sent Roosevelt his famous message, 'we shall go on paying dollars for as long as we can, but I should like to feel reasonably sure that when we can pay no more you will give us the stuff all the same'.

In the circumstances it was not surprising that Britain, once Argentina had accepted sterling, should have had as objectives both the suspension of the right of convertibility of the £1.5 million per year for Argentina's debt in the US, and the alteration of an exchange guarantee that immobilised gold.

It was inevitable that the future of the British-owned railways in Argentina should enter into the discussions. Their nominal value was very high, about £250 million, and there had been a constant Argentine interest in buying them. During the 1930s the Conservative government had bought the Cordoba Central, and more ambitious plans had to be abandoned when Argentina's financial position deteriorated in 1938.

The Governor of the Bank of England, Montagu Norman, kept a careful eye on the situation of the railways, which were one of the biggest of Britain's investments abroad. In June 1940 he took a very active interest, and wrote a letter to the Chancellor of the Exchequer on the subject. He enclosed a memorandum in which the maize surplus and the railways were linked, and discussed the future of the railways: 'The present time may be the last favourable opportunity, politically speaking, for dealing with the British Argentine Railway question'. He thought that in the last two years of his Presidency, Ortíz would not tackle such a big question, and that by the time that his successor came into office the expiry of the relevant clauses of the Mitre Law (exempting the railways from paying most taxes) would be close. This would seriously weaken the bargaining position of the railways. What he wanted was to use the Argentine preoccupation with the maize surplus to solve the railway question. He mentioned that Britain could buy 10 million tons of maize in two years if Argentina committed itself to buy the railways, paying a certain amount every year: 'What is important, from the British point of view, is that the present preoccupation about the maize should be taken advantage of and the psychological opportunity of tackling the railway question not be allowed to slip.'[18]

In order to achieve this, it was necessary to convince Argentina *not* to buy back its own National External debt, but to devote its sterling balances to the purchase of the railways. It was not only important that the Republic did not purchase railway shares piecemeal in the market; what was necessary was for Argentina to agree to a scheme by which it would commit itself to buying the entire railway system. This was necessary for two reasons: one was that the value of the railways on the stock exchange was at the time very low, and a general scheme had a much better chance of obtaining a more satisfactory price; the other was that it was important to have a long-term arrangement that would solve payments questions for many years. With the very fluid political situation in Buenos Aires, it was quite likely that a new Minister of Finance, if not bound by an agreement, could reverse the order of buying shares piecemeal.

The Bank of England was thinking much more clearly than the rest of Whitehall; and what the Bank understood in mid-1940 was accepted by other departments months, and in some cases years, later. One month later there was much discussion in Whitehall on the need to encourage the repatriation of South American securities and to get a peso loan. It was left to Niemeyer to point out to Waley that it was much better to enjoy the 'interest free loan' represented by the sterling balances than to surrender 'exchange bringing assets'.[19] The next day Waley confessed that his idea had not been very bright and added, 'I appreciate the difficulty of taking butter out of a dog's mouth, but I feel that in future we should not offer the best butter when the dog looks like being quite content with margarine' (Waley to Niemeyer, 18 June 1940).

The long negotiations that followed between Britain and Argentina were about the level of British purchases and the concessions that Argentina would make if British purchases rose above a certain level. The British line was that if no help were given, British purchases would be low; they would be willing to buy more (especially cereals) only if financial concessions were made. What was asked for was a suspension of the £1.5 million in gold for payment of Argentine external debt in third countries, favourable rates of exchange for public utilities and for some British exports, and finally a modification in the gold-set-aside clause. Britain needed this gold and offered instead to guarantee the gold value of the sterling balances. This simply meant that if the pound were devalued by say 15 per cent in terms of gold, Britain would put 15 per cent more sterling in the account of the Banco Central. Although apparently similar, it was profoundly different. Had the gold been free, Argentina could have used it for purchases in any country. In fact it was not free, as there had been an agreement that it had to be resold to the Bank of England. But its status was much better than blocked sterling. It will be seen that it made a big difference in the priority given by Britain to exports to Argentina.

Britain's line was very hard and by now she was asking for concessions even if she were buying on credit: 'It seems to me that we are in a strong position to bargain with Argentina and that we should be inflexible, if necessary showing them the door in the practical certainty that they will give in.'[20]

V

Once Argentina had agreed to enter into a situation that was de facto identical to a clearing agreement with Great Britain, she found herself powerless. The strange world of clearing agreements, as many European countries had discovered to their cost in their economic relations with Germany, was dominated by very different rules to those that had prevailed in a world of freely convertible currencies.

As Argentina had imposed no ceiling on the amount of sterling she was willing to accumulate, it was not urgent for Britain to send exports to Argentina. At the same time, very high prices could be charged; this helped to achieve the aim of shifting the terms of trade in Britain's favour. Not surprisingly, this had been a long-standing aim of British officials. 'My essential point was that we shall, and indeed have, to shift the terms of trade in our favour whether one calculates in pesos or in pounds', wrote Hutton, and he explained that 'Our objective, obviously, is to see that a certain proportion of Argentine savings is effectively transferred to us.'[21]

Later, when *de facto* clearing existed, this was not difficult to achieve. It was left to the discoverer of the multiplier, Richard Kahn, to explain matters to officials attending a meeting of the Inter-departmental Committee on Central and South America:

> Mr Kahn suggested that where payments agreements had been concluded the price level of our export products ceased to be an important factor. The countries concerned had to choose between buying our goods and holding blocked sterling (with a gold guarantee), thus in effect giving us a loan. He could see no point in a payments agreement if gold could be withdrawn, and if gold could be withdrawn there was no necesssity to promote exports.[22]

The Treasury representatives did not like discussing such delicate matters too openly; they were alarmed that someone from such a lowbrow department as the Board of Trade could express things so clearly. 'The Treasury were of the opinion that the present meeting was too large for adequate discussion of this matter', records the minute of the meeting.

With time, as British exports dwindled, it became more and more clear that the situation was dangerously unbalanced; 'It would be most unfortunate if a public outcry, fomented possibly by German propaganda, were to arise against parting with good meat against apparently useless sterling', wrote the President of the Board of Trade to the British Ambassador in Buenos Aires.[23]

Notwithstanding all the assurances regularly sent from those British officials in Buenos Aires who were in frequent contact with the Argentine authorities, London found it hard to believe that such a situation could continue indefinitely, especially because of the inflationary consequences for Argentina:

> As you know, we are buying from Argentina far more than we can ever hope to pay for by exports. You have told us, and Jerram has

repeated it, that at present the Argentine government is not worrying about their rapidly increasing sterling balance. I wonder how long that will remain true if we have to cut our exports still more drastically. It is true that *in the long run* the Argentines may feel that they can use their sterling to acquire British-owned public utilities, but in the meantime they will have to face the fact that they will be parting with their foodstuffs and raw materials in exchange, chiefly for the means of inflating their currency.

The fact that pesos were issued locally against blocked pounds[24] was contrary to all the rules of sound central banking and created constant puzzlement in London. In a minute of mid 1941, Mather Jackson of the Foreign Office commented on

> a remark made by Mr Jerram at a meeting on 2 August which astonished Mr N Young, Mr Powell and myself. We have been discussing surplus Argentine sterling at the Bank of England. Some had described the sterling as being, for the present at any rate, 'useless'. Mr Jerram didn't agree. When we asked him why, he said 'Because the Central Bank uses that sterling as backing for an increase in the fiduciary issue.' Is this a sign of unqualified faith in our ability not only to win the war but to be financially in good health after doing so? Or is it as gross an example of covert inflation as one could want?[25]

VI

What is of interest at this point is to discuss who benefited in Argentina from this state of affairs.

In London there was a clear knowledge of the redistributive effects in Argentina of accumulating sterling balances. This emerges clearly in a discussion at the Foreign Office in September 1942 arising from the remark of a senior official that it was 'most repugnant' to appease the Argentine government,[26] to which someone added that it was equally repugnant to pay exhorbitant prices for meat, enriching in this way 'the *estancieros*, who are by no means our [Britain's] best friends in Argentina'. The senior officer of the Department intervened at this point with a very pertinent observation,

> But are not the objections to paying more materially negligible (whatever they may be morally) or even unreal, since we shall, presumably, be paying in sterling for which no use can be found by

Argentina who is accordingly giving us the meat for nothing *at present*? (minute by Perowne, 15 September 1942)

Butler, who did not grasp the point, remained entirely unconvinced. He objected (and in doing so used an interesting verb that would have caused great offence in many land-owning families in Argentina) – 'if our sterling is of negligible value it seems odd that the *estancieros* should be jewing us for more of it' (Butler, 15 September 1942). Mather Jackson scribbled the explanation on the margin of the page: 'The *estanciero* gets pesos: the Argentine Central Bank, sterling.'

This was a key feature of all clearing agreements: exporters were indifferent to the technical clauses that involved the Central Banks; what they wanted was a good price in the local currency for their products, and this the clearing agreements did achieve. The experience of the countries of south-eastern Europe with Germany in the 1930s had shown that exporters usually did have enough political power to implement such agreements. In Argentina there were many who accepted the arrangements because they thought it to be in the long-term interest of the country; there were others who did so because they benefited directly from it.

The Argentine government had no qualms about its preference for the wealthier groups of the rural classes. In a very interesting official memorandum sent to the British government that dealt with sterling balances, it talked about 'the rural classes which form the most solid and stable nucleus of the social organisation of the Republic'.[27]

When he received this memorandum, the British Ambassador sent a telegram to London with a summary; he condensed the spirit of the paragraph in the following way: 'a solution can, it is thought, be found which will enable the social structure of the Republic, based as it is essentially on the rural classes, to be preserved'.[28] Although exports brought nothing in return and increased the inflationary pressure in Argentina, they enriched the *estancieros* and consolidated their political power. The issue was explained concisely in an internal minute at the Foreign Office:

> It can be argued, of course, that the maintenance of meat exports is more in the interest of the cattle owners who receive high peso prices than of the country as a whole which at present receives only blocked sterling in return. But the meat interests are so well represented in the government and influential circles that private are to a large extent likely to predominate over public interests.[29]

VII

As has been seen, Argentina accumulated an interest-free credit on Britain instead of buying back its own sterling debt. This was a mistake, but perhaps it could be justified given the uncertainty at the time as to the future balance of payments with the Sterling Area. Had there been a deficit, it could have proved onerous to issue a loan in war-time, especially in terms of the favours that would have been inevitably asked. In this perspective, the interest-free credit could be seen as a rather expensive insurance for an unknown future.

There was, however, another opportunity that was inexplicably wasted: for a time Britain was willing to allow Argentina to buy sterling with Argentine dollar bonds held by British residents. Had this opportunity been pursued Argentine exports to the Sterling Area would have reduced Argentina's dollar liabilities, thus improving significantly the balance of payments.

A certain part of Argentina's dollar debt was in the hands of British residents, and in May 1940, foreseeing an acute dollar shortage for 1941, Argentina raised the possibility of buying these bonds with sterling.

> It has occurred to them that His Majesty's Government might be disposed to assist by selling to the Argentine government for pounds their Argentine dollar bonds requisitioned from British bondholders. It is perfectly realised that His Majesty's Government thus surrender a potential dollar asset but it is thought that in practice the realisation of such an asset might be long and difficult.[30]

Niemeyer was favourable to the proposal as 'from a general point of view we do not, I think, want the pressure on Argentina for dollars to become more acute than we can help' (Niemeyer to Rowe Dutton, 23 May 1940). The total amount of Argentine dollar bonds registered by British residents was about $15 million; a telegram was sent to Meynell accepting Argentina's request, but as a last hope it was asked whether what was wanted was for the Treasury to buy periodically for the sinking fund or for the Treasury to buy as many bonds as possible. The astonishing reply was that the idea of the Argentine government was 'only to acquire Argentine dollar bonds with blocked pounds in amounts sufficient to cover sinking fund as and when due' (telegram from Ovey, 31 May 1940).

Not only did this mean missing a most favourable opportunity when the outlook for dollars in Argentina looked particularly grim; the proposal had serious administrative difficulties. 'I do not think we could contemplate clearing the very considerable mass of Argentine Bonds held by British owners in order to dole them out in small quantities, as and when required for sinking fund', wrote a Treasury official (Rowe Dutton to Niemeyer, 4 June 1940). At the Bank of England they were in agreement: 'But vesting for just each half-year separately is clearly absurd and not, anyway at the moment, very convenient' (Niemeyer to Rowe Dutton, 7 June 1940). It was proposed to Meynell that the British government should vest these dollar securities for the sinking fund of the next two years while the Argentine government would pay simultaneously the market price in sterling (telegram 198 from Foreign Office to Buenos Aires, 11 June 1940). It should be noted that this proposal was more favourable to Argentina than she herself asked. Events were moving very fast in the rest of the world, and it was becoming very clear that the fall of France was leaving Argentina in a very weak position.

> Had it not been for the great change in the situation caused by the French defection, I think this would be sound, but in the present circumstances it is obviously less attractive. Nevertheless, I think we might take up the sinking fund amounts for a period of six months only. (Rowe Dutton to Waley, 17 July 1940)

Waley's reply was very clear 'I agree. We are already committed. Next time we should be tougher.'

A most favourable opportunity to strengthen Argentina's balance of payments had been lost. Not only would Argentina soon lose the possibility of having gold set aside in her name and of receiving £1.5 million in gold to pay her external debt in dollars; from the end of 1940 she supplied dollars to Britain through her dollar external debt, part of which was in British hands.

VIII

It has already been mentioned that currency questions were intimately linked with British export policy. The war effort was the overriding priority, and unnecessary exports could mean wasting productive resources. Exports that produced or saved dollars or gold were most useful, as they increased the amount of goods and weapons that could be bought in the US and were indispensable to winning the war. At the other extreme were exports to colonies. In this case, exports were wasted in that they did not increase the amount of goods that Britain could use for her war effort, but rather decreased them as these exports required machinery and manpower. Their only result was a reduction in the sterling balances held by these colonies.

Objectives had sometimes to be modified. It could happen, for example, that workers in colonies would refuse to work in plantations if with their money they could not buy textiles. In such cases, currency considerations had to be abandoned, and exports were sent where they were necessary to obtain crucial imports. However, by and large the policy was maintained especially in the first three years of the war.

This could pose a difficult problem for countries exporting to Britain. Demanding payment in dollars or gold made it possible to buy goods in the US, at least until the end of 1941, and it ensured a high priority in the destination of British exports. But it could also mean not being able to sell at all. Britain could afford to spend very few dollars in countries other than the US, and would have switched to the utmost her sources of supply in favour of countries willing to offer easier methods of payment. On the other hand, accepting sterling without any limits meant receiving less British goods, and therefore having to buy more in the US, thus aggravating the strain on convertible foreign exchange reserves and gold.

British export policy inevitably changed with circumstances. In a first phase there was optimism about the future level of exports, and as there was still unemployment, the opportunity cost of non-engineering exports was not deemed high. As the war effort became more acute, and British gold and dollar reserves dropped at an alarming pace, it became essential to give priority to currency considerations when setting up lists of export priorities. Finally, after Lend Lease, when dollars were no longer scarce, exports were no longer guided by currency considerations but by the need to use them to obtain imports from countries that demanded goods in return, and not sterling or even dollars.

Exports to Argentina were considered important when the Banco Central demanded gold to be set aside in its name. This was the situation at the beginning of the war and until the last months of 1940. During this period Argentina as a market was of the 'highest importance' to the UK.[31]

A few months later the situation was slightly changed. At that time the Bank of England hoped to alter the Payments Agreement with the Banco Central in such a way as to cease setting gold aside. Argentina was placed with Bolivia in the group that was 'difficult till we make (or revise) the Payments Agreement'. This was at a lower level of priority than the US, Canada, Japan and Iran.

In November 1940, that is after the Banco Central had agreed to alter the gold guarantee into a guarantee of the gold value of sterling, there were three grades of priority for British exports: Group 1 was those countries that demanded gold; Group 2 were 'countries that hold sterling balances and do not ask for gold'; Group 3 were countries that were short of sterling and to which exports were usually discouraged.[32] Argentina, by being accommodating on sterling, had moved down the list.

In the list published in January 1941, which was circulated to many Departments, Argentina was in Group 3 out of 5. Group 1 was composed of the US, Sweden, Switzerland and Canada, all countries that demanded payment in dollars or gold. Group 2 consisted of countries like Portugal and Egypt that demanded part payment in gold. Bolivia, which was paid partly in gold, was in this group, and had thus parted company with Argentina. Argentina was in a group of very low priority, together with India. As it became clear that Argentina's sterling balances would grow quickly, a certain uneasiness became widespread about putting Argentina so low in the list. The Banco Central was not making trouble, but others could get restive.

> I suggest that Argentina should go to Group 2, not 3. We feel over here that this is necessary, especially in view of the clientele of the list. We are unlikely to be able to send much coal or tin plate and are cutting down on cotton exports, etc. The feeling here is that Argentina would be too low as 3, that we must keep up to the market reasonably well, that if we do not the accumulation of sterling, high already, will lead to a pressure for dollars or other trouble, and that the prospects of a securities deal are not so hopeful as to be helped along by a reduction of physical exports. (unsigned minute for Grant and Turner, 20 May 1941)

The result of such worries was that in the second edition of the directive on Direction of Exports of June 1941, Argentina was moved to Group 2. It is clear that the more troublesome the country with regard to sterling, the better treatment it was likely to get. It was impossible for British officials in London to know exactly what was the most effective method of allocating scarce exports. A quite sensible method was to wait for protests; if a country kept quiet it was reasonable to assume that it was unnecessary to supply her with more exports: 'Generally speaking we are inclined to leave it to overseas countries to complain as the position becomes more difficult, as the Dominions are now complaining of the insufficiency of their quotas of cotton piece goods.'[3]

The problem for Argentina was that her authorities did not complain enough. During the third year of war, it was foreseen that Britain would have a big deficit with Argentina and that this would 'swell the enormous sterling holdings of Argentina. We have not yet got Argentina to agree to exchange canned beef for idle sterling! Exports of cotton goods to Argentina can hardly be cut.'[34] In theory the imbalance with Argentina was very worrying. In a minute dated 3 September 1941 Richard Kahn questioned the wisdom of giving priority to exports to the US, Canada and South Africa. With Lend Lease the US was no longer a problem; South Africa was now willing to sell gold in order to purchase her securities, and Canada was willing to accept some sterling.

> If there is a real danger of the Argentine refusing to sell to us the quantities of meat, etc. which we want to buy from her, may this not mean that Argentine currency is now more difficult than the currencies of the USA, Canada and/or South Africa?[35]

The reply to this question is illuminating. 'The Argentine point has never been overlooked. There are dangers there but so far they have not come to anything and according to Mr. Jerram, our C-S [Commercial Secretary], they are not likely to come to much.'[36] Whenever consulted anxiously from London on the likelihood of Argentina continuing to accept sterling in unlimited amounts, they always gave a reassuring reply, which was in great part determined by the attitude of the Central Bank. Opinion at the Board of Trade was similar to that of the Ministry of Agriculture: the Treasury was afraid 'that Argentina will object to the accumulations of a surplus balance of at least £14 million of sterling, but so far as I know the Argentines themselves have not as yet shown much anxiety on this score.'[37]

IX

Up to this point my paper has been concerned with negotiations and based on official files. This method can present some drawbacks (interdepartmental differences included): what will now be done is to discuss one preconception of British officials which was probably wrong, and to put the problem of sterling balances in its proper perspective by using some statistics.

One basic assumption widely held in Whitehall was that sterling balances produced inflation. Although Keynes, Kahn and many others were more subtle in their views, a simple quantity theory of money was accepted by many. According to this view, an export surplus, by increasing the amount of money in circulation and decreasing the amount of goods available, was inevitably inflationary. It is important to remember, however, that given certain circumstances, an increase in exports can have a very positive effect on output. At the beginning of the war, Argentina was suffering the effect of a downward swing in world economic activity that had started in 1937; the price of Argentine wheat in Liverpool in June 1939 was lower than in any previous year of the disastrous decade of the 1930s.

At the Banco Central, 'Keynesian' ideas were probably more widely held than at the Bank of England. Those who wanted to work at the Office of Economic Research at the Banco Central had to take an examination that included questions such as: 'Do you think that the quantity theory of money is in some way valid in Argentina? Do you remember any case in which this theory has been verified? Do you think that under a gold standard the quantity theory is true for Argentine currency?' As Prebisch told an audience at the Banco de México in 1944 this was the sort of question that, beyond testing a good grasp of theory, 'indicates whether the applicant has thought about these problems and whether he is able to think for himself, to judge matters in his own head'.[38]

From phrases of Prebisch's such as 'orthodox virus', it is clear that he himself thought that the quantity theory of money was not very relevant to a country with excess capacity.[39]

There is no doubt that he understood the functions of a Central Bank to include the attenuation of business cycles. In this he had already disagreed with Niemeyer in the 1930s,[40] but the actions of the Banco Central had obtained wide acclaim for its successful anti-cyclical actions in 1936–8. This is how Nurkse summarised his judgement in his study of the international monetary system between the wars: 'The most striking and successful example of such a policy was given during the same period by the newly founded Central Bank of the Argentine.'[41]

In 1944 Prebisch himself recalled how economic ideas had changed under the impact of the world crisis; he also stressed that from the outbreak of the war until 1941 the main economic problem for Argentina was to sustain the level of economic activity while demand from abroad was falling.[42]

This is important for understanding a curious circumstance: reading British files one might get the impression that during this period inflation was rampant in Argentina. It should be noted, however, that British officials talked about actions which they thought would create inflation, never of actual inflation itself. As a matter of fact, during the first years of the war, inflation in Argentina was moderate. Import prices had increased markedly from the beginning; although the Banco Central had produced a memorandum on the subject, nothing effective could be done in this respect.

What *could* be done, however, was to control monetary expansion, and so it was. An international comparison at this point is instructive. Of the 20 main countries selected by the Bank for International Settlements (*Thirteenth Annual Report*, 1943), Argentina was the one that least expanded her note circulation. Other neutrals like Switzerland, not known for monetary laxity, followed a more permissive policy. As for Latin America, a study by the Federal Reserve Board on monetary developments describes the increase in the money supply and in the cost of living for the main 14 countries of the area. It covers the period between 1939 and 1944; although by this last year Argentina was accumulating sterling at a vertiginous rate, only Venezuela and Uruguay had had a lower increase in the money supply, while only Peru had had a lower percentage increase in international reserves.[43] Of the 128 per cent increase in the money supply of Argentina, 116 per cent was due to increased holdings of international reserves; this can be compared with 208 per cent and 79 per cent respectively for Brazil, 269 per cent and 160 per cent for Mexico, and 153 per cent and 66 per cent for Chile.

While (seen from London) Argentina's accumulation of sterling balances seemed inflationary, seen from the point of view of the Banco Central, the situation looked very different, at least until 1941 (see Table 9.1).

TABLE 9.1 *Variations in means of payments, 1939–44 (millions of pesos)*

	1939	1940	1941	1942	1943	1944
Internal factors	113	34	593	482	−56	462
External factors	148	−78	458	496	1 364	1 288
of which blocked £	11	56	53	206	559	655
Other blocked currencies	13	−5	−39	−61	12	−5
Internal plus external	261	−44	1 051	978	1 308	1 750

SOURCE Banco Central, *Memoria Anual* for 1944, p. 10.

In 1941 blocked currencies including sterling contributed less than 2 per cent to the original expansion of means of payments and were therefore significant from the point of view of inflationary pressures. By 1943 this had changed dramatically and the accumulation of sterling balances accounted for over 40 per cent of the original variations in the means of payments, that is, before deducting means of payments absorbed in time deposits, etc.

X

Anglo-Argentine financial relations must be seen in perspective, although it should be remembered that they formed part of a larger picture; this was true not only for Britain but also for Argentina. Many other countries ended up accumulating sterling balances, even if their motives could sometimes be very different. The comparison with Brazil, for example, a country which usually had a balance of payments deficit with Britain, is particularly interesting.[44]

A broad outline can be found in a document written by Keynes towards the end of the war, where he discussed the implications for the rest of the world: 'From the earliest days of the war we have tried to avoid incurring debts in foreign currency or in gold. In this we have been successful beyond any expectation which would have been reasonable before the event.'[5]

These were the Jesse Jones loans in US dollars, and a Canadian loan, without interest, in Canadian dollars, but both were covered with securities of those countries; finally, there was a gold liability to Portugal which was being renegotiated. Keynes continued:

> Apart from these we owe the outside world nothing but sterling; and it is pretty well understood by those concerned that they are in our hands and cannot successfully claim to use this sterling except in accordance with principles to be agreed with us hereafter (their chief anxiety is to learn as soon as possible what these principles are going to be, their present mood – and that is all to the good – being one which will, we hope, prove to be over-pessimistic). On such conditions, by cunning and kindness, we have persuaded the outside world to lend us upwards of the prodigious total of £3000 million. The very size of these sterling debts is itself a protection. The old saying holds. Owe your banker £1000 and you are at his mercy; owe him £1 million and the position is reversed.[46]

Most of these sterling balances were in the hands of members of the Sterling Area, in particular India. The accumulation of sterling by these countries often followed different rules; frequently they arose not from ordinary commercial transactions as in the case of Argentina, but from the financing of troops. However, in a sense Colonies were perhaps more protected than Argentina in that British officials could sometimes feel a degree of responsibility for the welfare of colonial subjects that was naturally absent when dealing with an independent and relatively rich country like Argentina. This can be seen clearly in the plea of a Treasury official, Dunnett, at an inter-departmental meeting on Argentina in mid-1940:

> Mr Dunnett suggested that Argentina and the Colonies had similar problems in respect of surpluses but the Colonies differed in not being able to lend us money. . . . Mr Dunnett pointed out that payment for the surplus products of the Colonies could not be made in blocked sterling as the inhabitants were too poor.[47]

What he wanted was to get a loan from Argentina even if the balance of payments between the two countries turned out to be in equilibrium, so that exports might be redirected to the Colonies.

> It is most unlikely that the Colonial producer can to any appreciable extent accept payment in money which cannot be quickly converted into cotton goods or other things. In other words, it is much easier to get a credit from the Argentine than from the African, and exports which would do for the Africans ought not to be sent to the Argentine.[48]

This was a personal position and not the policy of the British government; in the end the Colonial producer did not get much. Still, it is indicative of a widespread attitude at some extreme moments.

It should not be forgotten that during this period British officials were in the middle of a war. Their offices and houses were being bombed, and although they managed to keep on writing witty minutes, their friends and relatives were being killed. Niemeyer, to take one case among many, had a son killed in action while the negotiations described above were taking place.

The duty of these officials was to get goods on credit from Argentina for the prosecution of the war; it was also to look after Britain's post-war economy. This was the objective; what kind of Argentine government was prepared to accede was of secondary importance. After all, British officials were used to the oscillations of Argentine politics; they were also prepared for them. An official at the Embassy in Buenos Aires, reviewing a long period of Argentine politics, ended his note with a quotation:

> Finally, it was Manuel Quintana who said over 30 years ago 'La política argentina siempre ha oscilado entre el caudillaje y la revolución inevitable que aquél provoca. Epílogo: la amnistía.'[49]

NOTES

NB: The files of a number of British Ministries were consulted for this paper. The following initials are used in the notes: PRO for the Public Record Office (London), and MP for the papers of Henry Morgenthau at Hyde Park, New York. Among the PRO references the following sub-divisions will occur: FO (Foreign Office), BT (Board of Trade), T (Treasury), MAF (Ministry of Agriculture and Fisheries). When quotation marks are used without a file reference, the document cited is in the same files as the preceding document (unless it is a part of the same document quoted in the following footnote).

1. A good example of the confusion to be experienced in Argentine publications on such questions is Irazusta's *Perón y la crisis Argentina*. Irazusta is one of the few authors to discuss sterling balances at all, devoting a whole chapter to the subject. He concludes that 'Argentina's credits on Britain (£150 million) and on the USA ($500 million), placed us in a position inferior only to the United States in the world economic scale, and they promised us an immediate prosperity and a foreseeable future, both brilliant': Julio Irazusta, *Perón y la crisis Argentina* (Buenos Aires, 1966 edn) p. 45.
2. W. K. Hancock and M. M. Gowing, *British War Economy* (London, 1953 edn) pp. 101–2.
3. Bank for International Settlements, *10th Annual Report for 1 April 1939 to 31 March 1940*, p. 19.
4. 4 Sept. 1939: PRO, T160.1266.F18218/1.
5. R. S. Sayers, *The Bank of England 1891–1944*, vol. 2 (Cambridge, 1976) p. 518; A. Plumptre, *Central Banking in the British Dominions* (Toronto, 1947) pp. 147–8.
6. Niemeyer to Waley, 9 Oct. 1939: PRO, T160.1266.F.18218/1.
7. Hancock and Gowing, *British War Economy*, p. iii.
8. Leith Ross to Waley, 21 Nov. 1939: PRO, T 160.1266.F.18218/1.
9. Waley to Niemeyer, 24 June 1940: PRO, FO 371.24200.
10. 9 July: ibid., p. 313.
11. Hutton to Waley, 5 July 1940: ibid., p. 376.
12. See Keynes's elegant treatment of the issue in the *Economic Journal* (March

1929) pp. 1–7. For the more classical position that argues that by solving the budgetary aspect of the problem its transfer aspect is also solved, see J. Rueff, 'Les idées de M. Keynes sur le problème des transferts', *Revue d'Economie Politique* (1929) pp. 1067–81.
13. R. S. Sayers, *Financial Policy 1939–45* (London: HMSO, 1956) p. 338.
14. J. M. Keynes, 'Foreign Exchange Control and Payments Agreements', 29 July 1940: PRO, FO 371.24200.
15. David Dilks (ed.), *The Diaries of Sir Alexander Cadogan, 1938–45* (London, 1971) p. 292.
16. Note by Hutton on his visit to London, 14–18 July: PRO, MAF 83/1067.
17. Pavel Egoroff, *Argentina's Agricultural Exports during World War II* (Stanford, Calif., 1945) pp. 9–11.
18. Norman to Wood, 10 June 1940: PRO, T 160.1266.18218/2.
19. Niemeyer to Waley, 17 June 1940: PRO, T 160. 1143.F.16707/2.
20. Fraser to Waley, 11 Oct. 1940: PRO, T 160.1266.F.18218/2.
21. Hutton to Jopson, 6 Feb. 1940: PRO, FO 371.25702.
22. 12th meeting of the inter-departmental committee: PRO, BT 1395.C.R.T.8089.
23. 12 Aug. 1941: PRO, FO 118.705.
24. Telegram 207, British Embassy to Foreign Office, 28 March 1941: PRO, FO 371.25714.
25. Minute, 2 Aug. 1941: A. 5856/1/2, in PRO, FO 371.25701.
26. Butler, as quoted by Mather Jackson in minute dated 14 Sept. 1942: A.8650/159/2, in PRO, FO 371.30317.
27. Memorandum of the Argentine Ministry of Foreign Affairs, 7 Oct. 1941, point 11: A8998/125/2, in PRO, FO 371.25715.
28. Telegram 679 from Ovey to Eden, 8 Oct. 1941: A.8128/125/2 in ibid.
29. Minute by Gallop to Scott, 7 Aug. 1942: A.7163/2442/51, in PRO, FO 371.30510.
30. Telegram 275 from BA, containing Meynell's telegram of 17 May 1940: PRO, T 231.28.E.C.9.
31. FO to Embassy, 19 Dec. 1939: PRO, BT 11.1395 (it was 'most anxious to stimulate exports to Argentina').
32. Waley to Willis, 23 Nov. 1940: PRO, BT 11.1373.
33. 'Assessment of Overseas Requirements', 19 Feb. 1942: PRO, BT 11, 1895.
34. Owen to Col. Llewellyn, 1 Aug. 1941: PRO, BT 11.1503.
35. PRO, BT 11.1373.
36. Minute by Shannon, 14 Sept. 1941: in ibid.
37. Minute by Knight, 24 July 1941: PRO, MAF 83/1067.
38. R. Prebisch, 'La inspección de bancos y la oficina de investigaciones económicas. Conversaciones en el Banco de México', 7 Mar. 1944, in *La creación del Banco Central y la experiencia monetaria argentina entre los años 1935–1943*, vol. 2 (Buenos Aires, 1972) p. 621.
39. 'La moneda y los ciclos', in ibid., pp. 131–3.
40. Interview (subsequently) with author, Milan, 9 Apr. 1983.
41. 'International Currency Experience', in League of Nations, *Lessons of the Inter-War Period* (Princeton, N.J., 1944) p. 136.
42. *Creación del Banco Central*, vol. 1, p. 386.
43. *Federal Reserve Bulletin*, vol. 31 (June 1945) pp. 523 and 529.

44. The essential reference is to Marcelo de Paiva Abreu, 'Brazil and the World Economy, 1930–45' (unpublished Ph.D., University of Cambridge, 1977).
45. Keynes, *Collected Writings*, vol. XXIV, p. 257.
46. Ibid., p. 258.
47. Minutes of inter-departmental meeting on Argentina, 15 July 1940: PRO, T 160 1266 F.18218/2.
48. Minute by Dunnett, 16 July 1940.
49. 'Argentine Politics: a Few Elementary Considerations', 26 Feb. 1941: PRO, FO 118.703.

10 The United States, Britain and Argentina in the Years immediately after the Second World War

C. A. MACDONALD

I INTRODUCTION

Following the Argentine elections of February 1946, both London and Washington were forced to accept the existence of Perón's regime with its policy of economic diversification. The questions faced by Britain and the US were the degree of industrialisation which was to occur and the method by which the policy was to be pursued. A division appeared to exist amongst Perón's advisers on these issues and two broad groups could be identified, struggling for control of economic policy. 'Moderates', such as Bramuglia, the Foreign Minister, and the technicians at the Central Bank, were believed to favour a policy of gradual industrialisation in cooperation with Argentina's major trading partners. Their economic strategy embraced free enterprise at home and 'reasonable' prices for Argentine produce in world markets. 'Extremists', such as Miranda, head of the Economic Council, rejected this approach, arguing that Argentina must not allow the pace and direction of industrial development to be dictated from abroad. Miranda advocated rapid industrialisation under State control financed by high prices for agricultural exports. He was uninterested in the impact of such policies on Argentina's trading partners, emphasising instead the overriding need to establish economic 'independence' as soon as possible.[1] The 'extremists' were identified abroad with what became known as the 'Third Position', – the creation of an Argentina which renounced dependence in favour of independent national development, and which could therefore pursue its own international policies free from dictation by the great powers.

The struggle between 'moderates' and 'extremists' was closely followed in Washington and London. 'Extremist' policies in Argentina conflicted with the British desire to attain speedy postwar recovery which would allow Britain to retain its position as a great power. By charging high agricultural prices, attacking foreign interests and erecting tariff barriers, Miranda could impede British recovery. By contrast the 'moderates' seemed to offer the prospect of saving at least some remnant of the Anglo-Argentine 'connection' which had benefited British interests in the past.

The US was equally hostile to 'extremism'. A 'Third Position' which attacked US interests within Argentina and which proclaimed the existence of a middle way between capitalism and communism conflicted with the US aim of creating a united hemisphere against the Soviet threat. Moreover, after 1945 Washington defined British recovery as central to US global objectives and was unwilling to allow Argentina to 'profiteer' at the expense of an ally.[2] Washington believed that its purposes could best be served by an Argentine policy which renounced the 'Third Position' and aligned Argentina behind US aims inside and outside the hemisphere. In their attempt to achieve this end, officials regarded Bramuglia as an ally and deployed US influence behind his approach. The emergence of the US at the centre of the world economy after 1945 meant that policy-makers had the power to make their preferences felt, and it was primarily the economic weapon which was used to contain 'extremism'.

Thus the area of manoeuvre for Argentina was circumscribed from the start by the existence of an Anglo-American axis based on hostility to economic nationalism. After 1945, the US propped up the sagging British economy at Argentine expense in the interests of containing communism in Europe and disciplining anti-American nationalism within the hemisphere. The ultimate aim was to discredit Miranda and to force Argentina away from the 'Third Position' at home and abroad. 'Moderate' economic policies at home were regarded by Washington as the prerequisite for Argentine integration into US global strategy.

II PHASE ONE: FEBRUARY 1946–SEPTEMBER 1947

Both during and after the Second World War, Argentina was defined by London as an important market for British goods and as an indispensable source of agricultural supplies. The importance of Argentina to postwar recovery meant that a high priority was placed on establishing close and cordial relations with the Peronist regime. After the coup of 1943 which displaced the oligarchy, it was realised in London that the old relationship, based on the existence of a dependent class at the head of Argentine affairs which would defend British interests, could not be revived. Argentina had entered a nationalist phase, and Britain would have to deal with this unfamiliar situation if its position were to be saved.

Rather than openly opposing new developments in Argentina, a policy which Britain realised it was too weak to pursue with any hope of success, London decided to save what it could by appeasement.[3] As the British Ambassador, Sir Reginald Leeper, remarked in September 1946, any attempt to resist the rise of nationalism could 'lead us to nothing but disaster'. Accordingly, Leeper's mission in Buenos Aires was to 'get as thick with the Argentine Government . . . as the political circumstances of the moment permit.'[4] The Foreign Office argued that the key to success with the new regime would not be to attempt to force the Argentines to go on paying for goods and services which 'rightly or wrongly' they felt they no longer needed, but to discover 'how we can substitute for such goods and services, goods and services they want, with a minimum of pain and loss to ourselves.'[5] The Board of Trade agreed. As one official noted, Argentina was determined to industrialise, 'whether it was desirable or not'. It would be worse than useless for Britain to 'kick against the pricks.[6] London therefore deferred to Perón's insistence on diversification and the repatriation of certain types of foreign investment. Britons were prepared to sacrifice investments in areas such as the railways in the hope of appeasing nationalism and gaining openings for British goods in the emerging industrial sector. It was hoped that a diversified Argentina would provide a better market for British exports than a largely agricultural economy. As the head of the South American Department remarked in January 1947, the emphasis in future Anglo-Argentine relations must be 'on trade, rather than, as hitherto, on safeguarding our historical position as owners of invested capital'.[7]

London hoped that its policy of cooperation and conciliation would encourage the 'moderates' in Perón's entourage at the expense of the 'extremists', thus limiting the impact of economic nationalism on the British position.[8] The prospect of the Five Year Plan under the total control of Miranda and his associates was viewed with horror. The preference of the 'extremists' for high food prices and tariffs was attributed to 'selfish nationalism' and to the desire of 'newly risen industrialists', such as Miranda, for protection against foreign competition. They represented the forces of 'ignorant isolationism' which had no conception of Argentina's proper role and were determined to exploit Europe's need for food.[9] In a despatch on the Five Year Plan, Leeper complained that the 'drivelling rhetoric' setting out the scheme showed no sign of 'dawning recognition that the traditional customers for Argentine primary produce may be . . . impoverished by these selfish designs, or that the costs of these unsound enterprises must eventually impede the republic's ability to maintain her agricultural costs at competitive levels'.[10] This was a frank statement of concern about the possible results of 'extremist' policies which it was feared would damage the prospects of British economic recovery based on imports of cheap food and exports of manufactured goods unrestricted by high foreign tariffs. The way to avert the threat posed by Miranda was to cultivate 'moderates' such as Bramuglia who had a 'realistic' appreciation of Argentine interests and opposed a policy of 'chauvinistic foolishness'. The Foreign Minister's repeated interventions with Perón in favour of Britain earned him the ultimate accolade from the Foreign Office when he was characterised as 'a reasonably sensible man for an Argentine'.[11] Through the influence of such 'moderate-minded' advisers, the 'extremists' could be neutralised and Argentine development conducted *in association* with foreign interests rather than *against* them. Britain would be guaranteed cheap food and a market for its products on the River Plate.

Appeasement of 'moderate' nationalists, however, was only one part of the solution to the problem posed by the 'extremists'. The second consisted of establishing a united front with the Americans to steer Argentine policy along 'rational' lines, lest Miranda play one power off against the other to his own advantage. According to Leeper it would be 'short-sighted' to attempt to score off the United States. In its effort to entice Perón away from 'excesses of nationalism', Britain would be greatly strengthened if it worked 'in close understanding with the United States'.[12]

It was a measure of the decline of British power that London considered calling the Americans to protect its interests in what had previously been regarded as a British preserve. It was realised, however, that in the changed circumstances of the post-war world, Britain would have to concede a dominant share of the Argentine market to the United States. Any attempt to resist US penetration could end only in disaster. London should appeal to American self-interest, arguing that as the two leading capitalist powers, Britain and the US would stand or fall together in Argentina.[13] In its appeal to Washington, Britain was not disappointed. The post-war period was to witness an increasing degree of US intervention on behalf of London in its economic dealings with Miranda.

In November 1945 Spruille Braden, Assistant Secretary of State for Latin American Affairs, made a speech in which he distinguished between two types of industrialisation. According to Braden the first was unsound and designed 'not to promote increased productivity and a higher real income, but to serve the purposes of autarchy, neurotic nationalism and military adventure'. He compared this approach to 'sound industrialisation . . . carried out . . . under the dynamic system of private and . . . competitive enterprise'. Braden announced that Washington would oppose the first type of industrialisation which he believed to be proceeding in Argentina, and promote the second throughout Latin America.[14]

In championing the virtues of free enterprise against statism, Braden merely echoed the statements of other members of the Truman administration, such as Will Clayton, Assistant Secretary of State for Economic Affairs, who made a similar statement at the Mexico City conference. Clayton remained concerned about the trend 'towards nationalisation of industry' in Argentina which he believed the US must 'follow very closely'.[15] Argentina was thus regarded as a dangerous example to the rest of Latin America and a potential threat to US hegemony in the area. Braden was identified with a policy of open opposition to Argentine nationalism, designed to prevent Perón from consolidating his control. In the period after Perón's election, however, following the failure of the *Blue Book* campaign, Washington gradually abandoned its hostility towards Argentina, moving instead towards an approach which broadly paralleled British policy. The US did not abandon the essential distinction between diversification based on 'neurotic nationalism' and 'sound industrialisation' under the free enterprise system, nor its concern with statist tendencies in Argentina. Instead Washington attempted to promote the second model at the expense of the first by working *with* and *through* Perón rather than *against* him. Open opposition to industrialisation was replaced by an attempt to mould Perón's strategy in ways which promoted American interests. This change occurred with the appointment of George Messersmith as ambassador to Buenos Aires and the emergence of the Cold War as a primary US concern in 1946–7.[16]

Messersmith, fearing the possibility of war with the Soviet Union, was determined to solve the problem of Argentina which had plagued the US throughout the Second World War. Hemispheric unity must be guaranteed and Argentina firmly incorporated into the Pan-American system. In this approach Messersmith was supported by powerful elements in the Congress and the Pentagon. He also enjoyed the support of the business community which was anxious to break into the Argentine market, one of the few foreign markets undamaged by war.[17] Messersmith argued that the Five Year Plan offered the US a unique opportunity to create a new relationship with Argentina based on economic dependence. Perón was abandoning the traditional Argentine emphasis on Europe which had characterised the period of *estanciero* dominance and was turning to the US for the capital goods necessary to pursue a programme of industrialisation. If Washington failed to cooperate with Perón's strategy, the door would be left open to the USSR and Britain, which would use economic influence for political purposes if granted an opportunity.[18]

While emphasising, therefore, the anti-Soviet element in his approach to Argentina, Messersmith remained deeply suspicious of British influence in Buenos Aires. The ambassador adopted an economic interpretation of the Monroe Doctrine, believing that European commercial links with Latin America led to political influence, thus disrupting the hemispheric unity essential to the global projection of US power. In this respect the Anglo-Argentine 'connection' was as unacceptable as Soviet penetration; during the war it had allowed Argentina to pursue a foreign policy in opposition to the US. In his anxiety to contain possible rivals in Buenos Aires, Messersmith recommended that Washington should grant Argentina preference in access to supplies of scarce capital goods. This was rejected, however, on the grounds that wartime controls were being eliminated and that Argentina must take its chance with Europeans in an open market.[19]

While welcoming Argentine industrialisation, Messersmith remained as hostile to statism as Braden, and as wedded to free enterprise models. He did not deny that the Five Year Plan contained the seeds of a controlled economy, but hoped to avert this danger not by uncompromising hostility to change in Argentina but by a subtle policy of guiding change along lines acceptable to the US. By establishing a cordial relationship with Perón, Washington could persuade him to drop Miranda's strategy in favour of a more 'rational' approach. Messersmith maintained that with proper handling, Perón could be persuaded to diversify in association with foreign interests, establishing mixed companies even in previously jealously guarded fields such as oil.[20] His hold over the Argentine people would allow him to implement such moves over nationalist opposition. In pushing Perón along these lines, Messersmith counted on the assistance of 'the only man who understood what Argentine policy should be', Foreign Minister Bramuglia.[21] Messersmith's strategy therefore paralleled British policy, appeasing 'moderate' nationalism in the hope of maintaining control over the pace and direction of change. An example of Messersmith's influence was the arrival in Buenos Aires of a technical mission under two ex-military men, General Lord and Admiral Flannigan (February 1947). The mission was intended to provide expert advice on implementation of the Five Year Plan and to draw up blueprints for certain of its projects. Guided by American experts, the Five Year Plan was to evolve on the New Deal pattern of business/government cooperation rather than as an experiment in government coercion of industry, a line associated with Miranda. A corollary of US advice on implementation of the plan would be contracts for American firms and domination of the industrial infrastructure which emerged.[22]

While emphasising the dangers of British influence in Argentina, Messersmith realised that British cooperation was essential to contain the threat of 'extremism'. Moreover, he realised that if Britain were to play a key role in resisting communist expansion in Europe it must be assured of Argentine supplies and of access to a market which would allow it to pay for such essential imports. Messersmith was not opposed to legitimate British trade relations with Buenos Aires, so much as the old exclusive 'Anglo-Argentine connection' which had blocked US influence in the past. There was room for some British trade provided the US was the dominant element in Argentina.[23] The role of Britain in the global strategy of anti-communism meant that the 'extremists' must not be allowed to block British recovery. London and Washington must cooperate to move Perón towards 'rational' economic policies. Simultaneously, however, the US must guarantee its dominance over the free market which would emerge.

The British Foreign Office rightly characterised this policy as 'political cooperation and economic competition'. Messersmith was thus prepared to cooperate with Leeper in opposition to 'narrow and selfish nationalism'.[24] The most dramatic example of this unofficial collusion with the British was Messersmith's intervention at a crucial point in the Eady/Miranda negotiations of September 1946 when talks appeared on the verge of breakdown over Miranda's terms. Messersmith secured an interview with Perón at which he supported the attempts of Bramuglia to end the crisis. The result was that Miranda was overruled and Messersmith received fulsome praise from the British side.[25] He intervened to save the agreement because he identified the terms rejected by Britain with the 'extremists'. If a negotiated settlement on the railways failed it might be followed by 'violent acts of expropriation' in which US interests would suffer along with British. Moreover, Britain would lose a vital source of food necessary for its economic recovery.[26] On the other hand a reasonable settlement would assist 'moderate' elements while reducing British influence.

The railway deal symbolised the retreat of British economic power and the emergence of a vacuum which could be filled by the US, a process which Messersmith was anxious to facilitate. It was essential, however, that this retreat did not threaten British economic recovery which was necessary to containment of communism in Europe.[27] The Eady/Miranda agreement achieved both ends, liquidating a large bloc of British investment while guaranteeing meat supplies.

In this period, therefore, certain themes were emerging which were to dominate subsequent developments. The US was determined to subordinate Argentine industrialisation to European reconstruction, a fact which became evident when Clayton rejected Messersmith's plea for favoured access to American goods. In this respect the Five Year Plan was already suffering from the Cold War tendency to put Europe first in the global struggle with the USSR. As a source of capital goods, Britain was an unreliable alternative. By early 1947, London was already experiencing difficulties in supplying the classes of goods demanded by Argentina in return for food.[29] Tension was growing over British demands for the licensing of imports considered by Miranda to be 'inessential'. As Miranda complained in January 'what he needed was coal and raw materials such as caustic soda and soda ash. Argentina could not live on whisky and lipstick'.[29]

This complaint was to be the theme of subsequent Anglo-Argentine negotiations. Britain was unable to supply a high volume of capital goods or scarce raw materials because of shortages at home.[30] As long as sterling convertibility under the terms of the Anglo-American loan agreement of 1945 continued, Miranda could at least convert current export earnings into dollars and buy on the American market. British economic difficulties, however, clearly foreshadowed the suspension of convertibility in August 1947 which was to leave Argentina dependent for export earnings on a country with inconvertible currency, unable to supply the goods required by the Five Year Plan and determined to dump 'inessentials' on Argentina to promote its own recovery. In addition to these unfavourable circumstances, Miranda was faced by the determination of Britain and the US to dictate the pace and nature of Argentine economic development. The suspension of sterling convertibility and the emerging Argentine dollar shortage were to grant them a powerful lever with which to achieve their goals. As Escudé has argued, this international perspective should not be neglected in discussing the economic crisis into which Argentina had entered by the end of the decade.[31]

III PHASE TWO: SEPTEMBER 1947 JUNE 1950

The trends already visible during the first phase were accentuated during the second period which was dominated by the US attempt to rebuild the economies of Western Europe through the Marshall Plan as a barrier against communism. Argentina hoped to benefit from this development, regarding ERP dollars as a substitute for sterling convertibility. The policy of the Economic Cooperation Administration (ECA), however, denied Argentina the opportunity to benefit from Marshall aid. Washington insisted that Europe pay for its Latin American imports as far as possible through exports and the expenditure of soft currencies in blocked accounts, saving ERP dollars for commodities in short supply. The bulk of such scarce supplies was to be found in the US, and in this respect ECA policy represented an attempt to subsidise US exporters as well as European reconstruction. Latin America was thus left without dollar reserves to purchase US goods. Industrialisation in the area was clearly at the bottom of the US priority list, a fact which was confirmed by the institution of an export licencing system in October 1947 that covered goods and raw materials in scarce supply. The priority under this system went to Europe.[32] ECA policy therefore insisted that, in Latin America, production of raw materials for European recovery should come first. By supporting Europe, Latin America would assist in the containment of communism and speed the return of multilateralism from which it would reap ultimate benefits. US policy had immediate implications for the Five Year Plan. In September 1947, Perón complained to Messersmith's successor, James Bruce, that industrialisation was being held back by difficulties in obtaining the necessary equipment from the US.[33]

While discriminating against Latin America in general, ECA was hostile to Argentina in particular. US opposition focused on IAPI which it was claimed restricted agricultural production and, by artificially high prices, attempted to profiteer at the expense of European reconstruction. It was argued that Washington could not subsidise an inefficient government monopoly with taxpayers' money. In administering the Marshall Plan, ECA deliberately punished IAPI. Where dollars were available for Argentine agricultural surpluses, they were switched away to the US, Canada and Mexico. As one ECA official observed, this was designed to 'beat to its knees' Miranda's policy of State trade. ECA was determined that Argentina should sell its exports to Europe at 'reasonable prices' and accept 'reasonable quantities' of European goods in return before authorising the expenditure of dollars on any remaining surplus.[34] Behind this approach were powerful domestic factors quite as important as international economic considerations. Dependent on the Congress for appropriations, ECA hesitated to alienate the US agricultural lobby which opposed any subsidy for what it regarded as a major competitor in world markets. There was nothing to balance this pressure. US businessmen, important advocates of a settlement with Perón in 1945–6, were disillusioned by 1947 because of tightening economic controls that year. Moreover, the prospect of European revival now beckoned. The White House and higher levels of the State Department also focused their attention on Europe and neglected Latin America. Only desk officers and the embassy remained directly concerned with Argentina, and for a time they too went along with ECA policy. As a result, even when Perón promised to peg Argentine prices at parity with US and entered a series of agreements with Britain and others which furthered the goal of European recovery, no ERP dollars were forthcoming.[35] As in the past, the agricultural lobby dictated the nature of US/Argentine economic relations.

American policy after September 1947 consolidated the alignment with Britain in Argentina which had emerged under Messersmith. London quickly grasped the implications of sterling inconvertibility for the future of the Five Year Plan. As Shuckburgh, of the South American Department, remarked in September 1947:

> The fact is that Argentina will now be forced, whether she likes it or not, to curtail her imports from the US and spend the proceeds of her foodstuffs in those countries which buy from her.... This will mean ... that her grandiose five year industrialisation plans will have to be postponed either until Great Britain can supply the capital goods needed for it or until we are in a position once more to allow sterling convertibility. She will be compelled on the one hand to build up sterling reserves for future use ... and on the other hand to buy goods from us which in her present mood she regards as luxuries and is excluding.[36]

In the negotiations for a new economic agreement taking account of sterling inconvertibility, Britain insisted that Argentina dismantle its import licensing system and accept 'inessential' items such as textiles, whisky, cars and household goods.[37] In an attempt to force Britain to supply scarce commodities such as steel and oil or a guaranteed dollar ration, Miranda resorted to threatening the British meat supply. According to Miranda he was 'in a position to starve the British Isles at will . . . England has to have Argentine products . . . and . . . will get them at a price that suits him'.[38] In an attempt to weaken Miranda's position, the British appealed to Bramuglia who took a more 'reasonable' line on issues such as meat prices and the licensing of 'inessentials'. They also expressed the hope that the Americans would support their negotiating position since any injection of ECA dollars into Argentina would encourage Miranda to tighten the screws on London.[39]

Washington was prepared to assist London in its negotiations with Argentina. As the embassy noted in December 1947, 'we . . . assume that the success of the British Mission is very important to the Marshall Plan'.[40] US officials therefore would assist the British negotiators informally by hinting to the Argentines that a reasonable settlement with London was the prerequisite for the expenditure of ERP dollars in Argentina. The embassy concluded that 'the Argentine financial situation gives England a fighting chance to obtain concessions from Miranda . . . any immediate negotiation on our part would only strengthen Miranda's hand through actual or implied competitive bidding for favours'.[41]

US assistance went beyond mere refusal to request dollar expenditure in advance of the conclusion of the Andes agreement. The embassy was kept informed about British progress in the negotiations so that Bruce could intervene with Perón in the event of deadlock. According to Bruce

> Sir Stafford Cripps cabled the British Ambassador . . . to show me all their cables . . . no matter how confidential, and to treat me with the same freedom as if I were part of the British government . . . with the result that the two British negotiators, Sir Rex Leeper and Sir Clive Baillieu, were in my house until 4:30 one morning (me in a bathrobe and the distinguished Britishers not even in their striped pants). I then saw Bramuglia at the Foreign Office at 8 and the agreement was signed around noon.[42]

The conclusion of the Andes agreement therefore was based on an alignment of the US, Britain and Bramuglia against Miranda's demands.[43] It was also made clear to Perón that a prerequisite for ECA funding would be maximum utilisation of soft currencies and acceptance of a high volume of European goods.⁴⁴ This obviously encouraged him to repudiate Miranda and to support Bramuglia. Both embassies believed that the Foreign Minister's influence was decisive in securing the Andes agreement, and hoped that he would consolidate his position in the regime.⁴⁵

It was believed in the State Department that the worsening dollar position in Argentina would eventually allow Washington to write its own 'ticket' for a settlement with Perón. A precondition for any solution acceptable to the US was the removal of Miranda and of curbs on IAPI, the instrument through which he pursued his obnoxious policies. Expenditure of dollars in advance of Miranda's fall would merely consolidate his influence by persuading Perón that he was the man who could 'get things done'. The Americans believed that the removal of Miranda would be followed by the introduction of 'reasonable' economic policies. Argentina would abandon statism in favour of free enterprise and fair treatment of foreign interests.⁴⁶ The organisation of the domestic economy was regarded as the basis of foreign policy. Renunciation of 'economic independence' was thus the necessary preliminary to abandonment of the 'Third Position' abroad and the alignment of Argentina behind US goals inside and outside the hemisphere.⁴⁷

London had always expressed reservations about the Five Year Plan; in the aftermath of sterling inconvertibility, it argued that Argentina must abandon an industrial future, at least in the short-term, in order to promote British recovery. Many of the goods which Britain had to sell conflicted with precisely those types of import substitution fostered by the Argentines, hence the repeated clashes with Miranda over licencing of 'inessentials'.⁴⁸ In the wake of the European crisis of 1947, Washington adopted a similar line. The US demanded a form of development which emphasised the role of American companies in areas such as assembly and extraction, particularly oil where the Yacimientos Petroliferos Fiscales (YPF) monopoly was unpopular.⁴⁹ This would tie Argentina closely to a Pan-American system dominated by the US and prevent it from becoming a regional power, challenging American policy in the Southern Cone. For this reason, Washington had long opposed the creation of a significant heavy industrial base in the country outside the control of US interests. The free enterprise model, however, while offering immediate openings for US companies, was necessarily a long-term form of development as opposed to the 'forced industrialisation' associated with the Five Year Plan. In the past, Argentina had remained a producer of raw materials while developing an industrial sector in association with foreign capital, a situation which Washington wished to continue. In effect, therefore, US policy parallelled British, demanding curbs on diversification in favour of the production of raw materials for European recovery.[50] For this reason both powers were hostile to IAPI because of its pricing policy and supposed impact on the level of agricultural production. The Anglo-American approach demanded that Perón should continue to live with the world division of labour for the time being, and subordinated Argentine development to the recovery of the European industrial economies which were being rebuilt as a barrier against communism.[51]

In pursuit of its ends Washington attempted to support what were characterised as 'the pro-United States and pro-free enterprise elements in the Argentine government [against] the more anti-United States and nationalistic groups'.[52] It was hoped by the embassy that once Perón repudiated Miranda, ECA would authorise the expenditure of Marshall plan dollars in Argentina to revive triangular trade and encourage the 'moderates'. It was believed that this point had come in the summer of 1948, following Miranda's defeat over the Andes agreement and an apparent readiness on behalf of the Argentines to meet US grievances by discussing the problems of American firms and modifying the role of IAPI, at least in the import trade.[53] However, despite the fall of Miranda in January 1949 and the announcement of a new policy placing greater emphasis on agriculture at the expense of 'forced industrialisation', ECA refused to authorise dollars for Argentina. The result was a bilateral five year trade agreement between Britain and Argentina in June 1949 which the State Department felt could have been avoided by a less rigid attitude on the part of ECA.[54] It was feared that the continuing lack of dollars would weaken Bramuglia who had been encouraged to believe that US funding would be placed behind his policies once the power struggle with Miranda had been resolved in his favour. It was argued that his influence with Perón to a large degree depended on his ability to solve the economic problems which had defeated his rival.[55]

In August 1949 Bramuglia followed Miranda into oblivion. The US embassy feared that his inability to deliver dollars had led to his downfall, and Bruce intervened with Perón expressing US confidence in the Foreign Minister and requesting his retention in office. Perón, however, refused.[56] Bramuglia's departure was a source of regret in Washington and London. His successor, Paz, was a nationalist intellectual with neither Bramuglia's political power nor his influence with Perón.[57] Economic affairs were left largely in the hands of a group of technicians who seemed reluctant to take dramatic decisions.

The failure of ECA to provide dollars for Argentina forced the State Department to consider the idea of an Exim Bank loan as an inducement for abandoning the 'Third Position' at home and abroad. By 1949 Perón was obviously desperate for US assistance despite his earlier opposition to the idea of an American loan. Even former 'extremists' such as Cereijo, head of the Economic Council, were changing their attitude in the hope of saving the regime by an injection of US funds.[58] In such circles it was realised that the denial of Marshall plan dollars and the prospect of a war which would force the US to stockpile Argentine products, gave the regime no option but to appeal to Washington despite the price the Americans would demand in return for aid. The State Department was anxious to promote a 'moderate' solution to the Argentine economic crisis. It was feared that if conditions grew worse, Perón might be overthrown and replaced by a military junta based on 'extremist' elements in the army, an outcome which the Americans wished to avert.[59] As Blanksten argues, US policy in 1950 was to intervene in favour of Perón but only in return for repudiation of the 'Third Position'.[60] In February 1950 Edward Miller, Assistant Secretary of State for Latin American Affairs, visited Buenos Aires to discuss US–Argentine relations.[61] While nothing concrete emerged during this trip, it paved the way for Cereijo's visit to Washington in March 1950 when Exim funding was requested to cover commercial indebtedness and to allow the purchase of agricultural equipment in the US.[62] Clearly US assistance was considered fundamental to the new economic strategy based on greater agricultural investment and cooperation with US companies in the industrial sector. When the Exim loan was discussed in Washington it was related to the adoption of the development strategy favoured by the US. According to an Exim Bank official, the Argentines were beginning 'to pay attention to the views of people who have economic and financial competence . . . this group realised the economic errors that have been committed . . . and they had to a striking extent slowed down the progress of overly accelerated industrialisation'.[63]

The State Department agreed with this analysis, noting with approval that 'The economic objective of the credit . . . is to assist . . . in the restoration of agricultural production for export to Western Europe'.[64]

The Exim credit of $125 million in May 1950 was therefore intended to consolidate 'moderate' influence, to contain 'extremism', and to integrate Argentina into US strategy inside and outside the hemisphere. According to the State Department, US assistance was justified because Argentina was abandoning 'erratic' nationalist policies and 'facing realistically foreign and domestic problems'.[65] It was recognised that in itself, Exim funding could not solve the Argentine crisis, but it was believed to be a first step along the road to membership of the IMF and the World Bank, which would further underline the retreat from the 'Third Position' at home and abroad.[66] As Escudé argues, the loan was a 'symbolic capitulation' to the US.[67]

IV CONCLUSIONS

It is clear in retrospect that between 1946 and 1950 Argentina suffered not only from the general conditions of the period, sterling inconvertibility and the US decision to accord the needs of Europe priority over those of Latin America, but also from the opposition of Britain and the US to Miranda's policies. There was little prospect of playing the two off against each other as long as Britain was defined as essential to US defence and Miranda appeared to be hindering British recovery. The Anglo-American alignment after 1946 left Argentina little room for manoeuvre. The attempt to establish a 'Third Position' came at an unpropitious time. It could not be allowed to stand against the Truman Doctrine which divided the world into the free and the unfree, the capitalists and the communists. In such a manichean system there was no room for neutrality or compromise. The ideological framework of the Cold War contained no place for a 'Third Position'. After 1946, Washington was prepared to use its unparalleled economic power to secure its global objectives and to bring Argentina into line. The trend was clear by 1950. Perón would have to accommodate his policies to the reality of US economic power which ultimately allowed Washington to dictate its own terms for a settlement with Argentina.

NOTES

1. On 'moderates' and 'extremists' in Argentina see Robert R. Potash, *The Army and Politics in Argentina 1945–1962* (London, 1980) pp. 54–72; Callum A. MacDonald, 'The US, the Cold War and Perón', in Christopher Abel and Colin Lewis (eds), *Latin America: Economic Imperialism and the State* (London, 1985).
2. Richard Gardner, *Sterling–Dollar Diplomacy* (New York, 1969) pp. 248–53.
3. Callum A. MacDonald, 'The Politics of Intervention: the US and Argentina 1941–1946', *Journal of Latin American Studies*, XII (Nov. 1980) 381–2.

4. Leeper to Bevin, 24 Sept. 1946, AS6228/22/2 FO371/51178 (all British official documents cited hereafter are in the Public Record Office, Kew, London).
5. Minute by Fox, ibid.
6. Hooper to Perowne, 30 Jan. 1947, AS960/16/2 FO371/61124. Lomax to Lintott, 30 Jan. 1947, AS1025/16/2 FO371/61124.
7. Perowne to Eggers, 4 Jan. 1947, AS6228/22/2 FO371/51778.
8. Leeper to FO, 26 Nov. 1946, AS7342/235/2 FO371/51818; Leeper to FO, 5 June 1946, AS3462/235/2 FO371/51815.
9. Leeper to FO, 3 Aug. 1946, AS4759/70/2 FO371/51794; Leeper to Bevin, 24 Sept. 1946, AS6228/22/2 FO371/51778.
10. Leeper to Attlee, 2 Dec. 1946, AS7799/22/2 FO371/51778.
11. Leeper to FO, 8 July 1946, AS3953/235/2 FO371/51815.
12. Leeper to FO, 12 Dec. 1946, AS7961/235/2 FO371/51819.
13. Leeper to FO, 30 Dec. 1946, AS114/1/2 FO371/61121.
14. 'Foreign Trade Reconstruction – The Americas', *International Conciliation*, 419 (New York, 1946).
15. David Green, *The Containment of Latin America* (Chicago, 1971) pp. 173–5; Howe to Clayton, 11 July 1946, Clayton Papers, Box 10, Harry S. Truman Library, Independence, Missouri (hereafter HTL).
16. MacDonald, 'The US, the Cold War and Perón'.
17. Ibid.
18. Messersmith to Clayton, 31 Oct. 1946: George S. Messersmith Papers, File 1815, University of Delaware Library, Newark, Delaware (hereafter Messersmith).
19. Messersmith to Acheson, 2 Oct. 1946: Messersmith, File 1811. Messersmith to Clayton, 24 June 1946: US Embassy file, Record Group 84, BA 1946, File 850, Washington National Records Center, Suitland, Maryland (hereafter WNRC). Clayton to Messersmith, 27 July 1946: RG84, BA1946, File 850, WNRC.
20. Messersmith to Byrnes, 15 June 1946: Messersmith, File 1781; Messersmith to Byrnes, 30 Oct. 1946: Messersmith, File 1814.
21. Leeper to FO, 8 July 1946, AS3953/235/2 FO371/51815.
22. MacDonald, 'The US, the Cold War and Perón'.
23. Messersmith to Acheson, 2 Oct. 1946: Messersmith, File 1811; Leeper to FO, 16 Dec. 1946, AS7987/235/2 FO371/51819.
24. Minute by Tebbit, 2 May 1947, AS2509/1/2 FO371/61123; Leeper to FO, 8 Sept. 1946, AS5460/2/2 FO371/51764.
25. Nicholas St. F. Bowen, 'The End of British Economic Hegemony in Argentina', *Inter-American Economic Affairs*, XXVIII (1975) pp. 1–24.
26. Messersmith to Clayton, 25 Sep. 1946, Messersmith, File 1806; Leeper to FO, 3 Sep. 1946, AS5366/2/2 FO371/51764.
27. Perón agreed that Britain was a 'bulwark against communism' – see Leeper to FO, ibid.
28. Hooper to Shuckburgh, 10 July 1947, AS4130/16/2 FO371/61126; Leeper to FO, 12 Mar. 1947, AS2828/16/2 FO371/61125.
29. Lomax to Lintott, 30 Jan. 1947, AS1025/16/2 FO371/61124.
30. Leeper to FO, 12 Mar. 1947, AS2828/16/2 FO371/61125; Cruickshank to Stirling, 22 Apr. 1947, AS2422/16/2 FO371/61124.

31. Carlos Escudé, 'Las restricciones internacionales de la economía argentina, 1945–1949', *Desarollo Económico*, 77 (Apr.–June 1980).
32. Tewksbury to Bruce, 25 Jan. 1949, PSF Foreign Affairs 'A', Argentina, Folder 3, Box 170, HTL; memo by Lovett, 11 Dec. 1948, *Foreign Relations of the United States 1948*, vol. 9, pp. 307–9 (hereafter *FR*); Jorge Fodor, 'Perón's Policies for Exports', in David Rock (ed.), *Argentina in the Twentieth Century* (London, 1974) p. 159.
33. Bruce to State Department, 12 Sep. 1947, Papers of the Office of American Republics Affairs, Box 20, National Archives of the United States, Washington DC (hereafter NA).
34. Tewksbury to Bruce, 25 Jan. 1949, PSF Foreign Affairs 'A', Argentina, Folder 3, Box 170, HTL.
35. MacDonald, 'The U.S., the Cold War and Perón'.
36. Memo by Shuckburgh, 5 Sep. 1947, AS5292/16/2 FO371/61127.
37. FO Memo, 23 Aug. 1947, AS4953/16/2 FO371/61127; memo by Lomax, 7 Oct. 1947, AS5835/16/2 FO371/61128.
38. Bruce to SecState, 24 Dec. 1947, State Department Records, 635.4131/12-2447 NA.
39. Memo by Attwood, 19 Jan. 1948, 635.4131/1-1948, NA; memo by Tebbit, 10 Oct. 1947, AS5799/16/2 FO371/61128.
40. Bruce to SecState, 24 Dec. 1947, 635.4131/12-2447, NA.
41. Memo by Attwood, 19 Jan. 1948, 635.4131/1-1948, NA; Leeper to FO, 29 Jan. 1948, AS639/1/2 FO371/68082.
42. Bruce to Truman, 23 June 1949, PSF Foreign Affairs 'A', Argentina, Folder 3, Box 170, HTL.
43. Ray to Dearborn, 12 Apr. 1948, 735.41/4-1248, NA.
44. Leeper to FO, 29 Jan. 1948, AS659/1/2 FO371/68082; Marshall to Embassy, 26 Jan. 1948, 635.4131/1-2648, NA.
45. Ray to Dearborn, 12 Apr. 1948, 755.41/4-1248; on Bramuglia's assistance in the Andes negotiations see Leeper to FO, 3 Feb. 1948, AS709/1/2 FO371/68083; Leeper to FO, 3 Feb. 1948, AS723/1/2 FO371/68083; Leeper to FO, 5 Feb. 1948, AS765/1/2 FO371/68084.
46. Bruce to SecState, 3 June 1948, *FR 1948*, vol. 9, p. 289; Tewksbury to Bruce, 14 Jan. 1949, RG84, BA1949, File 350, Box 273, WNRC; Bruce to SecState, 4 Jan. 1949, *FR 1949*, vol. 2, pp. 473–8; Ray to Tewksbury, 18 Feb. 1949, RG84, BA1949, File 350, Box 540, WNRC.
47. Attwood to Daniels, 19 May 1949, *FR 1949*, vol. 2, pp. 499–500.
48. Memo by Shuckburgh, 5 Sep. 1947, AS5292/16/2 FO371/61127. Miranda argued that nothing should be imported which could be produced locally, while Britain held that if Argentina wished to sell it must buy what its best customer produced. The Argentine consumer should have access to foreign luxuries, for example whisky and other 'inessentials' such as textiles, bicycles, etc. Privately, British negotiators admitted the weakness of the British 'export drive'. As Baillieu noted, 'if the Argentine government do not create for us the means of payment within the limits of our miserable capacity, we must . . . immediately drastically curtail our purchases in this market'[9]. This argument that Argentina must subsidise British recovery at the expense of its own programme was a powerful one given Argentine dependence on British markets. It was also the direction in which the US

hoped to push Perón. See Lomax to Board of Trade, 2 Feb. 1948, AS930/1/2 FO371/68086; FO to Baillieu, 10 Feb. 1948, AS880/1/2 FO371/68085; Baillieu to Chancellor of the Exchequer, 5 Feb. 1948, AS766/1/2 FO371/68084.
49. Bruce to SecState, 4 Jan. 1949, *FR 1949*, vol. 2, pp. 473–8; Ray to Tewksbury, 18 Feb. 1949, RG84, BA1949, File 350, Box 540, WNRC; on oil see Potash, *Army and Politics*, pp. 68–71.
50. Minutes of the 156th Meeting of the National Advisory Council on International Monetary and Financial Problems, 16 May 1950, *FR 1950*, vol. 2, pp. 720–1.
51. Ibid.
52. Attwood to Daniels, 19 May 1949, *FR 1949*, vol. 2, pp. 499–500.
53. Bruce to SecState, 6 July 1948, ECA Records, RG286, Argentina Box 265, WNRC.
54. Bruce to SecState, 10 June 1949, *FR 1949*, vol. 2, pp. 508–9.
55. Bruce to SecState, 25 Jan. 1949, RG84, BA1949, File 500, Box 274; Pawley to Connelly, 28 Feb. 1949 OF366, HTL.
56. Balfour to FO, 15 Aug. 1949, AS4100/1016/2 FO371/74290.
57. Balfour to FO, 13 Aug. 1949, AS4055/1046/2 FO371/74290. Balfour to FO, 15 Aug. 1949, AS4100/1016/2 FO371/74290.
58. Woodward to Connelly, 13 Apr. 1950, OF366, HTL.
59. Minutes of the National Advisory Council, *FR 1949*, vol. 2.
60. George I. Blanksten, *Peron's Argentina* (New York, 1967) p. 437.
61. Griffiths to SecState, 1 Mar. 1950, *FR 1950*, vol. 2, pp. 701–4.
62. Minutes of the National Advisory Council, *FR 1949*, vol. 2.
63. Ibid.
64. Ibid.
65. David Green, 'The Cold War Comes to Latin America', in Barton Bernstein (ed.), *Politics and Policies of the Truman Administration* (Chicago, 1970) p. 179.
66. Minutes of the National Advisory Council, *FR 1949*, vol. 2.
67. Escudé, 'Las restriciones internacionales'.

Postscript and Conclusions

GUIDO DI TELLA and D. C. M. PLATT

I

Argentina, over the last decades, has become the outstanding example of failed development. Paul Samuelson, in his presidential address to the International Economic Association (Mexico, 1980), admitted his alarm:

> If someone in 1945 had asked: 'What part of the world do you expect to experience the most dramatic take-off in the next three decades?', probably I would have given an answer something like the following: 'Argentina is the wave to the future. It has a temperate climate. Its density of population provides a favourable natural resource endowment per employee. By historical accident its present population is the fairly homogeneous progeny of Western European nations. And Argentina is in 1945 at that intermediate stage of development from which rapid growth is most easily expected.' How wrong I would have been. Is it farfetched . . . to fear that many of our mixed economies will begin to suffer their own version of the Argentinian sickness?

Unfortunately Samuelson was not alone in saying what he did; his thoughts merely reflect the conventional wisdom of the day, the beliefs of the great majority of developmental economists and economic historians.

When we (the editors) invited papers from the contributors to this book, we did not expect precise explanations of so complex a phenomenon, for which, in any case, non-economic factors were so often responsible. Rather than try ourselves to supply some general and inevitably simple answer, we feel that reflection on the whole period 1880–1950 is called for, as it is a period over which one can see the accumulation of so many of the elements that lay behind Samuelson's prediction.

The period begins with Argentina as the success story of the day, even compared with other regions of recent European settlement, and in a golden league, of sorts, with Canada, Australia and New Zealand. There are some similarities, even, with the greatest success story of all, the United States. Yet by the time our period ends, Argentina is on the brink of disaster, uncertain of its future. It had abandoned its former, export-led strategy based on constant additions to the agricultural sector, in favour of an inward-looking strategy of industrial development. Its old policies were surrendered reluctantly, and perhaps belatedly. Argentina's new direction, after the Second World War, towards extreme import-substitution, was not unique, and the deduction must be that some general elements existed common to the whole sub-continent. But in making this change much of the original dynamism was lost – whether inevitably or not is one of the subjects of debate – and it suffered even further from an unusually harsh period of disturbance which transformed the country from one of the most politically stable in the developing world into one of the most unstable. By the middle of the century, however, this change was only beginning to manifest itself; worse was to follow.

II

The first paper, by D. C. M. Platt, takes up a theme that has attracted little attention in the past, that is, the role of domestic capital in the financing of city development (in this case Buenos Aires). Fascination with such phenomena as changes in the distribution, management and ownership of land, the opening of new territories, the construction of railroads, the spectacular rise in landed fortunes, the export-led boom, has led us to forget the equally impressive development of the great city of Buenos Aires. An interest in agricultural development has always suggested a nation linked indissolubly with the European economy – a distant enclave of the metropolis. A 'view of the city' however, conveys an impression of a country that was much more self-contained. The hinterland was certainly significant, but so was the urban sector.

Buenos Aires was one of the largest cities in the Western world, expanding faster before 1914 than any other, faster too than Argentina's agricultural sector. Furthermore, heavy investment was required for the expansion and renewal of Buenos Aires, 1880–1914, and the greater part of this money came not from abroad but, in one form or another, from the Argentines themselves. As Platt puts it, 'we have fixed our attention too exclusively on the glamorous superficialities – the public utilities, the international loans, the Puerto Madero, the top 10 per cent for which money had to be found abroad.' The effect has been to omit the less spectacular 90 per cent – the paving, the building – which, if taken together, are much more important and expensive. The re-evaluation of the role of domestic finance can contribute to a more balanced view of what Argentina actually was, of the degree of foreign influence and control, and of the precise areas in which foreign investment and enterprise were felt.

The conclusion may be that some of the less outward-looking strategies of later days would have been more predictable if attention had been focused more on what was happening within Argentina itself, and less on the international position of the Republic.

III

The second contribution, by Joseph Tulchin, describes and comments on the characteristics of the different frontier regions. These are defined by historical and geographical criteria, and derived from a careful analysis of the 1914 census. At times the agricultural sector in Argentina has been seen as homogeneous, a view which might indeed be useful for some purposes but which can conceal the complex process of historical evolution for various regions. Tulchin's central subject is the analysis of the distribution of capital and labour, and its relation with the organisational differentiation of Argentina's society. Capital usage – including machinery and livestock – is analysed in connection with labour and land; it is broken down by size and distribution of holdings, and by the legal status of owner and tenant. Labour in turn is disaggregated (agricultural workers/wage earners, administrators and owners) and related to the employment of the different kinds of capital. The analysis is repeated, as it is for capital usage, region by region. Diversity, not homogeneity, is seen therefore as the main characteristic of Argentina's regional frontiers – diversity explained in terms of the different combinations of productive factors at the local level, the dominant mode of production, and the disparities of power (as shown, amongst other things, by diversity in access to credit).

IV

Halperín turns his attention to a subject of critical importance for Argentina, that is, the early recognition that land-based expansion must end – a recognition that long anticipated acknowledgement either by the Argentine authorities themselves or by the public at large. In fact, a gloomy undercurrent can be detected even at the height of expansion. It was founded on an awareness of the intrinsic weaknesses not only of cattle-raising but also of extensive agriculture, so long as they continued to be based on the abundance of land. Optimism and expansion were bound to diminish; land must become less abundant and hence more expensive; rents and the cost of production must rise to the point of exceeding the value of the agricultural product. This view is far removed from Samuelson. Halperín investigates both the economic and social changes introduced on the frontier as a consequence of agricultural expansion, and the need to develop new means of transportation and new ports. More striking still was the effect on land tenure created by the appearance on the one hand of the tenant-farmer, and on the other of the colonist. The social consequences of this development were permanent; side by side with the traditional landowners came the new *empresarios de colonización*, the farmers, tenants and hired hands, quite apart from those who serviced the new sector, in transportation, merchandising and credit.

The instability of the tenant-farmer in Argentina came to be one of the central issues of the day. The speed of expansion made tenant-farming the most expedient form of land tenure. The State intervened, but not to change the system so much as to reinforce it, since the aim was to maintain its viability and to ensure that the closing of the frontier and the consequent pressure on land would bring no deterioration of the position of the tenant-farmer, in higher rents and greater instability. By the 1920s the economic organisation of the agricultural sector was already established, and when someone like Bunge looked to the future he no longer sought solutions from more intensive agriculture. Bunge's attitude reflected the constraint created by social developments in Argentine agriculture. His view of the future was part-and-parcel of a change in the intellectual climate of the Republic that brought with it profound effects on the future course of events.

V

David Rock gives us an over-view of the position reached by Argentina just before the First World War. He considers the achievements of the previous 40 years, derived both from the demand for Argentina's exports, and from the international mobility of labour and capital – a powerful combination which gave Argentine development a character of its own.

Rock does not limit himself to the pampa – the region within which were concentrated most of the productive activities of the Republic and a very large proportion of its infrastructure. He turns his attention to the interior, less important for the Argentine economy but nevertheless of great political significance. He stresses the distinction between the two regions, so complete that two different modes of production can be said to have co-existed, the capitalistic mode in areas where industrial crops were being developed and processed, and the pre-capitalist mode in the mass of the interior (where something existed akin to indentured labour). Rock suggests that a kind of dual society and economy existed in Argentina, side-by-side but not really integrated.

The city of Buenos Aires receives separate treatment. Rock points to the size of its public investment, reinforcing a line of argument already developed in Platt's paper; he emphasises the complex social and economic structure associated with a city so large as Buenos Aires by 1914.

Rock ends by pointing out that by 1914 the pampas were nearing the peak of their development. Argentina experienced a diminishing potential for growth and less freedom of manoeuvre – a persistent theme in other contributions to this book (Tulchin, Halperín and di Tella).

VI

Arturo O'Connell's analysis of Argentina in the 1920s takes into account changes in world trade and their effect on the country. Furthermore, he considers that the 1920s were more significant as a dividing line than any later decade, but he suggests reasons different from those advanced either by Halperín or di Tella.

O'Connell argues that since the First World War (if not before), and most markedly so in the 1920s, protectionism of various kinds was introduced by the major countries. Thus, the free trade assumptions that had determined Argentine policies at the turn of the century were rather a passing phenomenon than a permanent trend. Discrimination and oligopolistic practices were a marked feature of the 1920s, reinforced by a depression in world agriculture which encouraged restrictive practices in the central countries both in the shape of tariff and non-tariff barriers (such as the sanitary embargo on Argentine beef). The origins may be traced to protectionism in the United States. But monopolistic intervention could be seen equally in the 1920s in the form, for example, of tied purchases by Britain in Argentina, and in the existence of a small group of large companies which handled Argentina's export trade. By the late 1920s Argentina was faced with discrimination and the beginnings of imperial preference.

VII

A rather different approach has been adopted by Peter Alhadeff who portrays the making and implementation of financial and economic policy during the Depression of the 1930s. In practice the policy-maker was called on to play two simultaneous, and sometimes conflicting, roles, that is, administrator of public funds and developer of the economy. In the early 1930s, when the fall in customs receipts and the absence of foreign loans required parsimony in the management of public finance, the Argentine policy maker was unlikely to be an agent of economic change – a task that was easier to fulfil when economic recovery opened up new possibilities for the financing of the private sector.

Alhadeff's paper suggests, in fact, that to understand the actions of the policy maker it is more fruitful to enquire into the problems with which he had to contend than to delve into his adherence to the economic ideology of the day. The distinction between 'orthodox' and 'heterodox', 'monetarist' or 'Keynesian', even if useful, implies that there was a fixed prescription as to how to deal with the problems of the economy, irrespective of time and place. It is too rigid to be of use to the pragmatist.

The central point is that a number of the writers who have used such categories, either explicitly or implicitly, have given a schematic representation of policy-making that does not recognise the element of continuity in the administration of the Argentine economy during the 1930s, and which ignores the link between the so-called 'orthodox' policies practised before 1933, and the more expansionary measures prevalent thereafter.

VIII

The next paper, by Guido di Tella, emphasises the fact that the expansion of the frontier ended somewhere between the 1910s and the 1920s. The fact that this was not fully understood (as Halperín says earlier) gave rise to impossibly high expectations for the future of the Republic. Argentina was popularly destined to become a latter-day version of the United States. In di Tella's opinion, the crisis of the early 1930s did not mark a dividing line; it was merely a passing phenomenon. On the other hand, the closing of the frontier was an irreversible process; it meant a transition from accumulation based on land rents to accumulation based on quasi-rents. Unfortunately, these were not of the Schumpeterian innovative kind; they were the consequence of collusion and protection. The process did not begin immediately after the closing of the frontier; it was delayed for 10 or 20 years. When it finally took place in the 1930s it was a matter of expediency to be repeated, involuntarily, during the Second World War.

IX

When we invited Raúl Prebisch to give a talk of Argentina's past, we were unsure of his reaction. His thoughts on fundamental aspects of growth are well known from his years as Director of ECLA; it would surely be impossible today to talk about the problems of Latin America and of the developing world generally without referring to his ideas. But Prebisch, because of the position he occupied at the head of an international organisation, has had to distance himself from the politics of member States. Thus he caused a sensation when, in his first words to the conference, he declared his own leading role in the controversial politics of the 1930s. Furthermore, he recalled the evolution of his thinking and of his collaborators', the crucial part played by Pinedo, and the way in which, little by little, the more orthodox attitudes were abandoned to be thought out, under force of circumstance, anew.

Prebisch discusses policy towards credit, determined fundamentally by the creation of the Central Bank, but also by that contemporary preoccupation with the need to reflate the economy while at the same time preventing a surge of inflation. Particularly interesting are his remarks on the need to play down industrial policies so as to avoid a reaction from certain political sectors in the opposition.

Prebisch deals also with the era of the Second World War, and with the difficulties experienced in negotiations with the United States. Then, turning his attention to 1955 and to his own *Plan de Emergencia*, Prebisch defends the latter against the allegation that it was designed as a disincentive to industry – an implausible accusation given his past record and later ideas.

We have decided to publish the discussion and the questions asked and answered at the time. Prebisch's answers were extraordinarily frank. He acknowledged a possible failure in negotiations with Britain in 1939–43. Some comments were made on his relations with various members of the governments that held power from 1930 to the coup d'état of 1943. The problem of the role of the United States was ventilated, and it prompted a very critical reaction from Prebisch. A final question gave Prebisch the opportunity to summarise his present thinking on the need for economic transformation, linked closely with the creation, appropriation, and distribution of the economic surplus.

There can be no doubt that this conference, and the book that has resulted from it, will be remembered for Prebisch's forthright opinions, and for the way in which he took full responsibility for the policies of the 1930s. These will add to the current re-evaluation of that decade (so evident in the papers of two others among our contributors, Guido di Tella and Peter Alhadeff). The critics must be prepared to think again. . . .

X

Jorge Fodor's contribution deals with the critically important period of the Second World War. He analyses the influential role played by the accumulation of sterling in the determination of Argentina's economic policies, particularly, as it happened, after the war when the country found itself with a run-down industrial base but with huge reserves of foreign exchange. A great part of these, however, were in the form of sterling balances which could be spent only in the Sterling Area. Furthermore, because of the precarious standing of sterling at the time, these balances were effectively blocked since not only was Britain unable to repay old debts but, to prevent further decline, it was in urgent need of *new* loans. For Argentina this created many constraints, to the point, for example, of making the nationalisation of the British-owned railways almost inevitable.

Fodor's intention is to show how the sterling balances came to exist and then to discuss whether Argentina, realistically, had other options. He focuses on the period beginning with the war and ending with the military coup of 1943. These four years in turn can be divided, first, into the interval before the fall of France, second, up to Lend Lease, and third the phase from Lend Lease to June 1943 during which Lend Lease had a marked effect.

Fodor's argument is that Argentina's policies were not best suited to its interests. On the one hand Argentina extended generous credits without asking either for a guarantee as to the date of repayment or for a limit within which it was prepared to lend. On the other, the Republic followed a foreign policy which implied support for the Axis at a time when in fact it was being much more helpful to Britain than many other countries. This was exactly the opposite of Britain's experience with the United States. The United States had demanded cash and had forced Britain to sell overseas investments at very low prices, while at the same time remaining politically most friendly to Britain. Fodor's main conclusion is that Argentina might have been much better treated if it had had both a firmer economic policy towards Britain and a more supportive foreign policy.

XI

The last contribution, by Callum MacDonald, follows on from Fodor's analysis of Argentina's international relations. MacDonald focuses on the triangular relationship between Britain, Argentina and the United States during those important first years of Peronist rule. By so doing he is able to explain the nature of cooperation and conflict between Britain and the United States, the different interests and policies of the two countries, and the shift in power. MacDonald shows also the differences between the 'extremists' led by Miranda, and the 'moderates' under the Argentine Foreign Minister, Bramuglia. He explains the ways and means exercised by the United States to put pressure on the Argentine government.

The United States tried to prevent Argentina from moving towards a 'Third World' position – that is, an excessive reliance on domestic capital and increased State intervention in foreign trade and in basic services and industries. From 1946 to 1950 Argentina suffered from two different sets of problems, on the one hand sterling inconvertibility, and on the other the priority given by the United States to the reconstruction of devastated Europe. Furthermore, Argentina experienced an outright hostility to its Third World aspirations which flew in the face of the Truman policy – a policy that divided the world between capitalists and communists. Then, while the United States wished to avoid any excessive advantage being taken by Argentina in its dealings with Britain, it did not look with favour on the 'special relationship' between the two countries. Washington was prepared to use every scrap of power in its possession to achieve these ends, but in doing so it provoked a deep resentment in Argentina which, in the long run, had serious consequences.

XII

Although we have now suggested the direction and focus of the ten papers which make up this volume, it might be worth emphasising, even at the risk of repetition, some of their common themes and differences. One of the more obvious distinctions is between those that lay stress on internal factors and domestic developments, and those, like O'Connell's, Fodor's and MacDonald's, that attach paramount importance to pressure from abroad. Among the former, Platt takes exception to the conventional view that foreign influence was paramount in Argentina; domestic ability and national resources may well have been of greater significance. Paradoxically, Platt's view can play into the hands of the nationalists even if his intention is to confound the 'internationalist' obsessions of nationalists and 'dependentistas'. An emphasis on domestic capacity is popular with nationalists, and if foreign interests were not that significant, the concessions that O'Connell and Fodor allege to have been made to Britain by Argentina would have been even less justifiable than they were. A similar preoccupation with local, domestic peculiarities as determinants of the shape of Argentine development can be seen in Tulchin, Halperín and di Tella. All three call particular attention to the special characteristics, and unique role, of the agricultural sector.

The importance that Tulchin attaches to regional diversity, as measured by differences of capital and labour intensity, is echoed by Rock, although Rock arrives at his point from a different direction. Rock attempts to deal not only with the pampa but with the country as a whole; he puts forward a more comprehensive view of the kind of country Argentina had become by 1914. Halperín and di Tella remind us of the impossibility of indefinite growth based simply on the expansion of agriculture. Doubts in this respect, as Halperín shows, can be detected from early in the history of Argentine growth, and di Tella points to one of the more unfortunate consequences of the transitory nature of frontier expansion – a shift in the source of accumulation from land-rents to industrial profits (quasi-rents). Argentina was able to rely only on those rents that were derived from protection rather than innovation. The outcome is the observation that some of the extraordinary expectations of the beginning of this century proved unwarranted, which may in part lie behind the disappointment expressed by Samuelson and of those similarly inclined.

Turning to the 1920s and 1930s, O'Connell and Alhadeff reach opposite conclusions as to the adequacy of the country's response to foreign influence. O'Connell is highly critical of the policies pursued, while Alhadeff finds the Government's reaction well-attuned to domestic and international conditions in the 1930s. The disagreement may partly be explained by a different way of looking at things, but it is also one of emphasis and period. The effect of Alhadeff's argument, and likewise of di Tella's for the same period, is to take much of the steam out of conventional criticisms of government policy and to reinforce what Prebisch has to say. Prebisch identifies the rationale of the more important measures of the 1930s and early 1940s, and the lack of real alternatives. He acknowledges not only the major part he himself played in policy formation over the whole period but explains, very forcibly, the reasons and constraints which lay behind the measures actually adopted.

The last two papers, which discuss the relations which existed between Argentina, Britain and the United States during and immediately after the War, also differ in their conclusions. Fodor, like O'Connell, is most critical of foreign interference (particularly British). He castigates the compliant attitude of Argentine policy-makers, masked by an independent foreign policy of an impracticable kind. MacDonald, who has had the advantage of seeing the American government papers, takes a more neutral position. Although he does not evade some of the more unpleasant dilemmas of the relationship, MacDonald is inclined to take a critical view of what he regards as an exaggerated reaction to all things foreign. Again the difference between Fodor and MacDonald is not only a reflection of personalities but rather of a change in Argentine attitudes which, in less than a decade, have moved from one extreme to the other in their perception of the role of foreign interests.

The arguments of the contributors to this volume convey a sense of the evolution of Argentina. In a half-century Argentina moved from an acknowledged place as one of the economic marvels of the world, destined (so it seemed) to become one of its greatest countries, to a modest position, one among many. Argentina after the Second World War was still important, but it had fallen victim to a faltering rate of growth, short-lived booms and longer slumps. Extraordinary expectations were not fulfilled, partly because they were wrongly based, exaggerated and impossible to fulfil, partly because of the difficulties experienced in making the inevitable switch from an open, agricultural (land-using) strategy to one which employed capital both in the agricultural sector and in the new areas of industry. At this delicate moment Argentina had to withstand foreign pressures, British and American. To what extent these were pernicious, or Argentina's reactions adequate, is still, evidently, a matter for debate.

By the middle of the twentieth century Argentina was in the midst of an ambitious programme of industrial development, although restricted to domestic capital and the local market. High hopes survived, even after the period with which we are concerned. But an inward-looking strategy of the intensity of Argentina's was bound to encounter diminishing returns. This book, however, stops with Perón, and what follows is another story. . . .

Index

Agriculture, Department of (US), 85
Agriculture, Ministry of (Argentine), 31, 44, 45, 57
Agriculture, Ministry of (British), 175
Alberdi, Juan, 31, 40, 124
Alfonso, Salvador, 1, 3
Alhadeff, Peter, xi, *95–119*, 206, 208, 210, 211
Alvear, President Marcelo T. de, 57, 89, 90, 129, 146
Alvear, Torcuato de, 1, 6, 7, 9
Anales (Sociedad Rural), 90
Anchorena, Joaquín de, 11
Andes agreement, 193, 194, 195
Arcondo, Anibal, 50
Argentine Confederation of Commerce, Industry and Production, *see* Confederación Argentina del Comercio, de la Industria y de la Producción
Armour Co., 68
Armour (Research Foundation), 129
Australia, 77, 78, 84, 98, 160, 202
Azara, Felix de, 41

Bahia Blanca, 19, 22, 62, 63, 69
Baillieu, Sir Clive, 193
Balfour Committee, 83
Banco Central, *see* Bank, Central
Banco de México, 176
Banco de la Nación, 28, 30, 34, 66, 105, 112, 134, 136, 137, 147, 165
Banco Hipotecario Nacional, 8
Banco Nacional, 66
Bank, Central (Argentina), 106, 107, 111–13 *passim*, 127, 128, 138, 139, 143–8 *passim*, 155–9 *passim*, 163, 165, 167, 169, 170, 173–7 *passim*, 183, 207
Bank, Central (Canada), 144
Bank, Central (South Africa), 144
Bank of England, 157, 158, 161, 163, 166, 167, 172, 173, 176
Bank, Export–Import (Exim), 139, 196, 197
Bank for International Settlements, 177
Barcelona, 6
Baring Brothers, 61, 158
Baring crisis (1890–1), 8, 65
Baring, Evelyn, 115
Belgium, Evelyn, 115
Belgium, 64, 69, 77, 164
Beveraggi Allende, W., 98, 101
Blanksten, George I., 196
Bolivia, 64, 173, 174
Bollini, Francisco, 7
Bolsa (Buenos Aires), 5
Bolsa de Comercio, 102
Braden, Spruille, 187, 188
Bramuglia, Atilio, 183, 184, 186, 189, 193, 194, 195, 209
Brazil, 64, 65, 68, 70, 98, 177, 178
Britain, 4, 64–8 *passim*, 74–7 *passim*, 83, 84, 85, 89, 90, 91, 98, 128, 131, 141–6 *passim*, 154–67 *passim*, 170, 171, 173, 175, 178, 179, 183–97 *passim*, 206, 208, 209, 210, 211
Bruce, James, 191, 193, 195
Buenos Aires, 1–12 *passim*, 16, 18, 21, 22, 27, 32, 33, 35, 61, 63, 66, 69, 104, 107, 115, 134, 135, 158, 166, 168, 172, 180, 185, 187, 188, 189, 196, 202, 205
Buenos Aires (province), 16, 18, 19, 20, 33, 41, 45, 52, 53, 55, 62, 63, 67, 70
Bülow, von, 82
Bunge, Alejandro, 57, 58, 75, 76, 89, 99, 123, 124, 131, 134, 204

Cadogan, A., 164
Campolieti, Roberto, 44, 45, 53
Canada, 69, 77, 78, 87, 143, 144, 145, 155, 156, 163, 174, 175, 178, 192, 202
Cárcano, Miguel Angel, 43
Casares, Alberto, 3
Castillo, Ramón, 147, 148
census, agricultural (1937), 35

213

Index

census, Buenos Aires
  (1887), 5
  (1904), 5
  (1909), 5
census, second national (1895), 4, 63
census, third national (1914), 20, 21, 35, 36, 37 n.6, 63
Cerijo, Ramón A., 196
Chamberlain, Joseph, 84
Chicago, 67, 68
Chile, 177
Chivilcoy, 41, 42
Churchill, W., 165
Clayton, W., 187, 190
Cleveland, Ohio, 8
Cobbold, 160, 164
Committee, Ways and Means (US House of Representatives), 80
Confederación Argentina del Comercio, de la Industria y de la Producción, 75, 102
Confédération Nationale des Associations Agricoles, 82
Conference, Colonial
  (1887), 84
  (1902), 84
Conference, Imperial War (1917), 84
Conferencia Segunda Económica Nacional, *see* Congress, Second National Economic
Congress, First National Economic, 75
Congress, Second National Economic, 75, 90
Congress of Livestock Producers of the River Plate (1926), 90
Consejo Nacional de Postguerra, 131, 132
Conversion Board, 62
Conversion Law (1899), 66
Conversion Office, 102, 103, 104, 105, 112
Coolidge, President (US), 81
co-operative movement, 24, 48, 51
Córdoba province, 16, 18, 19, 24, 26, 29, 33, 40, 45, 52, 53, 62, 63, 64
Corporación para la'Promoción del Intercambio, 129
Corrientes province, 67
Cortés Conde, Roberto, 53
Customs Law (Argentina, 1905), 88

D'Abernon agreement, 91
debt
  floating, 3, 101, 102, 111, 112, 113
  Municipal Floating, 5, 8
  National External, 166, 167

Delledonne, O., 82
devaluation
  of the dollar, 104
  of the peso, 104, 105, 113, 116, 137–8, 141, 149, 150
  of sterling, 135, 155
Díaz Alejandro, Carlos F., 87
Dickmann, Enrique, 105
Duhau, Luis, 90, 104, 105, 137
Dunnett, G. S., 179
duties, McKenna, 83

Eady/Miranda agreement, 189, 190
ECLA (Economic Commission for Latin America), 138, 140, 150, 207
Economic Action, Plan of (1934), 105
Economic Association, International, 201
Economic Co-operation Administration (ECA), 191, 192, 193, 195, 196
Economic Council (Argentine), 183, 196
Economic Research, Office of (Central Bank), 176
Economic Research Unit (Banco de la Nación), 134
Economic Warfare, Ministry of (British), 165
Education, National Council of, 108
Egypt, 174
Entre Ríos province, 18, 33, 36, 67
Escalante, Wenceslao, 45, 50
Escudé, Carlos, 191, 197
Estudios y Conferencias Industriales, Instituto de, 130
Exchange Control Commission, 104, 115
Exchange Equalisation Account, 157

Fair Trade League, 84
'Farm Block' (US), 78
Federación Agraria Argentina, 52, 56
Federal Reserve Board, 177
Ferrer, A., 96, 106
Ferrocarríl del Sud, 18, 19; *see also* railways
Finance, Ministry of (Argentine), 111, 113, 115, 148
Flannigan, Admiral, 189
Fodor, Jorge, xii, 143, 144, 145, *154–82*, 208, 209, 210, 211
Food Defence Plans Department (British), 157
Food, Ministry of (British), 161, 162, 165
Fordney-McCumber Act (US, 1922), 80, 86

Index

Foreign Office (British), 164, 169, 170, 172, 185, 186, 189, 193
France, 64, 66, 81, 89, 160, 163, 164, 172
free trade, 74–94 *passim*, 136, 138
Friedman, M., 152

García, Eugenio, 6
George, Henry, 50
Germany, 64, 66, 71, 81, 82, 143, 146, 155, 156, 161, 162, 167, 170
Gibson, Herbert, 48, 49, 56
Girola, Carlos, 45
gold premium, 61, 62
gold standard, 62, 103, 155, 176
Grant (Bank of England), 174
Great Britain, *see* Britain
Groppo, Pedro, 100, 148

Hall-Patch, E. L., 159
Halperín, Tulio, xi, *39–59*, 203, 204, 205, 206, 210
Harding, President (US), 86
Haussman, Baron, 3
Hawley-Smoot Act (US, 1930), 81, 86, 91
Holland, *see* Netherlands
Holm, Hert T., 51, 52
Hoover, President (US), 81, 86, 98
housing, 1, 3, 4, 12, 127, 128, 139
Hueyo, Alberto, 107, 111, 112, 115, 116, 137, 147
Hutton, M. I., 162, 168

IAPI (Instituto Argentino para la Promoción del Intercambio), 191, 194, 195
IMF, 197
immigrants, 21, 29, 36, 48, 53, 60, 68, 70, 71
immigration, 19, 30, 46, 63, 64, 121, 125
imperial preference, 76, 84–6, 89, 90
income tax, 96, 107, 108, 127, 134, 147, 160
Income Tax Agency, National, 127
India, 174, 179
Indian(s) (Argentine), 18, 19, 20, 21
wars, 19
Infante, J. Daniel, 55, 57
Institute for Mobilizing Frozen Bank Investments, 112
Italy, 64, 81, 82

Japan, 71
Jerram, Bertram, 168, 169, 175
Johnson Act (US, 1934), 156
Johnson, Hugh S., 80

Juárez Celman, President Miguel, 60, 65
Jujuy, province, 63
Justo, President Juan B., 50, 51, 52, 54, 55, 108, 110, 134, 146, 147

Kaerger, Karl, 48
Kahn, Richard, 164, 168, 175
Kautsky, Karl, 50
Kennedy, J. F., 147
Keynes, J. M., 144, 163, 164, 175, 178
Klein, Guillermo W., 127, 147

Lahitte, Emilio, 45, 46, 47, 48, 50, 54
land value, 5, 6, 8, 22, 26, 32, 36, 44, 53, 78
Lascano, M. R., 98
Leeper, Sir Reginald (Rex), 185, 186, 189, 193
Leith-Ross, Sir Frederick, 81, 142, 160
Lend Lease, 156, 173, 175, 208
List, Friedrich, 131
Liverpool, 176
Llanos, Doña Eulogia, 39, 40
loan(s), 3, 9, 156, 157
 of 1882, 3
 of 1884, 7
 Canadian (to Britain) 178
 domestic, 4, 8
 Exim, 196, 197
 foreign, 114, 139, 156
 government, 102
 Jesse Jones (to Britain), 178
 long-term, 7, 104
 municipal, 6, 7, 9, 11
 Patriotic, 102, 105, 137
 public, 65
 Roca funding, 104, 114, 115, 116
 short-term, 27
Lobería, 27
Lobos, Eleodoro, 43, 49, 50
London, 7, 104, 114, 158, 163, 168, 169, 170, 174, 175, 177, 183–95 *passim*
Lord, General, 189
Lloyds Bank, 68, 69

Macdonald, Callum, xii, *183–200*, 209, 210, 211
Machado, Antonio, 133
McNary–Haughen bills (US, 1927–8), 81
 plan, 80
Malaccorto, Ernesto, 107, 127
Mandelbaum, W., 83
Martínez, Alberto B., 4
Mather Jackson, 161, 169, 170
Mendoza, province, 64

216 Index

Messersmith, George, 187, 188, 189, 190, 191, 192
Mexico, 177, 192
Meynell, E. C., 158, 171, 172
Miller, Edward, 196
Miranda, Miguél, 183–90 *passim*, 192–7 *passim*, 209
Mitre Law (1907), 66, 166
Mitre, President Bartolomé, 40, 41, 58
Molinas, Florencio T., 47, 48, 50
Monick (French Embassy), 159
Monroe Doctrine, 188
Morales, Carlos, 10
Morgenthau, Henry, 144
Mussolini, Benito, 81

Nación, 91, 134
Netherlands, 64, 69, 77, 164
New Zealand, 84, 160, 202
Niemeyer, Sir Otto, 112, 157, 158, 159, 161, 162, 166, 167, 171, 172, 176, 179
Norman, Montagu, 159, 166
Nurkse, Ragnar, 176

O'Connell, A., xi, *74–94*, 141, 142, 205, 210, 211
Ortega y Gasset, José, 124
Ortíz, Roberto, 146, 147, 166
Ovey, Esmond, 171
Oyhanarte, Horacio, 91

Pan American Union, 107
Paraná River, 16, 18, 39
Paris, 3, 4, 6
Patagonia, 66
Paz, Hipólito J., 195
Peek, George N., 80
Pellegrini, President Carlos, 60, 61, 66, 122
Peña, President Luis Sáenz, 60, 61
Peña, President Roque Sáenz, 51
Peréz, Enrique, 107, 111, 112, 116
Perón administration, 132, 149, 154, 183, 185
Perón, President Juan, 56, 138, 148, 183, 185–9 *passim*, 191–7 *passim*, 212
Peronism, 146, 148, 149
Peru, 177
Phelps, V. L., 103
Pinedo, Federico, 95, 100, 101, 104–9 *passim*, 111–16 *passim*, 127–30 *passim*, 133, 135, 136, 139, 146–8 *passim*, 207
Plan, Emergency (1955), 140, 150, 207
Plan, Five-Year (Argentine), 185, 186, 187, 188, 189, 190, 192, 194

Plan, Marshall, 191, 193, 195, 196
Plan de Reactivación Económica (1940), 128, 129, 139
Plata, La, 67
Plate, River, 18, 68, 186
Platt, D. C. M., xi, *1–14*, 141, 202, 210
Playfair (Treasury), 164
Portugal, 174, 178
Powell (Bank of England), 158, 169
Prados Arrarte, J., 105
Prebisch, Raúl, v, xi, 103, 107, 113, 127, 128, *133–41*, *141–153*, 155, 176, 207, 208, 211
Prensa, 108, 134
protectionism, 76, 79, 81–4, 85, 87, 88, 89, 134, 138

Quintana, Manuel, 180

Radical
  government, 125
  opposition, 129
  party, 56, 57
railroad, *see* railway(s)
railway(s), 18, 19, 20, 40, 51, 52, 53, 57, 60, 61, 62, 65, 66, 68, 69, 121, 123, 127, 149, 158, 159, 165, 166, 185, 190, 202, 208
  Córdoba Central, 165
  Ferrocaríl del Sud, 18, 19
Republican Party (US), 79
Review of the River Plate, 113
Revista de Economía Argentina, 131
Rioja, La (province), 63
Roca, Julio R., 115
Roca funding loan, 104, 114, 115, 116
Roca–Runciman Agreement (1933), 110, 114, 115, 116, 128, 142
Rock, David, xi, *60–73*, 204, 205, 210
'Romero Deal', 61
Roosevelt, F. D., 98, 147, 165
Roosevelt, T., 51
Rosa, José Maria, 2
Rosario, 18, 39, 40, 62, 63, 69
Rosas, Juan Manuel de, 41
Rowe Dutton, Ernest, 171, 172
Ruiz Guiñazú, Enrique, 5
Rural Society, *see* Sociedad Rural Argentina
Russia, 77, 81, 187, 188, 190

Salado River, 18
Salera, V., 105
Salta, 69
Samuelson, Paul, 201, 204, 210

Index

San Alberto, fray José Antonio de, 40
San Luís, province, 19, 64
Santa Fe, province, 16, 18, 19, 22, 24, 33, 36, 45, 52, 55, 62, 63
Sarmiento, Domingo, 40, 41, 51
Savio, Manuel, 130
Schacht, H., 146
Seeber, Francisco, 9, 10
Shuckburgh, John, 192
Smithfield market, 142, 143
Social Assistance, 108
Socialist party (Argentine), 50, 105, 127, 134
Sociedad Rural Argentina, 86, 90, 91, 102, 142
South Africa, 155, 175
Soviet Union, *see* Russia
Sweden, 143, 144, 145, 174
Swift Co., 68
Switzerland, 174

Tandíl, 27
tariff(s), 51, 71, 79, 81–91 *passim*, 107, 108, 121, 134, 184, 185, 186, 205
  Act (US, 1913), 79
  Bill, Emergency (US, 1921), 80
  Commission (US), 80
  Law (Argentina, 1892), 89
  Laws (Germany, 1925), 82
  Law (Italy, 1921), 83
  Méline (France, 1892), 88
  McKinley (US, 1890), 89
  reform campaign (Britain), 84
  Revision (France, 1927), 81
  see also duties, McKenna (Britain)
Taussig, F. W., 80
tax, 9, 10, 47, 49, 56, 61, 108, 109, 136, 140, 163, 166
  on land, 47, 49, 50
  reform, 109, 134
  see also income tax
Taylor, A. D., 77
Taylor, H. C., 77
Tecnología Agropecuaria, Instituto Nacional de, 141
Tella, Guido di, xi, 75, *120–32*, 134, 141, 205, 206, 207, 208, 210, 211
tenancy, forms of, 21, 22, 31, 34, 45, 46, 48, 56
tenant farmers, 31–6 *passim*, 43, 45, 48–56 *passim*, 65, 204

Thünen, von, 131
Torino, Damián M., 49, 50
Tornquist, Ernesto and Co., 7
Trade, Board of (British), 168, 175, 185
trade unions, 141, 149, 153
Treasury (British), 157, 159, 160, 161, 162, 168, 171, 175, 179
Treasury (Argentine), 161
Truman
  administration, 187
  doctrine, 197, 209
Tucumán, 64
Tulchin, Joseph s., xi, *15–38*, 203, 205, 210
Turner (Bank of England), 174

unemployment, 125, 126, 135, 137, 138, 139, 173
Unión Aduanera del Sud, 129
Unión Industrial Argentina, 86, 102, 126, 130
United Kingdom, *see* Britain
United States, 51, 65, 67, 68, 69, 71, 75–81 *passim*, 84–90 *passim*, 98, 138–47 *passim*, 155, 156, 165, 172, 173, 174, 175, 178, 183–97 *passim*, 202, 205, 207, 208, 209, 211
Uriburu, E., 96, 98, 107, 108, 111, 112, 116, 136, 147
Uruguay, 18, 103, 177

Vegas, Harera, 89, 90
Venezuela, 177
Versailles, Treaty of, 82
Vieytes, Hipólito, 41
Villanueva, Javier, 95, 98, 109, 111, 116

Waley, David, 158, 160, 161, 163, 164, 166, 167, 172
Washington, 183, 184, 186, 187, 188, 189, 193, 194, 195, 196, 209
Wilson, President (US), 79, 80
World Bank, 197

Yacimientos Petrolíferos Fiscales (YPF), 194
Young, N., 159, 169
Yrigoyen, H., 91, 134

Zeballos, Estanislao, 39, 40, 42
Zymmelman, Manuel, 75